CRITICAL ACCLAIM FOR
LOIS DUNCAN AND
WHO KILLED MY DAUGHTER?

"Duncan's anguish and frustration surface on practically every page of this sad but intriguing mystery. Her forays into the realm of psychics and dreams are downright eerie."
—*The Plain Dealer* (Cleveland)

"What a story! . . . A tragic story for sure, but also a celebration of the psyche as it stretches beyond time and space to encompass loved ones."
—Dr. William Roll, Research Director, Psychical Research Foundation

"*Who Killed My Daughter?* is a story of sadness, frustration and hope. . . . It is an emotional book that reads more like a novel than nonfiction."
—*San Antonio Express-News*

"This book is especially well written, perhaps because Duncan's writing comes from her broken heart and anguished soul."
—*Library Journal*

"Ms. Duncan is an award-winning young adult novelist. She does a remarkable job of organizing the untidy events of real life into a cohesive, readable narrative."
—*The Atlanta Journal and Constitution*

BOOKS BY LOIS DUNCAN CURRENTLY IN PRINT

Young Adult Suspense Novels:
DON'T LOOK BEHIND YOU
THE TWISTED WINDOW
LOCKED IN TIME
THE THIRD EYE
STRANGER WITH MY FACE
DAUGHTERS OF EVE
KILLING MR. GRIFFIN
SUMMER OF FEAR
DOWN A DARK HALL
I KNOW WHAT YOU DID LAST SUMMER
A GIFT OF MAGIC
RANSOM
THEY NEVER CAME HOME

Young Adult Autobiography:
CHAPTERS: MY GROWTH AS A WRITER

Juvenile Fiction and Picture Books:
THE BIRTHDAY MOON
FROM SPRING TO SPRING
HORSES OF DREAMLAND
WONDER KID MEETS THE EVIL LUNCH SNATCHER
HOTEL FOR DOGS

The "Songs Of Childhood" series of Children's Audio Cassettes
(with music and vocals by Robin Arquette):
SONGS FROM DREAMLAND, DREAM SONGS FROM YESTERDAY,
OUR BEAUTIFUL DAY, THE STORY OF CHRISTMAS

WHO KILLED MY DAUGHTER?

LOIS DUNCAN

A Dell Book

Published by
Dell Publishing
a division of
Bantam Doubleday Dell Publishing Group, Inc.
1540 Broadway
New York, New York 10036

ISBN 0-440-21342-8

Reprinted by arrangement with Delacorte Press

Printed in the United States of America

Published simultaneously in Canada

March 1994

10 9 8 7 6 5

OPM

For Kaitlyn Clare Arquette
September 18, 1970—July 17, 1989
with love

"It is no measure of health to be well adjusted to a profoundly sick society."

Krishnamurti

Psychic Readings

Listed by Page Number for Easy Reference

Author's Note

Our teenage daughter Kaitlyn was chased down and shot to death while driving home from a girlfriend's house on a peaceful Sunday evening.

Police dubbed the shooting "random."

"You're going to have to accept the fact that the reason Kait died was because she was in the wrong place at the wrong time," they told us.

But to our family the circumstances didn't add up to "random," especially after we made the shocking discovery that Kait had been keeping some very dangerous secrets from us.

Some of those secrets were exposed by psychics.

Others by private investigators.

Others by an aggressive newspaper reporter who followed up on leads the police refused to look into.

After spending two years investigating Kait's death our family has managed to accumulate enough information to form a fragmented picture of what may have happened to her, but the jigsaw puzzle still lacks the few key pieces that could nail the identity of her killers.

It is my hope that reading Kait's story will motivate potential informants to supply us with those pieces.

Tipsters can address their letters to:

Lois Duncan, Author of *Who Killed My Daughter?*
c/o Dell Publishing
Dept. LD
1540 Broadway
New York, NY 10036

PROLOGUE

Once upon a time, in a faraway land, there dwelt a man who was a teacher of things strange and wonderful.

He taught that the soul could leave the body and fly, and that people could foretell the future, and that healing could be accomplished by love and by touch, and that the spirits of those who moved on to other dimensions could communicate with the living through visions and dreams.

Such teachings were considered heresy in that time, so the teacher was forced to conduct his classes in secret. He met with a small group of students in a garden by a fountain and continually cautioned them never to reveal what he taught them.

Among those students there were three strong-willed young men who were very excited about the things they were learning and desperately wanted to share this knowledge with others.

The first went off to teach in a foreign country so as not to endanger his teacher and fellow students.

The second absorbed, not only the lessons of the teacher, but his fears and paranoia as well. Cautious and conservative, he monitored the safety of the group and struggled to keep the others under control.

But the third young man was a rebel who would not be

intimidated. He considered himself invincible, but his judgment was poor, and he trusted all the wrong people. His actions brought disaster to himself and his teacher.

This took place long ago in a faraway land.

Centuries later it happened again.

1

Our daughter, Kaitlyn Arquette, was murdered in Albuquerque, New Mexico, on Sunday, July 16, 1989.

They got her at night.

I have lived that evening over so often in dreams that by now it has become an extension of myself. When I go to bed it runs through my head like a videotape, the images sharp and precise, the dialogue unchanging, except that with each repetition there are new things I notice.

The setting is always the same, of course; it's our family room. Although we no longer live in that house, I can picture it perfectly. The rug, a rich rust color, muted by pet hair, as our cat and cocker spaniel shed in the summertime. The brown-and-white couch and love seat with cushions molded into irreversible slopes and hollows by years of accommodating the bodies of sprawling teenagers. Bookshelves, lined with albums that are filled with photographs chronicling ski trips, camp-outs, Christmases, graduations, and birthday parties. A television set across from the sofa. A Navajo rug on one wall. On another, a painting by my stepmother that depicts my late father—white haired, bearded, shirtless—on the porch of a beach cottage, baiting a fishing hook for a grandson.

I am a writer by trade and am practiced in recreating

scenes. It is easy for me to place myself back in that room again. Beyond the bay window there lies a tree-shaded yard, and, beyond that, an unkempt rose garden. When I peer out through the glass, I can see that it's raining, and the soft gray drizzle produces a premature twilight.

Now that I have set the stage, I will bring on the players.

Kaitlyn, eighteen, comes into the house. I hear the slam of the front door and the sound of her footsteps in the hallway and immediately know this is Kait and not one of her brothers. Her tread is solid and purposeful and distinctly her own.

My husband Don and I have just settled ourselves on the sofa to watch *60 Minutes*. I raise my eyes from the television screen and call, "Is that you, honey?"

"Who else?" Kait answers, and materializes in the doorway. "I thought I'd stop by and say hi on my way to Susan's."

"The bad penny returns!" says her father. "You were here all morning. We see more of you now than we did before you moved out!"

"The rain's depressing, and Dung's out with his friends," Kait says. "The apartment feels weird tonight and I don't like being there."

She comes into the room and perches on the arm of the sofa. She is dressed in a short black skirt and a black-and-white striped blouse, and around her neck there hangs a chain with a tiny gold cross. She is wearing the sand-dollar earrings I brought her from Florida the last time I visited her sister, Robin. The earrings are rimmed with gold, the same burnished shade as her hair, which she is still determinedly trying to grow back to one length after last summer's disastrous asymmetrical cut.

Each time I rerun the scene, new details leap out at me.

For instance, how perfect her teeth are, straight, white, and even. Her complexion is perfect also, unmarred by the adolescent acne that torments her friends, totally unblemished except for an odd little hollow on the ridge of her left cheekbone. When I caught my first sight of her in the delivery room, I gasped, "My baby has a hole in her face!" but the obstetrician assured me that the dent wasn't permanent. As it turned out, it was, but we came to regard it as a misplaced dimple and jokingly referred to it as "God's fingerprint."

Kait flashes her mischievous smile, but something doesn't feel right to me, and I regard her suspiciously. Her eyes are red, and the lids are abnormally puffy.

"You've been crying." I make it a statement rather than a question.

"Like I told you, the rain depresses me," she says defensively. "Besides, I'm pissed at Dung, and I always cry when I'm mad."

"Have you two had another fight?"

"Not another one since last night, if that's what you mean," Kait says. "The reason I hung around here so long this morning was because I didn't want to have to go home and talk to him. This living-together business is a crock. Things were a whole lot better when we were just dating."

"Why don't you move back home, then?" Don asks reasonably. "There's no sense staying in a situation where you're miserable."

"I'm not about to crawl back into the womb," Kait responds with characteristic stubbornness. "I love my apartment, I'm just sorry I ever let Dung move in. His weirdo friends are over there all the time. I feel like I'm running a crash pad for half the Vietnamese in Albuquerque."

"Ask *him* to move out," I suggest. The solution seems so simple.

"I have, but he won't," says Kait. "He says it's his place, too, but it isn't because the lease and utilities are in my name. He still doesn't understand how things work in America. He says that in Vietnam women do what men tell them. I've told him I'll let him stay until the end of the month, but then I want him out so Laura can move in with me."

"What's suddenly gone so wrong between you and Dung?"

"I don't want to get into it now, it's just too heavy. I'll tell you about it sometime, maybe later tonight even." She glances at her watch. "Well, I'd better get going. I've never been over to Susan's, and it may take time to find it. I thought I'd stop on the way and pick up some ice cream. She's cooking the dinner, so the least I can do is bring dessert."

"Where does she live?" Don asks.

"It's down around Old Town. I'll either spend the night there or come back here. If Dung calls trying to find me, don't tell him where I am."

"That's cruel!" I exclaim, shocked by this display of callousness. "You may be breaking up with him, but you've been going together for a year and a half, and whatever your problems are, you know Dung cares about you. If you don't come home, he's going to think you've had an accident."

"Mother, you don't understand—"

"I *do* understand! What *you* don't understand is how horrible it is to worry about somebody!"

I consider myself an authority on that subject. Even after our five children were all bigger than I was, I insisted that Don and I dovetail our business trips so that one or the other of us was always home to keep an eye on things. When Kait was an infant, I was chronically reeling from sleep deprivation from checking her crib throughout the night to make sure she was still breathing, and despite the fact that my fears were never substantiated, I didn't get any better when the children became teenagers. They knew that if they missed their curfew by as much as ten minutes, they could expect to find me pacing up and down in the entrance hall, fighting hysteria as I pictured a blazing car wreck with beloved bodies mangled and strewn across the highway.

I'd expected my paranoia to diminish once the nest was empty, but now, as Kait starts toward the door, I realize that it is stronger tonight than it has ever been. Here in this familiar room, on a damp, sweet summer evening that couldn't be less threatening, I am suddenly overwhelmed by such a surge of panic that I can feel the pounding of my heart in my fingertips. I sense the vibrations of a tidal wave rolling toward us as we stand on a peaceful beach with our backs to the ocean.

"Don't go out! Something terrible is going to happen!"

"What did you say?" Kait can't believe she has heard me correctly.

"Something terrible is going to happen!" I repeat irrationally, and grasp for some way to make the statement less preposterous. "We don't even know this girl Susan. Who is she, anyway? Daddy and I haven't met her. Why hasn't she ever been over here? She certainly doesn't live in a good part of town."

Kait glances across at her father. *Can you believe this?*

"The reason Susan hasn't been over here is—if you'll remember, Mother—this isn't where I live now." She addresses me with exaggerated patience. "She's a very nice girl who sells snow cones in front of Pier One. I met her on a

lunch break, and we got to be friends. We've been trying to
get together to see a movie or something, but our plans
keep falling through because of my work schedule. And
what do you mean about Old Town's being a bad area? You
and Daddy have friends who live there. It's not like it's one
of those creepy barrios like Martineztown."

"I won't let you go," I say firmly.

Then I leap from the sofa and grab her before she has
time to take in what I've said and flee from the room.

Kait is a big girl, taller and heavier than I am, but that
doesn't matter; she's no match for the crazy middle-aged
woman who bears down on her. I shove her onto the sofa
and pin her arms at her sides with a powerful viselike grip
that cannot be broken.

"Get me some rope!" I shout.

"Rope?" Don repeats blankly, shifting his gaze from Dan
Rather to zero in on the battle scene. He has never seen me
like this, and he's obviously horrified. He is looking at a
woman gone suddenly mad.

"There's a coil of rope in the garage! I saw it there yesterday! Hurry and get it, I can't hold her down forever!"

We've been married so long that Don responds automatically. He jumps up from the sofa and takes off at a run for
the garage.

Kait struggles to break my grip, but the same bony, long-
fingered hands that buckled her into her car seat and
snatched her away from hot stove burners and steadied her
two-wheel bicycle when she took off the training wheels
have developed incredible strength when it comes to her
safety. There is no way in the world that she can break my
grip on her.

"Is this being taped by *Candid Camera*?" she asks, half
laughing, half crying, trying to pretend it is a joke. "It isn't

as if we're going to be doing something dangerous. We're going to eat dinner, and then we're going next door to decorate Susan's boyfriend's apartment. He's out of town, and she wants it to be a surprise for him."

"I'm sorry," I say. "This isn't the evening for you to do that."

Don reappears with the tow rope we use for water skiing and makes an attempt to hand it to me.

"You're going to have to help me," I tell him. "Wind it around her shoulders and work your way down. Make it tight, but be careful not to cut off her circulation. All we want is to keep her from going out tonight."

Don takes the rope and starts looping it around Kait's body, doing his best to ignore her shrieks of outrage. It takes us a while, but the job is finally completed. With our daughter securely cocooned, I test the knots to make sure they will hold.

Kait lies on the sofa, glaring up at me in impotent fury.

"I will hate you for this forever!" There is venom in her voice.

"That's all right," I say gently, stroking her hair.

I sit by her side and guard her the rest of the night.

That is the way the scene plays when I run it in my dreams. In truth, of course, that is not what happened at all. Common sense took precedence over instinct, and I confined my admonishments to telling Kait to drive carefully.

"I always drive carefully," she said.

That wasn't true, and we both knew it. Kait was an aggressive driver, given to risk taking, but traffic was light on Sunday nights, and it wasn't as if she was going to be driving on the freeway. The easiest route to Old Town was straight down Lomas, an east-west street that ran one block south of our home. There wouldn't be many drunks on the road on a Sunday, and her plans for the evening were certainly simple and harmless.

She's going to be fine, I told myself. I'm being ridiculous.

Still, I said, "I want you to leave us Susan's phone number. That way, if you don't come back, we'll know where to start looking for you."

"Honestly, Mother, there are times when you're just *unreal!*" She indulged me by scribbling a number on the back of a magazine. "Now, *you* do something for *me*. I want you to promise that if Dung calls here you won't tell him I'm at Susan's."

"I promise," I said reluctantly, with the mental reservation that, while I wouldn't divulge Susan's name, if Dung did call, frantic with worry, I would tell him that Kait was all right and was sleeping at a friend's house.

Kait raised her hand in a comical half salute.

"Later! I'll see you guys later!"

Those were the last words we were ever to hear her speak.

The call from the emergency room of the University of New Mexico Hospital came just before midnight. The woman who called said Kait was there and had been injured but would give out no further information over the telephone.

Don and I threw on our clothes and drove to the hospital. I sat in the passenger's seat with my hands clasped tightly in my lap, the nails of one making gouges in the back of the other, living a nightmare eighteen years in the making. I wanted to pray, but I didn't know what to pray for. I hated to press my luck by asking God for too much and offending Him with my greediness, so I couldn't ask for the call to have been made by a prankster or for Kait to have suffered nothing more than scratches.

I finally decided to confine my prayer to the request that she not have a head injury. Two years ago my stepsister's teenage son had been in an accident that had left him brain damaged, and Kait had gone into hysterics when she learned about it.

"Poor Andy!" she'd gasped through her tears. "He was always so *smart!*"

Kait's tough, I told myself. She can deal with almost anything—fractures, disfigurement, even with life in a wheelchair—*but, please, oh, please, don't let anything have happened to her brain!*

The space in front of the emergency room was reserved for ambulances, so Don dropped me off at the door while he took the car across to the visitors' parking lot. The nurse who had called us was standing in wait in the doorway, and I knew that it had to be bad when she took me in her arms.

"You're sure it's Kait?" I whispered. "There's no chance it's a mistake?"

"It's Kait," the woman said. "There was a picture ID in her wallet. She's alive, but in critical condition. You need to prepare yourself for the fact that you may lose her."

"A car wreck?" I couldn't conceive of any other possibility.

"Your daughter's been shot in the head," the nurse said quietly.

The sand of the beach slid out from under my feet, as the tidal wave struck the shore and I was sucked under.

Kaitlyn Clare Arquette, age eighteen, in the spring of 1989, the year of her death

2

Don and I sat in a small private waiting area off the emergency room, side by side on a green vinyl couch, propped against each other like Raggedy Ann and Andy dolls. If one of us had moved, the other would have fallen over.

After a while Don said, "We should call the boys."

"Please, not yet," I implored him. Once we started informing people I would no longer be able to tell myself this was a fragment of a fever dream. "There's no sense dragging them down here at this hour of the night. It's not as if there's anything they can do here. Let's wait until we have something definite to tell them."

I could tell that Don didn't agree, but he didn't make an issue of it, and we continued to sit there, staring out into the hallway, waiting for somebody with authority to come in and talk to us.

At one point we saw Kait being wheeled past our doorway on the way to the X-ray room. Her face was slack and waxen, and her head was swathed in bandages. If we had not been told who she was, we would not have recognized her. We jumped up from the couch and trailed the gurney down the hall until the green-clad orderlies shoved it through a set of double doors into an area designated for doctors only.

Then we went back to the waiting room and sat back down again.

We didn't feel alone, because hospitals are busy places even on Sundays, and there was a steady flow of traffic in and out of the emergency room. Somebody brought us coffee that we couldn't force down, and we let it grow cold on a table piled with magazines. A nurse came in with Kait's purse and a plastic jar that contained the items removed from her person when she arrived at the hospital—her watch, the chain with the cross, the sand-dollar earrings.

The next person to visit us was a detective from the Homicide Department. He asked us when we had last seen Kait.

"She left our home at around six-fifteen to go to a girl-friend's house for dinner," I told him.

"I've spoken with the friend, Susan Smith," the police officer told us. "Her address and a hand-drawn map were in Kait's car. Susan said Kait was planning to spend the night with her and then suddenly remembered she had to study for a test tomorrow."

"She's taking two college classes in summer school," I said. "She's going to be attending full time in the fall."

"Is her home address the one on her driver's license?"

"No," Don said. "That's the family home. Kait lives at the Alvarado Square Apartments. She moved out on her own a month before she graduated."

"Not quite on her own," I said. "She lives with her boy-friend."

"Dung Nguyen? We got his name from Susan. Is there anything we ought to know about that relationship?"

"It's pretty much over," I said. "They've been fighting a lot lately. Dung's going to take this hard, though, so break it to him gently."

The detective left, and a doctor came into the room to give us the results of the CAT scan.

"It doesn't look good," he said. "Kaitlyn's head wounds are massive. One bullet struck her cheek, and another entered her temple. We've placed her on life support, and if she survives the next forty-eight hours, we might want to consider surgery to relieve the intracranial pressure. Aside from that, there isn't much more we can do for her."

"Is she in pain?" Don asked him.

"I'd like to believe not."

"If she survives, will she ever be well?" I asked.

"It's possible, but not probable, that she'll regain consciousness," the doctor said. "Miracles do happen, and we never totally rule them out. The one thing I can tell you with certainty, though, is that if she does live she will never again be Kaitlyn as you knew her. Too much of her brain is gone for that to be possible."

"What should we pray for?" I asked him.

"I don't know what to tell you."

The future rolled out before me like a thin gray carpet—days, months, years spent taking care of Kait's body, an empty shell with the kernel of awareness removed from it. I experienced an unforgivable moment of self-pity. For the rest of my life I would be cast in the role of caretaker—bathing, diapering, spoon-feeding, exercising a vegetable. Unable to work, to travel, to visit my out-of-state children and grandchildren, I would live out the rest of my days with Kait's body as my jailer.

"I can do that," I said.

Don turned to stare at me.

"I can do that," I repeated, and amazingly I meant it. There were plenty of people with heavier burdens to carry.

My love for Kait wasn't based upon her level of intelligence; with or without a brain she would always be my daughter.

"It's time to tell the boys now," Don said firmly. This time I gave him no argument.

We called our older son first. At twenty-eight Brett was still a swinging single with a party-boy life-style who sported a single earring and a three-inch ponytail. Although it was two A.M., we didn't expect him to be asleep and were not surprised to find that his line was busy. After several attempts to reach him, during which we continued to get a busy signal, we decided he was probably entertaining a girl and had taken the receiver off the hook. Since he lived only blocks from the hospital, we drove over to get him.

When we pulled up in front of the house Brett shared with two other bachelors, we found him standing in the driveway.

"How badly is she hurt?" he demanded, getting into the car.

"It's bad," Don said. "Very bad. How did you know?"

"I had a call from a girl named Susan," Brett said. "She said the police had been over at her place questioning her. They wouldn't tell her what happened, but from the kinds of things they were asking her, she thought Kait must have been in an accident. She tried to call you, and when she didn't get an answer, she decided to try the only other Arquette in the phone book. I thought you'd be headed over here, so I came out to wait for you. If you hadn't turned up soon, I was going to start checking out hospitals."

"She wasn't in a wreck," Don said. "She was shot."

"Kait was *shot*!" Brett exclaimed incredulously. "You mean in a holdup?"

"We don't know what happened," Don said. "All we

know is she's critical. Now, let's get Donnie, so we can get back to the hospital."

Donnie, our twenty-one-year-old, had recently moved into his own apartment. We phoned him from Brett's and drove over to pick him up. When he saw the headlights of our car turning in through the gate, he started to run toward us across the parking lot, his mane of wheat-colored hair flying out behind him.

I got out of the car and held out my arms, and he threw himself into them.

"I'm so *mad*!" he sobbed. "I'm so *mad*! It's just not *fair*! Kait's so *nice*! Why would anybody hurt *Kait*?"

"It wasn't on purpose," I said. "It has to have been an accident. Some crazy idiot was playing around with a gun."

I got into the backseat with him and tried to haul all six feet one of him into my lap, rocking him back and forth as if he were a baby and I was the Mighty Mother with magical powers who could kiss away hurts and make everything right for everybody. I felt his tears on my neck and longed to cry with him, but everything inside me had turned to stone.

Back at the hospital we were taken up to the intensive-care trauma ward to which Kait had now been transferred. She lay motionless on the bed, encased in a network of wires and tubes that connected her body to machines that blinked and beeped like monsters in a *Star Trek* movie. A screen over the bed displayed wavering lines that we assumed had important significance, but none of us had enough courage to ask what they indicated.

I went down to the lounge to put through calls to our two older daughters. I first called Kerry, who lived in Dallas with her husband, Ken, and their two little girls. Our son-in-law answered the phone, so I gave him the news first. By the time he handed the receiver over to Kerry, she had overheard enough to begin to brace for what was coming.

"Kait's been shot," I said. "I think you should come."

"Shot *dead*?" Kerry asked, too stunned to show emotion.

"She's alive," I said, "but I think you'd better come soon, honey."

Then I called Robin in Florida. I'd saved that call for last because I dreaded it so much. Despite a sixteen-year age difference the oldest and youngest of our children had always been exceptionally close. Robin lived by herself and had no one to give her emotional support as Kerry did. I hated to give her the news when she was alone, but I didn't feel I could wait to call her at work. To my relief she managed to hold herself together and said she would make arrangements to come immediately.

When I got back to Kait's room, I found that Dung had arrived and was standing next to her bed, seemingly in shock.

"It's all my fault," he muttered under his breath.

"No," said Brett, who was extremely fond of Kait's boyfriend. He put a comforting arm around the younger man's shoulders. "So you guys had a fight, that doesn't make you responsible for what happened. You couldn't have prevented this, even if you'd been with her."

"It's all my fault," Dung insisted, pulling away from him. He crossed to the window and pressed his face against the glass, staring out at the dark silhouettes of the mountains that were rapidly taking form against a lightening sky. I went over to stand beside him, and we watched the clouds in the east turn peach—then gold—then puffy and white against a backdrop of blue. The rain was over, and the day was going to be beautiful.

I remember that long, strange day as a series of vignettes,

an assortment of images closer to dreams than reality. The shooting made the morning news shows, and friends began to turn up at the hospital. Susan Smith arrived and stood weeping in the hallway; I know we talked, but I can't remember what we said to each other. A group of Kait's coworkers at Pier One Imports trooped in with a get-well bouquet, and Kait's best friend, Laura, and her boyfriend and mother came also. There wasn't much conversation, but we were grateful for the emotional support of people who cared about us. One friend brought a sack of quarters so we could make calls from the pay phone. Another, assuming correctly that none of us had eaten, came with milk shakes. A neighbor we hardly knew volunteered to go over to our house to take care of the pets.

Kerry flew in from Dallas, and a friend picked her up at the airport and brought her to the hospital. Robin called to report that she had not been able to get the early flight she had tried for but would arrive that evening. She said to tell Kait to hang on until she got there.

One nurse told us that even though Kait was comatose it was possible she might be soothed by familiar voices.

"I know this sounds crazy," she said, "but there are people who have come out of comas and been able to report everything that happened in their hospital room while they were seemingly unconscious. They've said they were out of their bodies, floating near the ceiling, looking down and taking in everything."

Robin was a professional singer and songwriter. Knowing her voice was the one Kait would be most likely to react to, we put a cassette of her lullabies on a tape recorder and played it over and over throughout the day.

I sat by the bed and held Kait's broad, strong hand—so unlike my own hand, so unlike the long, slender hands of her sisters—and told her, "Robin is coming. Robin's on her way. You can't leave yet, you have to wait around for Robin." I watched the lines on the monitor, hoping to see some change in the sequence of patterns, but they stayed the same. Feeling foolish for doing so, I glanced self-consciously up at the ceiling, but if Kait's spirit was there, it wasn't in evidence.

The media descended upon us, and the hospital spokes-woman suggested that we hold a press conference so we wouldn't have to talk to reporters individually. A friend taped the television interview and gave us a copy. Don and I are shown seated at a conference table, holding hands and staring, glassy eyed, into the camera lens, as we struggle to answer a barrage of questions.

"No, we don't know who did this. It can only have been an accident."

"What is she like? She's pretty and funny and smart. She wants to be a doctor."

"No, she doesn't do drugs. No, she doesn't drink. No, she wasn't coming home from a party. No, she didn't have any old boyfriends who were mad at her; she's been dating only one person for a year and a half."

The one question that really registered with me didn't make it onto television and wasn't quoted in the papers. Just as the conference was ending, one reporter demanded, "Didn't you think it was dangerous to let a blond girl drive a red car in a city filled with Mexicans?"

"Of course not," I told her. "That *can't* have been the reason for this."

When we returned to the trauma ward, Dung was waiting at the elevator.

"Hurry!" he told us frantically. "Something's happening with Kait!"

We set off at a run down the hall, and when we reached Kait's room we found that it was crowded with doctors and Kerry was standing out in the corridor.

"The lines on the monitor suddenly started jumping all over," she told us. "I screamed for a nurse, and she sounded a Code Blue. They think the sudden acceleration in her heartbeat may have been caused by a massive hemorrhage in her brain."

Eventually the doctors filed out, and we were allowed in the room again. The lines on the monitor had now flattened out, and Kait's heartbeat appeared to have stabilized.

People from the organ donor program arrived to ask if we would consider donating Kait's organs for transplant. As a contributing editor for *Woman's Day* I had recently written an article about a woman who had given a kidney to her critically ill husband. Kait had responded to the story by getting a donor card. We agreed to donate her organs, grateful that she had spared us that painful decision.

We decided we needed to start spelling each other at the hospital, so Kerry and Dung kept a vigil at Kait's bedside, while the rest of us went home for a couple of hours' sleep. Don and our sons and I walked out into the parking lot to be confronted by a spectacular sunset. The heavens were blazing crimson and orange and gold, while a cloud-banked pathway of light fell straight to the earth like a stairway leading into the heart of the sun.

Kait will never see a sunset again, I thought, but Donnie surprised me by saying, "Look what a welcome they're giving her!" He had never shown any interest in organized religion, and I had not even realized he believed in an after-life.

Back at the house Don and I lay down to try to nap, but the phone kept ringing, and we were afraid to ignore it in

case it was a call from the hospital. After an hour we gave up
and decided to go back. Friends had been leaving food at
the house all day, and we loaded up a tray of casseroles to
take back with us.

This time, when we got off the elevator, it was Kerry who
was waiting.

"I've been trying to decide whether to call you or just
wait," she said.

"Then it's over?" I asked.

"Yes, Mother, I think it's over. That hemorrhage flooded
the brain stem. They think she's brain dead."

We stood in silence, waiting for a formal announcement.
Eventually a doctor emerged from Kait's room and told
us, "We have to make some final tests before it's official, but
there isn't much doubt but that she's gone."

One by one we went in to say our good-byes. I kissed
Kait's cheek, and it was warm to my lips. When I placed my
hand on her chest and felt it rise and fall to the steady
rhythm of the respirator, it was hard to believe that she
wasn't alive.

"Sleep well, my baby," I whispered. "Go with God."

We all made phone calls. First, we called Brett and Donnie and told them to come back to the hospital. Kerry called
Ken. I called my brother in San Francisco. Don called his
three brothers in Michigan and Ohio. Dung wanted to use
the phone, and I told him there was another at the end of
the hall.

We met again with the organ-donor people to sign papers.

"You can't take her yet," I told them. "You have to wait
until her oldest sister gets here. Her plane's due in at midnight."

"I don't know if that will be possible," one woman said

doubtfully. "The heart and lung recipient is already on his way. His parents are driving him down from Santa Fe."

"If you move her before Robin gets here, you can't have her organs," I said.

By now Kait's brothers had arrived and were standing in the corridor, weeping and hugging Kerry.

Dung stood a little way apart with his face to the wall. I went over and turned him toward me and put my arms around him.

"Why don't we call a friend to be with you?" I suggested, thinking he would want to be with someone who spoke his native language.

"I have no friends," he said brokenly.

I smoothed back the glossy black hair that Kait had so loved and caught a whiff of the cologne she had given him for Christmas.

"Then stay with us," I said. "We'll all be together to-night."

We took the food we'd brought over into a private consultation room and tried to force it down. Then our sons and Dung went back to our house, while Kerry drove with Don and me to the airport to meet Robin's plane and take her to the hospital.

Kait was still there, but obviously on borrowed time, as the transplant surgeon was pacing impatiently up and down the hall outside her room.

"So, I've got me another heart!" he said triumphantly when Robin went in to tell her sister good-bye.

"Yes," I told him, "you've got you another heart."

Robin stayed in the room fifteen minutes, while the doctor continued to pace and glance at his watch. When she emerged at last, she was pale, but composed.

"I didn't know a bullet could make such a big hole," she said.

"You don't mean they've taken off the bandages!" I exclaimed in horror.

"There was a bandage around the top of her head," Robin said. "The hole in the side of her face was the one that wasn't covered."

"Oh, honey!" I started to move toward her to take her in my arms, but she had already turned and was striding down the hall.

"I'm okay," she called back over her shoulder. "Don't worry about it."

When we were finally all assembled back at the house, I was struck by such a wave of exhaustion that, after organizing the sleeping arrangements, it was all I could do to stagger upstairs to our bedroom. I fell onto the bed fully clothed, and before long Don came up and lay down next to me. We slept the night as heavily as if we had been drugged, holding on to each other like survivors of a shipwreck, attempting to keep afloat in an ocean of darkness.

Even so, I was up at dawn to check on the children. Brett and Dung had bedded down in the family room, but both the sofa and love seat were now unoccupied, so I continued on down the hall to the room at the end.

Dung wasn't there, but our four older children were in Kait's oversized water bed, tumbled together like a litter of puppies in a basket.

But there ought to be five, I thought. Why aren't there five of them? One of the children is missing!

"It's the baby," I murmured inanely. "Something's happened to the baby."

I was too much in shock to ask the obvious question, "Who could have murdered our daughter?"

3

The day that began like a surrealistic nightmare continued on that way. We staggered around like zombies—bumping into each other, dropping things, making lists of things that needed to be done and then losing the lists—dependent upon kindhearted friends to guide and direct us.

The first of those friends to arrive on that terrible morning was a recent widow who knew firsthand how the grief process worked. She took one look at our faces, realized we were dysfunctional, and loaded us into her car to go shopping for a cemetery plot. Other friends took over our telephone, answered the doorbell, kept records of people who brought food and flowers, and offered to house out-of-town relatives who came for the funeral.

Kait's murder received extensive coverage by the media. Both our morning and evening papers ran banner headlines —HONOR STUDENT DIES FOLLOWING CAR SHOOTING and BRIGHT FUTURE OF SHINING TEEN DIES IN GUNSHOTS—with Kait's smiling senior picture prominently featured. Television cameramen materialized on our doorstep, targeting in on Kerry in particular. A former hostess for the *P.M. Magazine New Mexico* television show, she was well remembered in Albuquerque, and reporters threatened to trample each other down as they competed for interviews.

The police respected our grief and did not contact us. Like everyone else we learned the facts about the shooting by reading the newspapers:

Albuquerque Journal, July 18, 1989:

Eighteen-year-old Kaitlyn Arquette died Monday night of two gunshot wounds to the head. She was discovered in her car at about eleven P.M. Sunday by police officers investigating what they thought was a routine car accident on Lomas near Broadway NE, said Albuquerque police spokeswoman Mary Molina Mescall.

Mescall said someone apparently had pulled up alongside Kaitlyn's car as it was moving and fired three gunshots through the side window. Two bullets struck her head. The car went out of control, veered, and struck a telephone pole.

Kaitlyn, a University of New Mexico student who recently graduated with honors from Highland High School, had been returning home from dinner with a girlfriend.

Police, late Monday, had no witnesses, no suspects, no weapon, and no explanation for what appeared to be a random shooting.

Albuquerque Tribune, July 18, 1989:

The national test scores arrived on Monday. As expected, Kaitlyn Arquette had passed "with flying colors."

Teacher Jo Colvard tried to call the 1989 Highland High School graduate with the good news, but there was no answer.

Arquette was shot in the head Sunday night as she drove home from having dinner with a girlfriend.

The eighteen-year-old student whose mother writes critically acclaimed teen books under the name Lois Duncan died Monday night at University Hospital.

Police have no leads in the shooting.

"When these things happen you say, 'That person was probably involved in drugs,'" said Arquette's sister, Kerry, of Dallas. "Not Kait. She was a straight arrow. She worked throughout her senior year and still held down shining grades."

Kerry said her parents, Don and Lois Arquette, were "doing as well as could be expected—lousy."

Colvard, the Highland teacher, called the shooting "a freak thing, especially after those other traffic things."

There followed a list of fatalities that had occurred during physical conflicts over traffic disputes.

Don and I read the articles aloud to each other and tried to make sense of their contents. To us the terms *freak* and *random* seemed inappropriate for Kait's shooting. They implied that her death had been caused by an act of nature, like being struck by lightning or crushed in an earthquake.

"None of the deaths they're comparing it to were 'random,'" Don commented as he read through the list. "All of them occurred during fights. Kait didn't have enough time to get involved in a confrontation. She was shot just minutes after leaving Susan's house."

"And *three* shots were fired," I added. "That's too many for an accident. And the shots weren't fired from the sidewalk. Somebody pulled up next to her and fired from a vehicle." Although an empty Budweiser can had been found in the gutter next to Kait's car, the autopsy had turned up no trace of alcohol in her blood, and the fingerprint on the can had not been hers.

The fact that our world was a madhouse actually proved a blessing, because it allowed us more time to accept the unacceptable. The telephone rang nonstop; people streamed in and out of the house bringing casseroles and condolences; Don's brothers and their wives flew in from Ohio and Michigan, and my brother arrived from California. There were planes to meet, Kait's obituary to compose, a minister with whom to confer, and a funeral to orchestrate.

At one point I realized it had been hours since I'd seen my daughters. I went in search of them and found them in Kait's room, deep in conversation on the bed.

"What's going on?" I asked. "Is this a private conference?"

"Actually, no," Robin said. "We need to talk to you. Will you, please, come in and shut the door?"

I did as she asked and joined them on the bed.

"Mother, Robin and I have been talking and—well—the thing is, we don't think Dung should be staying with us right now," Kerry said.

"Why not?" I asked in surprise.

"There are some things that are bothering us. We have no idea who shot Kait, but we do know she was having problems with Dung. They were having a lot of fights, and she was looking for a new roommate."

"That's hardly a reason to suspect him of murder!" I exclaimed.

Robin and Kerry exchanged glances.

"There's something else," Robin said. "Something's come to light that makes us believe Dung's not the simple, honest person you seem to think he is. Tell her, Kerry."

"A friend of Kait's told me something weird," Kerry said.

"She said that back last summer Kait confided to her that Dung was involved in some sort of car-wreck scam in California. Kait didn't understand how the thing was set up, but Dung went out to L.A. with a bunch of his friends, and they staged wrecks in rental cars. Kait said she thought each of the guys was paid two thousand dollars."

"Who told you that?" I demanded.

"I don't remember her name. It was one of the girls Kait worked with."

"I can't believe anybody would be such a troublemaker," I said. "Especially at a time like this, when we're so vulnerable."

"But what if it's true?" Kerry persisted. "I know Dung's been over here a lot, but what do we really know about him? When Ken and I came for Christmas, there he was, scarfing down turkey like one of the family, but nobody ever told us where Kait came up with him."

I tried to recall exactly what Kait had told me.

"She met him at a coffeehouse across from the university. He hasn't had an easy life. He was one of the boat kids, and from what Kait told me, his journey to America was horrendous. He lived for a while in California, then he and his best friend, An, decided to move here. He has a sister who owns an import shop in Orange County. He and Kait stayed with her in March when they went out to do Disneyland during Kait's spring break. The rest of his family is still in Vietnam."

"How has he been getting his money?" Robin asked. "I know there was a long time there when he was out of a job, and the only reason he finally got one was because Kait wouldn't let him move in with her unless he was working."

"He did have a job when Kait first met him, but he got fired," I said. "Work isn't easy to find when you don't speak

the language well. Kait told us the Vietnamese take care of
their own. Dung's sister in California was sending him
money."

"Well, under the circumstances, I'm not comfortable
with it, and I think we should have him stay someplace else
until we figure this out," Robin said.

"You're being ridiculous," I told her. "And it's a moot
point, anyway. He's not here now, and he wasn't here when
we got up this morning. Brett said one of his friends came
by at dawn and picked him up."

"I thought Dung said he didn't *have* any friends," Kerry
said.

"Then, maybe an *acquaintance* picked him up. For God's
sake, girls, your sister is *dead!* Can't you find something
better to do than backbite her boyfriend?"

I got up off the bed and stalked out of the room, leaving
my daughters staring after me with stricken faces, and three
minutes later I couldn't remember why I was angry with
them.

The rest of the day went by in a meaningless blur as I
moved in a daze from one pressing demand to another. It
was late afternoon when I dropped down on the couch in
the family room and looked up to find Dung standing over
me.

"I got problems, Mom," he said in his awkward English.
"I just come back from the apartment. The manager
changed the locks so I can't get in. Will you tell him it's
okay that I still be sleeping there?"

"Of course," I said. "I can't believe he's done such a
thing. He had no right to change the locks. All your things
and Kait's are in that apartment, and I know Kait paid the
rent through the end of the month."

"I want to sleep in our bed again," Dung said softly. "I want to smell her cologne on the pillow like roses."

"Don't worry, I'll call and take care of things," I told him. "It's just a silly mistake that can be easily corrected."

I looked up the number of the Alvarado Square Apartments and put through a call to the manager.

"I'm Kait Arquette's mother," I said. "Her boyfriend tells me you've locked him out of their apartment. I'm calling to give our permission for him to continue living there until the lease runs out."

"I know this is a tough time for you, Mrs. Arquette," the manager said apologetically. "The last thing I want to do is to create more problems for you, but there's no way I'm going to let Mr. Nguyen back in there."

"Why not?" I asked in bewilderment.

"Because that guy's bad news. I rented the place to your daughter, not to him. Kait was a real sweet kid—both my wife and I thought the world of her—but Nguyen and his cronies are something else again. I don't know what was going on in that apartment, but there were times when Kait would come running over to our place, begging to sleep on our couch because she was scared. She asked me to change the locks to keep the guys out."

I couldn't believe what I was hearing.

"Did you do it?"

"Yes, but they smashed a window and got in that way. Another time she locked Nguyen out, and he kicked in the door. Now I've changed the locks again, and if Nguyen tries to tamper with them or goes in through a window or does any more damage to our property, I'll have him arrested. He can come get his things, if one of you people comes with him, but I don't want him in there unsupervised, and I don't want his friends there. If you'll come to the office, I'll give your family the new key."

"All right," I said, too shaken to put up an argument. "One of my sons will be over there in a few minutes."

I hung up the phone and turned to Dung, who was standing expectantly at my elbow.

"It's okay?" he asked. "Did he say he will let me go home now?"

"I'm sorry," I said. "It's more complicated than I thought. The manager tells me your name isn't on the lease, so legally you don't have the right to keep on living there."

"But I hear you say it's okay!"

"I guess I don't have the authority to make that decision," I said. "I didn't sign the lease, either, you know, only Kait. I think it has something to do with liability insurance. I'm sure we can straighten it out, but it won't be today. For now, it would be best if you stayed with one of your friends."

I asked Brett to take Dung over to collect his belongings and to drive him from there to wherever he wanted to go. When Brett came back I asked him what Dung had taken from the apartment.

"Not much," he told me. "Just clothes and some pictures of Kait. I brought back Kait's VCR. I thought we could use it to record the television news shows."

"Her VCR doesn't work."

"What makes you think that?"

"When Daddy and I went to San Diego in May, I asked Kait to record the final episode of *L.A. Law* for us. It turned out she couldn't do it because her VCR wasn't working, so she had to ask a friend to record it for us." I paused. "How is Dung holding up? I haven't really seen him today."

"He's a wreck," Brett said. "He loved Kait a lot. Last

night, he woke up crying and couldn't stop. He told me he'd had a horrible dream about Kait. She said she was lost in the dark and was scared and wanted him to save her. Just for the record, I think you're treating him rotten. First he gets kicked out of his apartment, and now *you* kick him out. Why won't you let him stay here until he finds a new place?"

"I have my reasons," I said. "We'll talk about them later."

That time didn't come until dinner was over that evening and visiting relatives had been dispersed to the homes of friends. Donnie had gone back to sleep at his own apartment, but I called the rest of the family together in the living room.

"We have things to discuss that are very disturbing," I told them, and repeated my conversation with Kait's apartment manager.

After I'd finished there was a long moment of silence.

It was Brett who broke it.

"That's a bunch of bullshit!" he exploded. "That guy must have something against Orientals! He fed you that crap as an excuse to force Dung out!"

"Wait, there's more," I said, and motioned to Kerry, who repeated the story Kait's friend had told her that morning.

Brett reacted with disbelief, but Don turned pale.

"My God!" he exclaimed. "Could that have been what that call was about?"

"What call?"

"It was back when Kait and Dung went to Disneyland. A rental car company called to say there'd been an accident. Kait had rented a car out there, and since the credit card was in our name, they had to inform us, even though the accident was a minor one. I didn't think much about it at the time, because they told me nobody was hurt and the wreck was just a fender-bender. After the kids got back, I asked Kait about it, and she said Dung and An went out for fast food, and somebody rear-ended them. They were covered by insurance, and the accident wasn't Dung's fault, so they took the car back to the agency and were given another one."

"Even if Dung was involved in some sort of scam—I don't buy into that, but let's just say he was—why would that be a reason to murder Kait?" Brett demanded.

"It wasn't just Dung who was involved in the wrecks," Kerry said.

"So you're accusing his friends of killing her? Kerry, get *real*! If that were the case, why not knock her off in California? Why wait until four months later and do it in Albuquerque?"

"Back in March, Kait wasn't breaking up with Dung," Don said. "As long as the two of them were solid, she wasn't a threat."

"Forget it!" Brett snapped. "I know Dung better than any of you. There's no way he could have killed Kait!"

"Of course Dung didn't kill her," I said. "But *somebody* did. Those shots didn't come out of nowhere. If Kait wasn't afraid of Dung's friends, why did she run to the manager asking for protection? Why did she have the locks changed? Why, on the night she was shot, was she so insistent that if Dung called looking for her we weren't to tell him where she was?"

"I'm going to call the police," Don said, getting to his feet.

"You're all crazy!" Brett insisted angrily. "It was a *random shooting*!"

"We'll let the police decide if we're crazy," Don said. "To

me, two well-placed shots in the head don't add up to 'random.' "

It was hours later before any of us got to bed that night. Detective Steve Gallegos and another detective from the Homicide Department came to our home and spent several hours listening to us. They were interested and attentive and took copious notes.

When they were getting ready to leave, Detective Gallegos told us that if we thought of anything else he wanted us to call him. Day or night or on weekends, he could be reached on his pager.

"Your input is very important to us," he said.

I locked that statement in my mind and didn't forget it, despite the fact that we never heard it again.

4

The day of the funeral was filled with frenetic activity. Friends poured in and out of our house all morning, bringing paper plates, covered dishes, and ice chests filled with soft drinks for the wake. It seemed as if every few minutes another delivery truck arrived with plants and floral arrangements. A woman from down the street came to mow our lawn and wouldn't even let us reciprocate with a glass of iced tea. Two of Kait's girlfriends, weeping as they worked, vacuumed carpets, dusted furniture, and hung clean towels in the bathrooms.

Family members went in different directions. Don sat out on the patio and conversed with his brothers, whom he hadn't seen in two years, while their wives kept order in the kitchen. Robin went to Kait's apartment and transferred her favorite songs from records onto a cassette that could be played before the service. Brett, who worked as a sound engineer for a rock band, drove to the funeral home to test their public address system. Donnie, discovering he had outgrown his only dress shirt, went to the mall to buy another. Kerry spent much of the morning on the phone with her husband, who had remained in Dallas with their two-year-old and four-year-old.

I drifted about the house, detached and disoriented, feeling strangely disconnected from all the activity. Occasionally I found myself glancing around for Kait, half expecting her to come popping out of her bedroom to ask me to iron a blouse or help fix her hair.

The previous day's sunshine had given way to rain again, and a slow-paced drizzle continued throughout the morning. Then it stopped, and a rainbow appeared above our house, so unbelievably vivid that neighbors called us out to look at it. I recalled how, four years earlier, when we were returning from my father's memorial service in Florida, a rainbow had suddenly formed outside the window of our plane, creating such a startling effect that Don had taken a picture of it. Kait had insisted it was her grandfather's way of telling us not to grieve for him, but I couldn't accept that fantasy, then or now. The dead were dead, they didn't send messages through rainbows.

When Robin returned from the apartment, she brought a frilly white dress for Kait to be buried in and some items she had found on her bedside table. Among those was a copy of my most recent teenage suspense novel, *Don't Look Behind You.* The story was about a family who informed on an interstate drug ring and were forced into hiding in the Federal Witness Security Program. Kait had been my model for the heroine, April, a headstrong teenager who considered herself invulnerable. I opened the book and saw the inscription I had written in it—*For Kait, my own special 'April.' Always be sure to look behind you, honey!* Horrified, I ripped the page from the book, crumpled it into a ball, and hurled it into the wastebasket.

I remember little about the funeral except that the chapel was jammed and people who couldn't find seats were standing in the aisles. Kait's body, now hollow as a broken piñata, was in a closed casket. The minister began the service with the Twenty-third Psalm, and I tried to picture Kait lying down in a "green pasture" or wading in the "still waters" of some heavenly pond, but the Shadow of Death was too dark for such visions to be of comfort.

After the service, people filed past us in an endless stream to offer condolences—neighbors, Don's colleagues from Sandia Laboratories, my writer friends, and the friends of our surviving children. Kait's classmates, some dating back to grammar-school days, embraced us and wept, as did many of her teachers and a large contingent of children she used to baby-sit. Dung came through the line, his arms filled with yellow roses, which he tenderly laid on the coffin. His friend, An Le, walked beside him with his hand on his shoulder.

Photographers from the media stood massed on the lawn as we left the chapel for the cemetery. The coverage made the evening television news shows, and the following day both papers ran lengthy articles:

Albuquerque Tribune, July 21, 1989:

Robin Arquette sang her little sister to sleep for the last time Thursday as her friends and family said their farewells.

Kaitlyn Arquette, a teenager who "had high hopes and great dreams for the future," was buried after a standing-room-only memorial service.

Dr. Harry Vanderpool, a retired minister who spoke at the service, played a tape made by Robin Arquette, who produces audio- and videocassettes for children. The tape was also played while Kaitlyn lay in a coma in University Hospital.

"For the last time her beloved sister will sing her to sleep," Vanderpool said. Mourners sobbed aloud as the soft voice of Robin Arquette filled the chapel at the end of the service.

"According to those who knew her best, Kait lived all of her life, however brief," Vanderpool said. "Kait had high hopes and great dreams for the future. She made the most of the eighteen years she had; she didn't stand around and watch the world go by."

He praised the attitude of the Arquette family, who, he said, had chosen to "celebrate the life she had rather than focusing on her death." He also talked about how her death had created life, for the family donated six of her organs, which went to five donor recipients.

Among those who grieved at the service was Dung Nguyen, who had dated Arquette for two years. They were living together at the time she was killed.

"I don't know what I am going to do with my life," he said, tears welling up in his eyes.

Albuquerque Journal, July 21, 1989:

Albuquerque police are searching for a beige Volkswagen they say may be connected to the shooting of Kaitlyn Arquette.

"We are not saying the Volkswagen is a suspect's car," Police Chief Sam Baca said during a news conference. "It was seen around the area around the time of the shooting."

The Volkswagen does not have an engine cover and has a loud muffler, Baca said.

During the news conference Ray Baca, a deputy chief administrative officer for public safety, said the general public is not in danger.

Chief Baca agreed, adding, "The overall crime rate is down. Most drive-by shootings are gang related."

Outside the funeral Kaitlyn's girlfriends filed past

Dung Nguyen, Kaitlyn's boyfriend, hugging and consoling him.

Later, he talked about the night Kaitlyn was killed.

"I waited and waited for her," Nguyen said. "But she never came home. Nobody called me. Nobody told me nothing. Then police came to the door. They started searching my house and going through everything. They asked my whereabouts that night. They asked if I had a gun. I kept asking them, 'What happened? What happened?' When they told me, I went down there, but she had already been taken to the hospital. I went to the hospital. It wasn't like her, it didn't look like her. I didn't know who she was."

The Albuquerque police were represented by six motorcycle officers, more than the usual escort complement.

"It is important that we come out and show that we do care," said traffic Sgt. John B. Gallegos. "This is just sad."

Many of the people who attended the funeral came back to the house afterward. Our living room and family room were filled to overflowing, and the crowd spilled out onto the back patio and into the yard beyond. A group of Brett's friends congregated on the front lawn, reminiscing about Kait, the tagalong kid sister, who had both delighted and exasperated them.

One young father wept unashamedly.

"Kait's diaper was the first I ever changed!" he sobbed.

Another friend recalled the boys' efforts to ditch Kait when she was a preschooler.

"She was always trailing after us, wanting to do everything we did," he remembered. "We kept trying to wear her out so she'd go take a nap."

Brett's eighth-grade girlfriend arrived with a wooden bowl painted to look like a watermelon. She'd recovered it from Pier One Imports where Kait had put it on layaway, intending to make it a Christmas present for Kerry.

People who knew Kait at different stages of her life remembered her differently. To an elderly neighbor she was the little girl who hung a May basket on her doorknob and hid giggling in the bushes. A junior-high classmate recalled her attempts to learn to water-ski—"She'd get up and fall down and get up and fall down, but she'd never give up." A nurse recounted how Kait worked one summer as a hospital volunteer and took a special interest in the elderly invalids —"After her shift was over, she'd still be there, sitting by the bedside of some shriveled old woman, listening to her rambling stories about her childhood."

Those perceptions of Kait, superimposed one upon another, supported the image of the "shining teen" portrayed in the newspapers. But there had been a second side of Kait. The toddler who trailed adoringly after her brothers was the same miniature daredevil who yanked her small hand out of mine and leapt into the deep end of a motel swimming pool. The twelve-year-old at the lake had not only water-skied with her friends in the bright summer sunshine, she had sneaked out at midnight to take the boat and explore the other side of the lake in the moonlight. And the teenager who had listened so patiently to the reminiscences of sweet old ladies was the same young woman who picked up hitchhikers because they looked "interesting" and coaxed them to tell her stories about their experiences on the road.

Despite a high level of intelligence Kait was lacking in judgment. In *Don't Look Behind You* there was a scene in which an FBI agent snapped at April, "You've still got a lot of growing up to do. You're a nice enough kid, but you're part of the Cinemax generation. You can't believe real life stories don't always have happy endings." I had made that same statement so often to Kait that, when she saw it on paper, she burst out laughing.

"Mother, you're something else! Won't you *ever* lighten up?"

That peal of laughter was still so vivid in my memory that for one crazy instant I thought I was actually hearing it. Then reality took over, and the sound was replaced by the voices of friends and relatives and the clink of glasses and silverware as Kait's farewell party accelerated.

The odors of food and coffee were making me nauseous, and afraid I was going to be sick, I set down my untouched plate and headed for the stairs.

Don and I passed each other in the hall and he stopped to give me a hug.

"You're doing great," he said approvingly. "I haven't seen a tear yet."

Don is by nature an introvert who keeps a tight rein on his emotions, while I let mine hang out for everyone to see. Oddly, though, it had been Don who wept in the hospital, while I had sat by Kait's bedside, dry-eyed and stoic, breathing in time with the respirator as I waited for her to die.

I was still working hard to keep my emotions in check. But how could I deny the guilt I felt? "I shouldn't have let her go out that night," I said.

"There was no way you could have known—"

"I felt it coming. I had a premonition that something was going to happen to her."

"That's ridiculous," Don said.

"I did have a *feeling*, though. If only I had listened to it!"

I went upstairs and stretched out on our king-size bed, while the wake churned on without me in the house below. Eventually Dung, who had been out in the front yard with Brett, came in and searched the house until he found me.

"Mom," he said, "I need pills to make me go to sleep tonight."

"I'm afraid I don't have any," I said. "I don't use sleeping pills."

"You got pills from the doctor for me that time I got my tooth pulled. Those made me sleep."

"Those weren't sedatives," I said. "They were very strong pain medicine. They're not meant to be used as sleeping pills."

"They made me sleep all night and all day," Dung insisted with surprising stubbornness. "They worked real good. They made me sleep and not dream."

"That was a side effect," I said. "It wasn't the reason for your taking them. Let me see if I can find you something less potent."

I went into the bathroom and rummaged through the medicine cabinet until I located a small vial of Valium. I started to hand it over to him and then thought better of it and shook two tablets onto his palm.

"Take one of these now and the other before you go to bed," I said. "You can have more tomorrow if you need them, but I want to make very sure you don't take too many."

"I'll be careful," Dung said. "I want to take home the bottle."

"No," I told him. "I'm keeping the bottle here."

Later I was glad that I made that decision. Dung didn't turn up at our house at all the next day, and it wasn't until

My father's rainbow, 1985

Kait's rainbow, 1989

that evening that we learned where he was. According to a television news report he had been taken to the hospital by ambulance after stabbing himself in the stomach with a four-inch knife.

5

We later received a more detailed account of Dung's suicide attempt from Detective Gallegos. This is his statement as it appears in the police report:

> Writer was contacted by APD Communications, who informed writer that Dung Nguyen was at Kirtland Air Force Base, and attempted suicide by stabbing himself. . . . Dung Nguyen was staying with Khanh Pham in his dorm.
>
> Also staying in the room was An Le, another friend of Dung Nguyen. . . . Khanh Pham and An Le left the room during the evening . . . and went to a restaurant to eat. Dung Nguyen did not want to go and stayed alone in the room, saying he was tired and wanted to sleep. When Khanh Pham and An Le returned to the room about an hour later, they noticed Dung Nguyen asleep in the bottom bunk bed. A short time later An Le and Khanh Pham went to bed and heard Dung Nguyen moaning. An Le and Khanh Pham got up, turned the light on, and found blood on the sheets of the bottom bunk bed where Dung Nguyen was lying.
>
> Upon further investigation they found a folding-type knife in the bed and a stab wound to Nguyen's stomach area. An Le and Khanh Pham then contacted medical personnel from the base. Arriving to the dorm were medical technicians . . . who treated Dung Nguyen on the scene and

then had him transported to the University of New Mexico Hospital.

Writer then interviewed both An Le and Khanh Pham separately. . . . Both suspects told writer that Dung Nguyen was very depressed and upset over the death of the victim. Dung Nguyen also felt that the victim's family and the police suspected him of committing the homicide, so he decided to commit suicide.

Writer transported An Le to the main police station, where writer interviewed him. An Le told writer that he liked the victim very much and has no idea who is responsible for killing victim. An Le went on to say that Dung Nguyen and victim have had arguments in the past, but was not aware of any serious problems between the couple. An Le also said he has no knowledge of Dung Nguyen staging any traffic accidents in California.

When we called the hospital to check on Dung's status we were told he was in satisfactory condition following abdominal surgery.

Kerry flew home the next morning, and Robin was scheduled to do so also, but she canceled her plane reservation. Then she disappeared for an hour and when she returned she called Don and me into the family room and told us to sit down.

"You'd better get braced, because you're not going to like this," she said. "I've been to see a psychic."

"You've *what*?" I exclaimed. "Are you crazy?"

"I wanted to know why Dung tried to kill himself," said Robin. "Was it grief or guilt? I felt that we had to know. Remember my friend Maritza? Well, we got to talking after the funeral, and she told me about this psychic named Betty Muench. She said this woman's a 'channel' who does automatic writing, and after Maritza's father died, Betty was able to contact him and find out all kinds of things. I couldn't see anything to lose by trying to reach Kait that way."

"How much did she charge you?" Don asked suspiciously.

"She doesn't charge for murders."

"I don't want to hear this," I said.

"Well, you're going to have to. First, though, I need to explain how Betty Muench works. I expected something exotic, but it wasn't; she's just an ordinary woman with an electric typewriter. She didn't want me to tell her about our suspicions. She just told me I could ask three questions and she'd type out the answers."

Robin started to read from the transcript:

BETTY MUENCH, 7/22/89

QUESTION: WHAT MAY I KNOW ABOUT THE WELL-BEING OF KAITLYN AT THIS TIME AND DOES SHE HAVE A MESSAGE FOR ME?

ANSWER: There will be this energy that will be as of the impact of a sword. This will be the energy of Kaitlyn and then there will be this energy of the one Robin which will be like a large chevron at the bottom of this image. There is in this chevron that which will seem like the expeditor. This will seem to allow that Robin will be informed and she will come to know what Kaitlyn is feeling at this time.

There will first be this sense of an impact and then a moving around of the head and an uplifting that will hold her to this left side, above which there will be a light at the point of an opening. The light is like a veil behind which Kaitlyn waits. There is a sense of her pushing back this light like a drape, and then she will appear in an agitated state and very angry. She is angry that she will not have been more angry before and that she will have been influenced by certain people to withhold her anger and that then she will have known that anger in the body might have saved her anger now.

There will be in this time this which she would say to Robin, and it will have to do with the manner in which she will have had information and did not understand the information and yet she will have handed it over and that will have been what will have stirred up a controversy. There is a sense in this then that this information will have been given over to someone who will have misinterpreted it. There will have been the sense that she knew more than she really did. There will be this which she will have done *just that night* and she will have held back this information so as to serve and assist another and indeed it did not and she will therefore have been used and betrayed, thus her anger now.

This is the intrigue in this event and she will know now the series of the events in which she will not fully have realized her involvement. There will have been in Kaitlyn this desire to give benefits and trust to those who will not have understood her ways and the methods of this system. There is this desire in her now to correct the anger and to allow that there will come the unfoldment so that all may know the series of events and her involvement in them.

There is much more to be revealed, and it will be for Robin to have a certain contact in a place in which there will be a certain advantage in the media system. There is this one who will be as a kind of undercover person and there will be in this then the ultimate knowing in this case. There is in Kaitlyn this energy which she has still which desires to be transferred with the knowledge she *will* have, and that can come to Robin in a transference of energy and truth. In this time this will show an affinity beyond sisterhood. They are more than sisters, they are soul twins, and this cannot be erased.

Robin paused to give us a chance to digest this.

"Betty said soul twins have spent many lifetimes together in lots of different relationships. For instance, there might have been a time when Kait and I were mother and daughter, and another when we were best friends, and another when we were cousins. Between those lifetimes we were together in the spirit world. Betty said Kait's still easy to reach, because she hasn't moved into that realm yet, which isn't unusual when people die violently. The soul goes into shock and won't accept what's happened. It keeps turning back and trying to continue to communicate."

When she saw Don and I were too shaken to comment, she continued reading:

QUESTION: WHAT MAY WE KNOW ABOUT KAIT'S RELATIONSHIP WITH DUNG—ABOUT HIS SITUATION AT THIS TIME AND OUR CONTINUING RELATIONSHIP TO HIM—ABOUT HIS INVOLVEMENT IN KAITLYN'S DEATH, IF ANY, AND ABOUT THE INVOLVEMENT OF HIS COMMUNITY, IF ANY?

ANSWER: There will be this which will show that Dung will be in a sense the instigator of this event. There will have been anger in this time and it will have stemmed from something very serious about which Kaitlyn will have been trying to urge him to take a certain action.

He will have resisted strongly, and he will have been encouraged in his resistance by others who will also have been involved. He will have tried to gain some assistance from her by telling her certain things, and she will have urged him to do other than he expected of her, and then he felt betrayed by her. There will have been this matter of right and wrong and it will have involved also the matter of cross cultures. Kaitlyn will have had something to do with an action not truly against the law but which interfered with the law, and there will have been much fear all around.

"That might be referring to Kait's letting Dung use your credit card to rent the car," Robin said.

"She did more than that," Don said.

We both turned to stare at him.

"I wasn't going to tell you this unless I had to, but yesterday when I was over at Kait's apartment draining her aquarium, Detective Gallegos stopped by. He said he'd followed up on the things we'd told him and had gotten the accident report from California. Kait didn't just rent the car for Dung, she was the driver."

"She wouldn't have done that!" I exclaimed.

"I don't think so either," Robin said. "She'd have covered for Dung, but she wouldn't have crashed a car. Besides, the reading explicitly says she didn't 'break' the law, what she did was something that 'interfered' with it."

"That's quibbling," Don said.

"The subtleties are important, Daddy."

She continued with the reading:

ANSWER: There is in the relationship of Kaitlyn and Dung that which shows that both feel a sense of betrayal. A sense of hiding information will still be prevalent, but the ultimate cause will not be that serious. Thus the anger in Kaitlyn again and the confusion in Dung as to why this had to happen over something which was not that serious.

The situation in which Dung now finds himself is born out of misunderstanding and confusion. It is not as if he will have been the one to do this, but he will seem to know who did it. There is something he is in denial of at this time, and he will know that this does not involve something so serious that this should have happened. His remorse is around that, not some prior argument or disagreement with Kaitlyn. There is a golden light on the right side of his head, which has to do with a form of devotion involved in this relationship. Yet his love for Kaitlyn was also tied to his image of his manhood, and some of the misunderstanding stems from that source.

"Betty says mature, well-balanced people have a spiritual light or 'aura' that's centered above their heads," Robin said. "Dung's aura is off to the right like the aura of a child. Betty said men like that have a little-boy quality that appeals to insecure young girls and maternal women because it makes them feel needed. Kait felt that she was the superior one in their relationship, and Dung resented that."

She continued to read:

ANSWER: There will be this that pushes the head down, and it will be as if there is a shame in this now for the Vietnamese community and there will be this which has many of them fearful and closed off. Many of them do not understand what took place, and thus then the potential for more misunderstanding is evident.

There will be those in that community who would want to come forth and tell what they know, and this would have to do with the feminine aspect. There will be this energy which they, the feminine aspect, will seem to deplore, and they will still feel that they are in the grips of their old world energy pattern. There will be this which is causing much fear and this fear blocks any cooperation. There is in this beginning evidence of something which was *not done right* and in which there will have been the instigating energy in all this. There will have been that which will be known by only a few and this event grew out of all proportions and thus one more reason why this is all so elusive.

"Betty says there are at least one or two women who know what happened," Robin said. "They liked Kait and want to come forward, but they're afraid to do it because the men in their lives don't want them to."

QUESTION: WHAT DO WE, THE FAMILY, NEED TO KNOW IN ORDER TO BEST UNDERSTAND THIS SITUATION?

ANSWER: It is for this family to take pity on Dung. There is this they can do in so far as his relationship to Kaitlyn is concerned and that is to forgive him his guilt in her name. She has not yet indicated any forgiveness from the other side, but if she were injured and in her body she would have forgiven him already and so must the family.

There is anger and sorrow in Kaitlyn and this cannot be denied. This need not be taken on by the family.

There will be ways in which to make contact with her in which then each member of the family can assist her to change her pattern so that she will be able to release this personality of Kaitlyn and seek to move within the dimension in which she is to reside now. There will be assistance on the other side, but for now the assistance still must come from the family in the manner of not giving in to anger and sorrow. For now this deed is done and it will be that there will come the unveiling of the truth. It will be found out, and then all the more sorrow at the seeming uselessness of it.

Kaitlyn was one who walked the cutting edge of life, but her purpose is not lost in this time. If it were it would lend all the more to the sorrow. She will have been true to herself to the end and this she also must accept. She will not have been one to give false encouragement to another, and thus then this event out of misunderstanding of cross cultures, and thus then the knowing of how there has to be much understanding in the mixing of cultures. The hidden fears and resentments come forth even in the love affairs of the people such as in this event, and thus it will take time to unravel.

For this time the family can seek to light white candles in the name of Kaitlyn to bring light to her spirit and to allow the hierarchy to find her and guide her within. They can proceed in the manner they have, with gentle understanding, so that the remorse is more quickly laid aside and they will pursue their own purposes in that time.

Robin folded the transcript and laid it aside. Neither Don nor I said anything.

After a moment Robin said hesitantly, "Betty thinks what this means is that we have to forgive Dung in Kait's name for anything he did that might have led to her death."

"We're supposed to forgive him when we don't even know what he did?"

"And it has to be done in Kait's name or it doesn't count."

To my astonishment Don got up and went to the telephone.

"I'm going to find out if Dung can have visitors," he said. He dialed and spoke for a moment to several different people and then held the phone out to me. "Nobody gets to see him unless he okays it. He doesn't want to see me, but I've got him on the line."

I took the receiver from his hand.

"Dung?" I said. "This is Mom. I'm worried about you, and I want to come see you. Would that be all right?"

Dung started to cry.

"Mom, come," he said. "Please, I want you to come!"

We drove to the hospital, left the car in the now familiar parking lot, and took the elevator up to one of the higher floors. To our relief we didn't have to face the trauma ward. Dung was in a private room, and the door stood open to the corridor. From the doorway we could see him in bed, lying on his back with his eyes closed. An Oriental orderly seated next to him was engrossed in a paperback.

"Are you sure you want to go through with this?" Don asked me, having second thoughts about what we'd gotten ourselves into.

"I want to go through with it."

"Remember, it has to be in Kait's name," Robin reminded me.

"I can do that," I said, and went into the room.

Dung sensed my presence immediately and opened his eyes.

I bent over the bed, and he put his arms around my neck. He was obviously heavily sedated.

"I'd like to talk to him in private, please," I told the orderly.

"I'm not supposed to leave him alone," he said.

"He won't be alone, and I promise I won't stay long."

"It's okay," Dung told him groggily. "This is my girl-friend's mom."

The orderly left reluctantly and positioned himself just outside the door where he could keep a watchful eye on what was going on. I sat down in the chair he had vacated and took both Dung's hands. I knew what I had to say, but I didn't know how to word it. The language barrier made a full explanation impossible, so I tried to reduce the message to its simplest form.

"Brett told me you had a dream about Kait," I said. "I had one too. In my dream Kait said she forgives you. She didn't explain what she meant, but she said you'd know. She wants you to know you're forgiven and she still loves you."

Dung's eyes were huge in his pallid face. For a moment I didn't think he had understood me.

"You do know what she means?" I asked, and he slowly nodded. I decided to go one step further. "Kait isn't in heaven yet. She can't get to God. You know what she said in your dream about being alone in the dark? She can't get out of the dark unless you tell us what happened to her."

"I didn't shoot her," Dung murmured, tightening his grip on my hands.

"I know you didn't," I said, "but you know who did. You have to decide if you love her enough to tell."

He sighed and closed his eyes.

"I know. I am deciding."

"I'm going to have to go now," I said. It was evident further questioning would be useless. "Don't hurt yourself again. It won't bring Kait back or make anything better for anybody."

I left the room, and the orderly returned to his station. Don and Robin were waiting outside in the hall for me.

"Did you do it?" Robin asked.

"I forgave him for Kait, not for us."

"Do you think he knows who killed her?"

"He knows something," I said.

I phoned Gallegos and told him what Dung had said to me.

"That's almost as good as a confession!" he exclaimed.

When Dung was discharged from the hospital, Gallegos asked me to come down to the police station to interrogate him. I asked if there was anything I needed to know to help me ask the right things, and he said, "No, just do the same thing you did in the hospital." He put me in a room by myself and sent Dung into me. This time he denied knowing anything about what had happened to Kait.

The next day a sister and brother-in-law came to get him and drove him back to recuperate in their home in Kansas City.

We had not been aware this set of relatives existed.

6

Grief progresses through predictable stages. The first of these is shock. Shock produces a blessed state of numbness that works like an anesthetic to dull the senses and make it possible for people to bear the unbearable.

I remained in that stupefied state quite a while. One month after Kait's death I still had not cried. On the surface I appeared to be functioning amazingly well. Friends marveled aloud at my "strength and resilience." I continued to perform my routine duties in a normal way, doing the grocery shopping, fixing meals, running laundry, handling business correspondence, taking the pets to the vet for their inoculations, although I routinely made a detour to avoid the intersection where Kait had been shot.

What I could not do was write fiction. My energy level was so low that I couldn't be creative, and my mind would not focus on anything other than Kait.

So, instead of writing suspense novels, I wrote unrhymed poetry that had no meaning for anyone but myself:

August 20:

I cannot look at it fully, straight on. Not yet.
Tiny sideways glances are all I can manage.

One image at a time. Her graduation picture.
Her record collection. Her lonely black cat.
A schedule of college classes spanning the next four
years.
The posters from her bedroom—a jigsaw puzzle, half
completed—
A romance novel with a bookmark at page 57.
A brown rose, carefully pressed—who gave her the
rose?
Lyrics from a love song, copied in a notebook.
Did somebody sing that song to her, or was she
waiting,
Dreaming away the years until she would hear it?

I cannot look at it fully, straight on. Not yet.
I focus on each small chore as a separate entity.
Clothes are sent to a cousin in California.
Teddy bears go to the children she used to baby-sit.
A metal vase for flowers is installed at the grave site
So she may have roses in summer, poinsettias in winter.
Maybe in the springtime I can bring her a hyacinth
If the frost doesn't kill it.

If I widen my eyes to take in the whole of it
I will shatter like aluminum foil in a microwave,
Taking the house down with me.

I was worried about the fact that I was experiencing
blackouts of memory. When I thought back upon Kait's
funeral service the only part I could remember was the
minister's recitation of the Twenty-third Psalm, and I had
no memory at all of the interment afterward. I had trouble
recalling the content of conversations and had totally
blocked out the name of the homicide detective who had
accompanied Detective Gallegos to our home on the night
we called him over to tell him about the car wrecks.

Fearing that something important was going to slip past me, I started keeping notes about everything that happened. Then every night after dinner I would sit down at my office computer and transcribe that day's journal entries onto a disc.

Don and I divided up the after-death chores. He retrieved the Ford from the holding yard where APD had had it towed and sold it to a salvage company.

"I probably could have fixed it," he said. "The engine wasn't damaged, but I didn't think I could stomach cleaning the inside of it."

For my part I dealt with the paperwork. The desk in Kait's apartment held a lot of correspondence, including letters to Dung written in Vietnamese and postmarked Orange County. I loaded everything into a sack and took it down to the police station. I told Detective Gallegos that if the police couldn't get the letters translated, we would have it done ourselves, but he said a man on the force was fluent in Vietnamese and would translate the letters and give us copies.

"Would you believe there are people in this department who still insist your daughter's shooting was 'random'!" he said, shaking his head incredulously.

"Was it?" I asked.

"Of course not."

On August 20 I was scheduled to fly to Craigville, Massachusetts, to teach for a week at the Cape Cod Writers Conference. I had committed to this engagement a year in advance, and the people who registered for the conference had done so under the assumption that I would be teaching the juvenile writing course.

When I was offered the job, I'd accepted enthusiastically, delighted by the idea of a week on the coast. I grew up on the Florida beaches, and as fond as I was of New Mexico, I was never as happy anywhere as I was by the water. Now, however, I dreaded the thought of leaving Albuquerque. I couldn't imagine going anywhere without Don, and the effort involved in teaching a class was overwhelming to me.

Still, I had made the commitment, and I felt I had to honor it.

The day before I left, a psychologist friend brought over a paperback.

"I think this might interest you," she said. "The author, Dr. Brian Weiss, is chairman of psychiatry at the Mount Sinai Medical Center in Miami. It took a lot of courage for him to write this. He's really putting his professional reputation on the line."

I thanked her for the book and, having no time to read it right then, absentmindedly stuck it in my purse.

My plane arrived at the Hyannis Airport in the late afternoon, and I rented a car to drive the short distance to Craigville. Even when I'm on top of things, I have no sense of direction, and since few of the charming, winding little roads had street signs, I soon became hopelessly lost.

As evening came on, the fog rolled in to intensify my problems, and by the time I finally stumbled upon the conference center I was so worn out and disgusted with myself that I was totally disoriented. I signed in at the office, drove to the inn where I was to stay, dumped my suitcase in my room, and went out to get dinner. When I got back I discovered that I'd lost my room key.

By then the office was closed, and I was stuck for the night. Registration wasn't due to start until the following day, and the inn was virtually unoccupied. I wandered about the vacant lobby in search of a place to lie down, but nothing looked promising. Eventually, I ended up in a chair on a porch overlooking the marshes. Beyond this ocean of grass the real ocean sighed and sucked at the sand of the Craigville Beach, and the sound of the waves took me back to my childhood in Florida. Insects buzzed and hurled hard, small bodies against the screen, and crickets chirped in the brush, and frogs emitted shrill mating cries from the ponds. Although there was no sound of traffic or of human voices, I had never experienced a more disquieting night.

At first I attempted to sleep, but the chair was uncomfortable, and I couldn't stretch out in it. Finally, I turned on the light and, remembering the book in my purse, took it out and opened it to the preface.

Despite my exhaustion I read straight through the night. *Many Lives, Many Masters* was the true account of how Dr. Weiss, at that time a traditional psychotherapist, placed a woman named Catherine under hypnosis to regress her back to childhood in an attempt to discover the cause of her recurring anxiety attacks. The book was based upon audiotapes of Catherine's therapy sessions. Dr. Weiss regressed his patient farther than he had intended, and when she began to recall the traumas that had produced her phobias, she described them as having taken place in a previous lifetime. Not only was she able to describe in detail an entire sequence of former lives, she channeled messages from "the space between lives," more traditionally known as "heaven," that contained intimate information about Weiss's deceased father and infant son.

Under hypnosis Catherine described seven planes of spiritual existence, one of which sounded like the plane Betty Muench had described to Robin. According to Catherine souls on that interim plane can use their psychic abilities to make contact with people who are still in their physical bodies. She said that souls are permitted access to that plane if their lives ended so abruptly that agreements were left unfulfilled and mysteries unsolved. It was not a plane on which anyone stayed indefinitely.

By the time I had finished the book, the sky was growing light in the east, and the first pale strips of pink were beginning to appear over the dark stretches of marshland. I got up from my chair and stretched, sore and stiff from sitting so long in a cramped position. Then I left the inn and walked down the access road to the beach. At this time of morning it was deserted and offered the same sense of peace and solitude I had known as a child when I had walked alone, mile after mile along the water's edge, planning my life. I had never had the slightest doubt about what direction it would take. I had always known I was going to be a writer. By the age of seven I was filling notebooks with poetry, and by thirteen I was selling fiction to national magazines.

The other thing I was sure about was the number of children I would have. Even when I was a child myself, I felt them tugging at my heart, trying to get my attention and make sure I was aware of them. After graduating from high school I entered Duke University, but at the end of my freshman year I dropped out to get married. It seemed like a waste of time to spend four years writing term papers when I could be bringing those five children into the world.

The marriage wasn't a good one, and after nine years my husband and I were divorced. Twenty-eight and the mother of three, I had no college degree or job experience, and the only way I could support the children and myself was by writing. I started grinding out stories for the women's magazines, and by the time I met and married Don four years later, I was earning a pretty good living at it.

The fact that we married was a surprise to everyone who

knew us, and the fact that our marriage was successful was even more of one. Don was an electrical engineer at Sandia National Laboratories, a major Department of Energy laboratory for weapons research and development. A bachelor in his mid-thirties, he appeared to have nothing in common with a divorcée with three children, and his friends predicted that my rattling typewriter, haphazard housekeeping, and rambunctious, strong-willed youngsters would drive him up the walls. My own friends, on the other hand, were certain that I would soon be bored stiff by a quiet, self-contained scientist who weighed each sentence before he spoke and whose IQ and education so outdistanced mine that we would probably have nothing to talk about except the weather.

Surprisingly, though, we turned out to be a good balance for each other. I added color to Don's life, and he stabilized mine. He put up with my idiosyncrasies with quiet good humor, and after my previous marriage to a silver-tongued philanderer, I was very happy to have a responsible, trustworthy husband who expressed his love by actions rather than words. Don encouraged me to go back to school to earn a college degree, to accept a part-time teaching position with the journalism department, and to make trips out of state to give lectures and do book signings. Unlike the husbands of some of my friends, who felt threatened when their wives' careers started to accelerate, he was unconditionally supportive of all my endeavors and seemed prouder of my accomplishments than he was of his own.

Don adopted my first three children, and we had Donnie and Kait as soon as we could. It was while I was pregnant with Kait that I wrote *A Gift of Magic*, a book about a twelve-year-old girl with extrasensory perception. This was a major milestone in my career, because it was the first of my books to involve psychic phenomena, a subject teenage readers embraced with delight. That book was so successful, I followed it with others. It wasn't that I believed in the subjects I was writing about—telepathy, precognition, astral projection—but they provided good story material for exciting novels, and a little dose of fantasy never hurt anybody.

Morning fell upon Craigville Beach like a benediction. The breeze was fresh in my face, and the seagulls screamed with thin, sharp voices, and the sun burst into the sky like a globe of gold. I took off my shoes and walked barefoot along the waterline, unable to tear my mind from the book I had just read. I'd never given much thought to the subject of reincarnation. The concept was strange, but I didn't find it unacceptable. If in our Father's house there were "many mansions," it was conceivable that some of the lesser of those might be our planet and that some of us might be required to reside there more than once before we became worthy of better accommodations. But I had a problem with the idea of any sort of afterlife. I wanted to believe in one, but it strained credibility. How could a mind exist apart from a brain, and what good was a soul if it didn't come equipped with a mind? New Testament references to eternal life were encouraging, but I'd done enough reading to know that the Bible had been revised and reinterpreted over many centuries and by now had become as much the word of man as the word of God. The fact that physical matter was continually being recycled made it logical to assume that mental energy was also, but it seemed reasonable that this energy would flow into some huge, universal melting pot in which individual personalities were lost.

Yet, Weiss's patient appeared to have retained her personality when she spoke from the "realm between lifetimes." And Betty Muench had presented Kait as we knew her. Her description of her "in an agitated state and very angry" had been so powerful and so in keeping with what Kait's reaction would be if tricked or betrayed that it had sent us barreling down to the hospital in a frenzy. And the rest of the reading had been just as strong and convincing. I had even started lighting white candles to "bring light to Kait's spirit," a ritual totally foreign to my upbringing.

Did Kait still exist? And, if so, was she able to communicate? I stared up at the sky, now clear and blue with the morning mists burned out of it, and impulsively shouted, "It's Mother! Can you hear me?"

The only response was from the gulls who had been circling overhead and now came swooping down expecting a handout. I didn't hear the sound of Kait's voice in the wind, and God didn't send me an angel with words on a tablet. None of the patches of sea grass burst into flame.

"Are you all right, lady?" somebody asked nervously.

I turned to find a gray-haired woman in Bermuda shorts, clutching a basket of seashells and regarding me as if afraid I would start frothing at the mouth.

"I was rehearsing for a play," I improvised hastily.

Feeling as ridiculous as I knew I must look, I hurriedly made my way back to the conference center and got into my car to go get breakfast. On the floor mat next to the accelerator I discovered my room key. Since I now had access to my room, I decided I would be doing my colleagues a favor if I took a shower and changed clothes before heading for the dining hall.

The office was now open, and as I passed it, the manager called out to me, "Ms. Duncan, you have a message! Your son Donnie called and wants you to call back. He said it's not an emergency, but it's very important."

The hands of my watch showed eight-thirty, and it was two hours earlier in Albuquerque. Donnie didn't have to be at work until eight A.M., and I couldn't imagine why he was up so early.

I went to the phone in the lobby and dialed his number. He answered on the first ring.

"I just saw Kait!" His voice was shaking with excitement. "I was just waking up, and I had this thing like a dream, but it *wasn't* a dream, it was real! We were having a party like the wake with hundreds of friends there. I was standing in the entrance hall, greeting people as they came in, when all of a sudden I turned and saw Kait standing next to me. Her hair was back to one length, and she looked just wonderful! I said, 'You can't be here, Kait, because you're dead!' That didn't seem to bother her. She just smiled and said, 'Everything's cool. Let's party and have fun.'"

"What a wonderful dream!" I exclaimed.

"It wasn't a dream," Donnie said impatiently. "Kait was *there*! She was *real*! I could even *smell* her! I thought you'd want to know that she's doing much better now."

He rode on that wave of elation for a very long time. To the rest of the family he seemed to be standing in a pool of ethereal light that prevented him from suffering in the same way we did.

I'm ashamed to say there were times when we very much resented this.

7

By the time I returned from Cape Cod the numbness had worn off, and the second stage of grief had taken over with a vengeance. The agony of my loss was so intense that there were times when I literally did not think I could survive it.

I longed to believe that Donnie's dream had been a visitation, but common sense told me otherwise. I knew how realistic grief dreams could be, because I'd experienced one myself after the death of my mother. Mother and I had been sitting in beach chairs in front of my parents' cabana, watching the sun go down over the Gulf of Mexico, when I suddenly realized that what I was experiencing wasn't possible.

"This is a dream," I told her. "You can't be here! You're dead!"

"I'm not dead to *you*," Mother said, leaning over to kiss me. "I'll never be dead to *you*, dear, because I'm *part* of you."

I had never before or since experienced a dream that involved so many of the senses. I could feel the salt breeze on my face and smell the faint film of perspiration on my mother's upper lip as she kissed me. That dream made such an impression that seventeen years later, when I wrote

Locked in Time, I included a similar scene between my heroine, Nore, and her deceased mother.

While Donnie was finding comfort in his "visitation," I looked for Kait in the cemetery. When I was alone there with nobody else within earshot, I would stand at her grave and *keen*. The first time I did this I didn't even know I was doing it. I was standing, stoic as ever, holding a chrysanthemum plant, when I became aware of an inhuman wail like the howl of an animal that has lost its cub, and when I glanced around for the source I discovered it was coming from my throat. The hideous sound continued until exhaustion overwhelmed me, and I sank down onto the grass, pressed my cheek against the grave marker, and let loose the flood of tears I'd held back for so long.

Then I got up, blew my nose, and drove to the grocery store.

And so the routine of family life continued. Don went off each morning to Sandia Laboratories. Donnie, who had moved back in with us when his roommates took off for other places, spent his workdays running a printing press and his evenings out with his friends.

I did everything I normally did except write.

Kait's mail was forwarded to us, and, as her bills came in, I paid them and closed out her credit accounts. One day, as I was writing a check to cover her final phone bill, I noticed that three calls to Santa Ana, California, had been made from her apartment only moments after she was pronounced brain dead. Two one-minute calls were to 714-664-1021; one two-minute call was to 714-662-3362.

I sat staring at the numbers, trying to make sense out of what I was seeing. Those calls had been made when Dung was with us at the hospital and the apartment should have been unoccupied. The thought crossed my mind that he

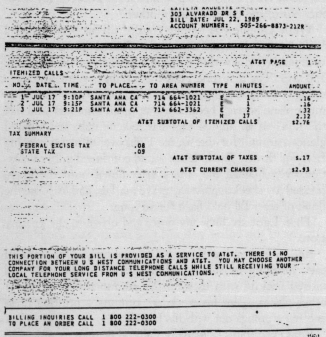

					AT&T PAGE	1

ITEMIZED CALLS

NO.	DATE	TIME	TO PLACE	TO AREA NUMBER	TYPE	MINUTES	AMOUNT
1	JUL 17	9:10P	SANTA ANA CA	714 664-1021	E	1	.16
2	JUL 17	9:15P	SANTA ANA CA	714 664-1021	E	1	.16
3	JUL 17	9:21P	SANTA ANA CA	714 662-3362	E	2	.32
					N	17	2.12
			AT&T SUBTOTAL OF ITEMIZED CALLS				$2.76

TAX SUMMARY

FEDERAL EXCISE TAX	.08		
STATE TAX	.09		
		AT&T SUBTOTAL OF TAXES	$.17
		AT&T CURRENT CHARGES	$2.93

THIS PORTION OF YOUR BILL IS PROVIDED AS A SERVICE TO AT&T. THERE IS NO
CONNECTION BETWEEN U S WEST COMMUNICATIONS AND AT&T. YOU MAY CHOOSE ANOTHER
COMPANY FOR YOUR LONG DISTANCE TELEPHONE CALLS WHILE STILL RECEIVING YOUR
LOCAL TELEPHONE SERVICE FROM U S WEST COMMUNICATIONS.

BILLING INQUIRIES CALL 1 800 222-0300
TO PLACE AN ORDER CALL 1 800 222-0300

See reverse for information on this bill.

Kait's final phone bill, hand-delivered to APD

might have phoned from the hospital and had the calls charged to their home number, but then I remembered that I hadn't been able to do that. When I phoned our out-of-state daughters and tried to bill our home number, the operator had told me that there had to be someone at our house to okay the charges, so I'd made the calls collect.

Who had been in the apartment the night Kait died? And who in Santa Ana had been informed of her death?

The second number seemed vaguely familiar, and when I checked our personal phone directory, I found it scribbled there in my own handwriting. When Kait had asked our permission to go with Dung to California, Don and I agreed on condition that she leave us the phone number of Dung's sister so we could reach her in an emergency.

The number she gave us was 714-662-3362.

I went to the police station in person to give the bill to Gallegos.

"The second number is Dung's sister's," I told him.

There was a moment of awkward silence while he processed that statement.

"Dung doesn't have a sister in California," he said finally.

"But Kait *told* us—" I started to object.

"She put one over on you," Gallegos said, not without sympathy. "That was before you knew they were sexually involved. Kait knew you wouldn't let her stay in a motel with her boyfriend, so she came up with this fictional 'sister' so you'd think they were staying with Dung's relatives."

"But this is the sister who sent him money every month!"

"I'm sorry, Mrs. Arquette, but she doesn't exist."

I couldn't believe that Kait had invented this person. It wasn't that she was incapable of lying; like any teenager, she could be sneaky. Don and I had grounded her on several occasions when, resentful of what she considered my "over-

protective mothering," she had fabricated stories to get
more freedom. But this time I didn't believe that this was
the case. She had been making casual references to this
sister for well over a year before the idea of a trip to Disneyland ever came up. It seemed more likely that *Dung* had lied
to *Kait* about the sister. But, in that case, who was it who
kept sending him money from California? Only so many car
wrecks could be lucratively faked. What had the man been
living on if he wasn't getting support checks?

There seemed to be nothing to be gained by pressing the
issue.

"Can you find out who these numbers belong to?" I
asked Gallegos.

"No problem," the detective assured me.

"And what about the translations of the Vietnamese letters? They may contain information about illegal activities."

"Those don't really matter now. We're pretty sure the
Vietnamese weren't involved in Kait's murder."

"But, remember, Dung said, 'I am deciding'? You said
that was as good as a confession."

"Dung has an alibi. He was out that night with friends,
the same two guys he was with the night he tried to kill
himself. They dropped him back at his place around ten
P.M."

"Kait wasn't shot until ten forty-five. He could have gone
back out."

"He didn't go back out. They dropped him off, and he
stayed there."

"How do you know?"

"The Vietnamese didn't do this, okay? The case is moving in another direction. We've found a witness to the chase
that led up to the shooting."

"The *chase*!" My breakfast surged up to fill my mouth. The idea that Kait had been terrorized had never occurred to me. I had pictured her cruising down the road with the windows rolled up, humming along with the radio, reliving her nice evening with Susan, when all of a sudden she was no longer thinking about anything.

That comforting illusion was now dispelled as I heard that her last conscious moments had been a nightmare. A truck driver named Eugene Lindquist had been making a delivery that night and had seen Kait chased at high speed by a gold Camaro. She had run a red light in her frantic attempt to escape and made a U-turn at the railroad tracks, but the Camaro had made one also and stayed behind her. Lindquist's window was down, and he heard the driver of the Camaro shout, "You fucking bitch!" with a heavy Mexican accent. The truck driver had continued on to make his delivery, and on his way back had seen police officers and rescue personnel around the area. He had at first assumed that this was the aftermath of a traffic accident, but later, after reading about the shooting in the paper, had decided that what he had seen had been the preface to murder.

"We're going to have him hypnotized," Gallegos told me. "We hope that way he'll be able to come up with more details."

Lindquist was hypnotized twice, once on Friday, September 15, and again on Monday, September 18. Under hypnosis he was able to recall that the fleeing car was a Ford Tempo and the Camaro was an old model low rider with gray primer spots on the right fender and a red-and-white license plate. Although he had not seen the face of the driver, he thought he had dark hair. He'd had a better view of the man in the passenger's seat, who was wearing gray

jeans and tennis shoes and had a rifle between his knees with
the butt on the floorboard.

"What about the beige VW?" I asked Gallegos.

"That was a false lead."

"How can you be sure?"

"Forget the beige VW, it was a gold Camaro. A couple of
Mexicans tried to come on to your daughter, and maybe she
threw them a finger. It made them mad, and they took off
after her to scare her. They were drunk and high and had a
gun in the car, and it went off. It's a terrible thing, but it
happens more often than you'd think."

He told me not to share this new information with anyone other than the family, because if a description of the
Camaro appeared in the newspaper, the killers would immediately get rid of the car.

I phoned Robin in Florida and told her about Lindquist's
testimony.

"It seems that the Vietnamese men may be innocent," I
said. "Gallegos agrees with the rest of the department now.
He thinks it's a random shooting."

"Not everybody in the department thinks that," Robin
said. "I talked with my friend Maritza yesterday. One of the
homicide detectives is a longtime buddy of hers, and he told
her there's just no way Kait's shooting was 'random.' He
said it has the earmarks of a professional hit. Maybe it's time
you went to Betty Muench for a reading."

"There's no reason for that," I said. "You've already done
it."

"But you might get something different from what I did,"
said Robin. "You'd be utilizing a different field of energy
and asking different questions. I only asked about Kait's
relationship with Dung. What I should have done was ask
for a description of her killers."

"I can't go to a psychic," I said.

"Why not?"

"I just can't, that's all. It makes me sick just to think about it."

When Kait was in junior high school, she and a girlfriend had talked me into taking them to a psychic fair. Everything about it had felt like a con to me, and I'd found the commercial aspect of the gathering appalling.

"If you won't go, then I'll have to do it," Robin said. "I used up all my vacation time for the funeral. If I make another trip to Albuquerque, I'll lose my job."

Her recording business had just started turning a profit, and her main source of income was an outside job at a credit bureau.

"That's blackmail," I said accusingly.

"It'll only take an hour."

"All right, I'll do it, but I warn you, it's not going to work." I resented being manipulated into doing something I didn't approve of and was sure that my negative feelings would be counterproductive.

I got out the phone book and looked up "Psychic Mediums" in the yellow pages. There were several listed, but Betty Muench wasn't one of them. I did find her in the white pages, though, and made an appointment. When I identified myself as Kait's mother, she recalled her session with Robin and told me to bring something with me that Kait had been wearing at the time she was shot.

Kait's purse and the plastic jar that contained her cross, watch, and earrings were in the top drawer of my bureau. The earrings were coated with blood, and I was tempted to wash them and then decided against it. After all, the blood was a part of Kait.

My appointment with Betty was for two P.M. On the way

to her house I stopped at a church, went into the chapel, and knelt in a pew near the altar.

This isn't my kind of thing, I told God silently. *If it is Your will that Kait communicate with me, please, help her to do it. And if this whole thing is a farce, don't let me make a fool of myself.*

When I left the church, I was feeling less apprehensive.

The moment I saw Betty Muench, I experienced a bizarre sense of recognition. It wasn't that I had met her before, I had *created* her; she was physically identical to the psychic detective, Anne Summers, in my novel *The Third Eye.* In that book I had described Anne as "unremarkable in appearance. She had a pleasant face, wide-spaced hazel eyes, and a mouth that was a bit too large to synchronize with her other features. Her hair was chestnut color and slightly frosted with gray."

I had written that description five years ago. Now an Anne Summers look-alike greeted me at the door, dressed in slacks and a pullover sweater, and I had the crazy feeling I had scripted the story of my own future.

Betty told me that, although she was a professional channel, she rarely worked on crime cases.

"It's too frustrating," she said. "The Albuquerque police won't accept information from psychics, and it's infuriating when they refuse to follow up on leads. Besides, there's usually so much anger coming from crime victims that it's a depressing experience to channel for them."

She said she'd done the reading for Robin only because she was a friend of Maritza's, but having gotten involved, she felt obligated to finish what she'd started.

Betty's small home office was lined with bookshelves and contained two chairs, a desk, and an electric typewriter. She motioned me into one of the chairs, sat down at the typewriter, and drew some long, slow breaths.

Finally she said, "I'm ready. You can ask your first question now. It seems to work best to start off by asking the deceased how she is and if she has a message for you. After that you can ask her about specifics."

I worded the first of my questions in the way she suggested, and her fingers started to fly across the keyboard. What she appeared to be doing was taking dictation.

QUESTION: WHAT MAY I KNOW ABOUT THE WELL-BEING OF KAITLYN AT THIS TIME AND DOES SHE HAVE A MESSAGE FOR ME?

ANSWER: There will be this initial energy which will feel like a kind of implosion. It will be as if the air is going out and there is this sense of energy over the ears and this will seem to be felt more strongly on the right side than the left. The right side holds the sense of the intellect, and there is now a kind of awareness in this intellect.

"Kaitlyn realizes you're trying to contact her," Betty said.

ANSWER: There will be then a white light which will show through a large keyhole and there is a sense of one peering through as if deciding whether or not to come through it. There will be this energy which is Kaitlyn, and it will show that she will be in this time now very wary and not so trusting.

There is, though, the assistance for her which would be hoped for. There is in this light that which is seemingly protecting her, and it will be that she will seem to open the curtain. There is this energy which will show that she is being guided in her thinking and there is the

desire on her part and *with approval* that she will be able
to convey that she will have known what will have been
happening to her and that there will have been this
which she can now understand but did not understand
at the time of her demise.

"The Deity seems to be encouraging her to respond,"
Betty said. "That's pretty unusual. Have you been praying
about this?"

ANSWER: There will be this that will show that she will
have known that night of one who will have been looking for her, and that one will have had others looking
for her. It will have had to do with some kind of message to be given to her which she did not want to hear.
She will not have wanted to confront a certain situation, and this will have been the end result. There will
be in this then the desire to have this also understood
by others. She will want her killers—more than one—
to come forth, and there will be a time soon in which
they will be exposed, and there will not be any way to
avoid this connection to her case.
    There will be this which will have been known by
her, and she will have known what was about to occur,
and she did not think that this could be as bad as it was.
Thus her trust was misplaced. There will be in this
time for her this kind of mistrust that was not there in
her before. She will now have learned to qualify all
things in her life, and thus her lesson was indeed
learned and her life fulfilled, but she will now be dealing with certain karmic patterns which she alone will
have to deal with. There will be those who will be
caught and exposed, and it will be for this family to

come to see and know what it is that she will have been dealing with in her final day.

It will be for Kaitlyn to allow that there is a certain light around her which is paralleled in this one mother, and this light will be the line on which they can communicate directly. There is still this line open between them. There will be this energy which will allow Kaitlyn to update and renew information as it becomes more clear to her. There will have been in this mother-daughter situation this energy which will have to do with truth and communication, and thus this does not end now. There will have been this work with trust that Kaitlyn will have had and thus she will move again behind her veil and seek to continue to work her own energy. The mother may seek her out in mental thought and make a space by which they can communicate again themselves.

"This seems to imply that when you become more emotionally stabilized and Kait learns how to transmit better, you won't need a go-between to help you communicate," Betty said.

ANSWER: There is an image of a straight line that will seem to come down and then there will be wakes out from either side of it as if to try to show motion. There will be this which seems to move through water, and there will be this which will seem to be moving very fast, and this would have something to do with the energy of one who is leaving, departing, and there is a far and urgency in this as if to leave and not return. A long trip over the water is indicated in this image.

"What does that mean?" I asked.

"I don't have any idea."

QUESTION: WHAT MAY I KNOW ABOUT THE CIRCUMSTANCES OF KAITLYN'S KILLING—ABOUT THE CAR AND ANY PEOPLE INVOLVED?

ANSWER: There is much light within on this. There is a kind of silver plate which will be seen lying down as though upon the hood of a car, and it will seem to have a kind of crisscross over it like some kind of embellishment. This is seen sideways and not straight on as a car might go. This image is transfixed in the head level of Kaitlyn, as if she will have perhaps seen this part of the vehicle just before she will have departed. There will be this that will show a kind of night image of two heads in the front of the vehicle and one short head in the back.

There is this sense of an image which she gets so briefly that it is almost nonreal. This will seem to evoke some sort of recognition in her, and it is as if she is not afraid, someone she will seem to recognize and know. There will be no panic in her at this moment. There will be this that will show this car turning off to the left as if to drive away.

Then there is an image of something which will be like the handle on a plastic brush. It is long with a square at the end. This seems to follow this car out the side, alongside this car moving away with it. This sense of recognition will have to do with something that is long-standing with her and thus no need to question this in her mind, no sense of any need to avoid or evade. Some recognition in this adds to her sense of frustration at her own misplacement of trust.

"The cross isn't a hood ornament," Betty said. "It's like metal stripping on the hood of the car. It's odd that Kait can see it, because she has to be looking down on it. That seems to indicate the car's low to the ground. It's one of those funny cars that bounce up and down a lot."

"You mean, a kit car?" I asked.

"No, I didn't mean that. It's one of those low-slung cars like the Mexican kids drive."

"A low rider?"

"That's it. That's what they call it—a low rider."

QUESTION: WHAT MAY I KNOW AT THIS TIME ABOUT THE ENERGY AND IDENTITY OF THE KILLER, SPECIFICALLY THE PERSON, LOCATION, AND PRESENT SITUATION OF THIS BE-ING?

ANSWER: There is a sense of three people involved and that there will be a kind of triangle and that these will be split up and going in many directions now. There will be this energy which will show that one is going west and one is going south and the other is going northeast. There will be this which will permit the overlay of a kind of triangle and this is some kind of protection by which they function. There is in this an energy of deceit and a different set of values about the meaning of life. There will be this that has not value of life in it. There is a hidden agenda in this and she will have been one to have come into this triangle in such a way that she will not have truly suspected the depth of the deceit. There will be in this then for her a lesson about trust. She will have had much to do in this time and she will have exposed herself at every turn. There will have been in her relationship with these three this which she will have not had a grasp on.

There is in the one going west a sense of going over the waters as if going over the seas. There is in this one going south that which will seem to stop at the border with a fear of entering into this southern nation of Mexico, as one who has a fear of the Mexican energy. There will be in the one going in the third direction, that one who will seem to have the least guilt in all this, a sense of going in the direction of Chicago. He would appear to have a contact there who would lend support, and there is no shame or even knowledge in this one. This one would then be able to involve others innocently again, and this could be perpetuated again.

"In other words, this isn't the end of it," Betty said. "Before this is over, somebody else may be killed."

ANSWER: There is no sense of this having now anything to do with this area of Albuquerque. There has been the elimination of the vehicle, which seems to be going with the one to the south. All are running now, and there is a sense that the one going over the waters is the one who will have the most guilt, and this will bring about the solution which ultimately this family will come to know.

Betty gave me the original copy of the reading and put the carbon in her file. Then she picked up, in turn, each of the items I had brought with me—the jewelry Kait had been wearing and some things from her purse—to see if she could "read" anything from Kait's "energy."

These were the impressions she got from the items:

KAIT'S SUNGLASSES: "These send prickles up my spine. I feel that Kait looked at her killer through these glasses. Since the shooting took place at night, she must have seen her killer on some previous occasion."

KAIT'S EARRINGS: "There's a sense of her head turning quickly from side to side. The earrings swing sharply. There's a last sensation of them having a kind of life of their own."

KAIT'S CROSS: "She falls forward, bending at the waist, and the cross also moves and gives a last sensation as it strikes her chin."

KAIT'S LIPSTICK: "Was there any indication that she was crying that night? Not in her final moments, but before that?"

KAIT'S WATCH: "I get a lot from watches. They absorb a great deal of energy, because people wear their watches all the time, not just on special occasions. Kait looked at this watch over and over that night. The time of nine o'clock was very strong in her mind. There's a sense of her knowing where she was going, a destination she wanted to reach by nine. There's a suggestion of a kind of setup. She will have been seemingly leisurely in her route, and then there is this overtaking and a sense of surprise, as if she expected one of these people to be somewhere else."

KAIT'S GRADUATION PICTURE: "I don't do well with photographs. What I get is vague and symbolic. There's an image of a door opening up partially to see who is there, as if someone is looking at Kaitlyn and does not open the door to her. It's an occurrence that happened that evening, a visit incomplete and information incompleted, a clue she was looking for missing and no cooperation."

"Don't expect the police to accept this," Betty warned me. "If you share it with them, they'll chalk you up as a crackpot. You're going to have enough problems establishing credibility without giving them that ammunition to use against you."

8

By the end of our session I felt certain Betty Muench was no charlatan. If I hadn't been convinced by her obvious sincerity and the fact that she wouldn't let me pay her, the speed with which she typed had allowed no time for composition. As a professional writer I was aware of the need to pause at the end of each sentence to word the next one. Betty had not paused once.

Although it supported the truck driver's statement that the car that chased Kait had been a low rider, the reading seemed to indicate Vietnamese involvement. Twice Betty had made reference to Kait's having recognized her killers, and the fact that one of them had fear of "Mexican energy" made it seem that he couldn't be Hispanic. But, while many of the statements in the reading were insightful, others were bewildering. Why would Kait have consulted her watch throughout the evening with the time "nine o'clock" in her mind, when she didn't leave Susan's until ten forty-five? How could she have had "much to do in this time" and "exposed herself at every turn," when she spent the whole evening with a girlfriend? And the part about someone moving "through water . . . very fast . . . leaving, departing . . . not to return" didn't seem to fit anywhere, especially when it came in response to my question "Does [Kaitlyn] have a message for me?"

I shared the reading with Don with trepidation. But despite his conservative nature he was surprisingly open to it.

"It's all that detail that makes it convincing," he told me.

Donnie, on the other hand, had no interest in reading it; he said he'd seen Kait "alive again," and that was enough for him. I mailed copies of the reading to our daughters, who found it fascinating, but when Kerry tried to discuss it with her husband, he became so upset that it created a rift in their marriage.

"I've never seen Ken so angry about anything," she told me.

Brett's reaction was almost as negative as our son-in-law's.

"It's like going to a witch doctor," he said with disgust. "I can't believe you and Daddy would buy into such a crock."

I phoned Steve Gallegos twice to find out about the numbers on Kait's final phone billing. The first time he told me identification had arrived in the mail that morning, but was "buried in the mess on my desk." The second time he said he had given it to his sergeant. I asked him if he could remember the names, and he couldn't.

In early November I was a keynote speaker at the "Courage to Write for Children" workshop in Santa Fe. Three longtime writer friends from other areas of the country were also on the faculty, and on the final night of the conference, as we lingered over dinner, I brought them up to date on the murder investigation and told them about my visit to Betty.

All three of them took this seriously.

"Have you given that information to the police?" one

friend asked, and I told him that Betty had advised me not to.

"She said they won't act on leads from a psychic," I said.

"Then you need to find some other way of getting it across to them," said a friend from New York state. "What about an anonymous phone call?"

"I couldn't pull it off," I told her. "I've never been good at lying. Besides, Detective Gallegos would recognize my voice."

"Then write them a letter," my third friend suggested. "That would be safe enough. Type it on a borrowed typewriter and misspell a lot of words."

"I could never do that," I said. "I despise anonymous letters."

The truth was, I didn't have enough nerve to play games with the police. I'd seen enough movies to know they had all sorts of sophisticated lab equipment at their disposal and could identify fingerprints on stationery and saliva on envelope flaps. For all I knew, they might even have specially trained dogs who sniffed such letters and identified the writers in lineups.

I was horrified when, several days later, I had a phone call from Sergeant Ruth Lowe of the Homicide Department, telling me she had received an anonymous letter from an informant who seemed to know a lot about the murder. Even worse, she insisted on reading it aloud to me:

KAIT ARQUETTE WAS NOT KILLED IN A RANDOM SHOOTING. SHE KNEW WHO DID IT. THERE WERE THREE OF THEM. AFTER THE SHOOTING THEY SPLIT UP AND WENT IN THREE DIFFERENT DIRECTIONS. ONE WENT TO STAY WITH FRIENDS OUT OF STATE. ONE WENT TO THE WEST COAST. ONE WENT SOUTH

WITH THE CAR AND WAS SUPPOSED TO GET RID OF IT
IN MEXICO, BUT MAYBE HE DIDN'T BECAUSE HE IS
AFRAID OF MEXICANS AND DIDN'T LIKE TO CROSS THE
BORDER, SO MAYBE HE DUMPED IT IN EL PASO OR
SOMEPLACE LIKE THAT. IT WAS NOT A VW LIKE YOU
THINK, IT WAS A LOW RIDER.

Obviously the note had been sent by one of my writer
friends. I didn't know which one, and I didn't want to know,
but I felt as guilty as if I had written it myself. Did Sergeant
Lowe suspect me, and was she trying to trap me? Was it a
criminal act to send an anonymous letter? If I took a lie
detector test, would it prove I hadn't done so, or would
"guilt by association" influence the results?

But Sergeant Lowe sounded friendly and nonaccusatory.
She said she was calling to see if the message made sense to
me.

"Kait's boyfriend went to Kansas City to stay with relatives," I said tentatively. "And the part about the man going
west—if he were one of Dung's friends, he might go there.
Those Vietnamese men have connections in the L.A. area."

"What sort of connections?" Lowe asked.

"That's where they have the car wrecks."

"What car wrecks?"

"The ones they stage to bilk the insurance companies."

As the conversation went on, I began to realize that Sergeant Lowe knew next to nothing about the things we had
told Detective Gallegos. Was she too overburdened to keep
track of the case? Or did people in the department rarely
communicate? When I mentioned the calls that had been
made to Santa Ana, she demanded to know why we hadn't
reported them to Homicide and then seemed surprised to
discover the phone numbers in the case file.

"We need to find out who those numbers belong to," she said.

"I thought that already had been done!"

"I see nothing here to indicate that."

"But Detective Gallegos told me he checked them out! He said he'd received the names and given them to *you*!"

"I don't know anything about these calls," said the sergeant. "They do seem rather suspicious. Maybe the men in the Camaro were Vietnamese, not Hispanic. It was dark, and the truck driver didn't see their faces, and he could have been mistaken about the accent."

I acknowledged that this was a possibility.

"Somebody out there must know who did this," she said.

I agreed that somebody must.

"I bet this letter was written by a friend of Kait's."

Or a friend of Kait's mother's, I amended silently.

Sergeant Lowe asked if I would be willing to appear on TV again to try to "stir up some action." I told her that I would be glad to.

Despite the discomfort I felt about the anonymous letter, it did seem to have had a revitalizing effect upon the investigation. There was an update of the case on the six P.M. news along with an announcement that there was now over $5,000 in the Kate Arquette Crime Stoppers Fund that would be paid for information leading to arrests. Everybody got into the act. Sergeant Lowe, who turned out to be an attractive woman, appeared on television to say, "We have reason to believe there is someone out there with information to share with us." A spokesman for Crime Stoppers added, "This person is probably afraid to come forth with information for fear that what happened to Kaitlyn will happen to him. I want to assure him it won't," and proceeded to explain how Crime Stoppers worked. I appeared

as the mother-of-the-victim, begging that person to come
forward "for our sake, for Kait's sake, and for the sake of all
the people out there who are afraid their own children will
be shot."

The presentation aroused local interest momentarily.
Then the case slid back into the woodwork. I called APD
several more times in an attempt to find out about the
phone numbers, but that information was never available.

That year brought a short, strange autumn with no fall
finery. The leaves must have fallen in the night without
bothering to change color, because one day the trees were
green and the next they were bare. Neighborhood children
scuffed their way through the gutters on their way to the
elementary school at the end of our street, and I watched
from the window, remembering how Kait, at their age, had
loved to play in the leaves.

Dung, now apparently fully recovered from his knife
wound, returned to Albuquerque. I called him at work and
told him we had his belongings stored in our garage and
asked if he wanted to come get them. He told me he did
and had his boss drive him over.

He was polite, but distant, and I had no opportunity to
talk with him alone, but I did stick a letter into one of the
boxes. He was later to give it to the police as evidence of
harassment:

Dear Dung,
Do you remember the dream you had in our den the night Kait
died? I have that same dream every night. In the dream Kait is
crying. She says she is all alone in the dark and can't get into
heaven until we know what happened to her. She says, "You

and Dung have to help me." I love her so much, but I don't know how to help her.

You knew Kait better than anybody. You know the things she did that she didn't want us to know about, and you know which people were mad at her. I know you didn't shoot Kait, because you loved her too much, but I think you are smart enough to find out who did.

If you find out, you won't have to talk to the police. You can write me a letter saying who did it and why, and not sign your name. Or you can phone me, and I will pretend I learned it from somebody else. Or, if you want the reward money, you can call 843-7867 and tell the people at Crime Stoppers. You won't have to give your name to them either. They will deliver money to you at a secret place, and no one will ever know you were the one who phoned them.

I know you never meant for this terrible thing to happen. If you did have anything to do with it, it had to be an accident. I promise I will make sure that nothing bad happens to you, just the way I would if you were one of my sons. But if you love Kait, please, try to find out who did this. She is afraid and alone, and she needs us to help her.

> Love,
> Kait's Mom

Soon after that friends of Donnie's reported seeing Dung with a new white girlfriend, and I realized the groveling letter had been an exercise in futility.

The end of November brought Thanksgiving, the first major holiday since Kait's death. The *Albuquerque Journal* ran an article about the thirty-six-year-old transplant patient who had received her heart and lungs. I had no regrets about our decision to donate her organs; still, it gave me an odd feeling to see a photograph of a man I had never met and know that a heart that had been formed in my womb was beating in his chest.

We made a great effort to have a traditional Thanksgiving. In keeping with family custom Don took responsibility for the turkey, and all day long we kept commenting about how wonderful it smelled cooking. When I went out to the kitchen to make gravy, I found a cold white carcass in the roasting pan. With the stress of the day Don had forgotten to turn on the oven.

By now it had been three months since the Albuquerque Gang Unit had been alerted to the existence of the gold Camaro, and they still had not found it. Since the car's description had not been released to the public, nobody else was on the lookout for it. Kait's murder had long since been replaced in the media by stories of more recent atrocities, and it appeared that the case was now part of the annals of history.

Crime Stoppers was a strong organization in our city, but for people who didn't speak English well, the concept was difficult to assimilate. I decided to put out a simply worded flyer that would explain that tipsters could be paid without revealing their names.

I tried to make it easy to understand:

THERE'S OVER $5,000 REWARD MONEY IN THE KATE ARQUETTE CRIMESTOPPERS FUND!

KATE WAS SHOT TO DEATH SUNDAY, JULY 16, 1989, AT ABOUT 10:30 P.M. ON LOMAS BLVD. NEAR BROADWAY N.E. SHE WAS DRIVING A RED FORD TEMPO. THE GUN

MIGHT HAVE BEEN A SMALL CALIBER RIFLE
OR AN UZI.

CRIMESTOPPERS WILL PAY FOR USEFUL
INFORMATION. YOU WON'T HAVE TO GIVE
YOUR NAME. REWARD MONEY WILL BE
DROPPED OFF IN CASH AT A SECRET COL-
LECTION POINT. NO ONE WILL EVER KNOW
YOU MADE THE CALL.

CALL CRIMESTOPPERS—843-7867

Since some of Kait's Vietnamese acquaintances might not
have known her by name but only as Dung's girlfriend, I
wanted to use a picture of the two of them on the flyer, but
for that I needed a black-and-white print, and the only
photos I had of them together were in color. Then, I remembered the mistake I had made on Kait's eighteenth
birthday. After shooting a full roll of pictures I had been
chagrined to discover that I had carelessly loaded the camera with black-and-white film. Kait was expecting color, and
since Brett had been snapping pictures, too, I didn't even
bother to process the ones I took. That roll of film still sat
on a shelf in my office, and I developed it in my small
darkroom at home. It was too old to be good, and only one
picture turned out, but it was the one I needed—Kait and
Dung stood together, smiling into the camera lens.

I first distributed the flyers by mailing them to gun stores,
pawn shops, movie theaters, video stores, convenience
stores, community centers, shopping malls, soup kitchens,
and Oriental restaurants, and asking the owners to post
them where customers would see them. Then, since Betty
had told us the "female element" was on our side, I sent
them to food stores, launderettes, child-care centers, and all
the Planned Parenthood clinics. After that I visited middle

schools and high schools throughout the city and spoke on
the intercoms to students to ask for their help in getting
flyers into teenage hangouts.

A narcotics agent at a school in an area with a large
Vietnamese population was especially sympathetic. As he
toted boxes of flyers in from the car for me, he told me he'd
never believed Kait's shooting was "random."

"As soon as I saw her boyfriend on television, I said to
myself, 'I bet that guy's got something to do with it,'" he
said. "The Vietnamese gangs in this city are vicious as hell.
They have their own people terrified, but the Vietnamese
community's a world of its own and the people don't squeal
on each other no matter how bad things get. The police
don't know how to deal with that, so they like to pretend
the only gangs here are Black and Hispanic."

The printing shop Donnie worked for offered to print
the flyers at cost, so I was able to get thousands run off.
Friends and neighbors helped distribute them, and I spent
my own days walking the streets with a staple gun, nailing
them to trees and telephone poles.

For the first time in our twenty-three years of marriage,
Don was not supportive.

"You shouldn't be running around with those things," he
told me.

"Why not?" I demanded, hurt and bewildered by his
attitude.

"You're asking for trouble. It could be dangerous."

"Asking for trouble!" I couldn't believe what I was hearing. "What are you afraid of—that I'll be arrested for litter-
ing?"

"Somebody might try to retaliate."

"For putting up flyers?"

"It's one thing to mail them to businesses, but it's another to be out there in person, taping them to walls."

"Why shouldn't I tape them to walls?" I shot back. "I'm Kait's *mother*! And you're her *father*, you ought to be out there helping me! How can you just sit there when we've got a whole city to be covered?"

"I do not 'just sit here,'" Don said with ice in his voice. "I put in a full day at work, and I'm trying my best to get my life back to normal. That's a whole lot healthier than what you're doing. You've gotten obsessed with this crusade. You can't talk about anything else; you're not able to eat; you can't stay awake past eight-thirty; you're totally *losing* it. If you need to see proof, just look at your hands!"

"What's wrong with my hands?" I glanced down at them and was surprised to find them covered with blood. The knuckles had been jarred through the skin by the jolt of the staple gun.

"Kait's dead," Don said. "There's nothing we can do to bring her back. We need to start rebuilding our lives. It's up to the police to find her killers."

"The police aren't doing a thing now!"

"There's no way for us to know that. We have to have faith in the system."

"I'm going to put up flyers from now until eternity," I said. "If you try to stop me, I'm leaving you."

I stomped out of the room and went upstairs to bed.

It was, after all, eight-thirty.

I'd once read that eighty percent of all couples who suffered the loss of a child were divorced within two years. At the time I hadn't been able to imagine how such a thing could happen to a loving, compatible couple with a solid marriage.

Now I understood perfectly.

THERE'S OVER $5,000
REWARD MONEY
IN THE KATE ARQUETTE
CRIMESTOPPERS FUND!

KATE ARQUETTE WITH HER BOYFRIEND

Kate was shot to death Sunday, July 16, 1989, at about 10:30 P.M., on Lomas Blvd. near Broadway N.E. She was driving a Red Ford Tempo. The gun might have been a small caliber rifle or an Uzi.

Crimestoppers will pay for useful information. You won't have to give your name. Reward money will be dropped off in cash at a secret collection point. No one will ever know you made the call.

CALL CRIMESTOPPERS
843-7867

9

December 1989:

She left her sister a watermelon bowl,
because it went so well
with her red-and-yellow kitchen.
She had it put on layaway for her sister for
Christmas.

She left her father and me her unhousebroken cat,
a tank filled with stupid goldfish,
and a house so quiet we hear the fish making bubbles
as they glide back and forth in the water.

I want a watermelon bowl.
I want to see the bowl in her strong, square hands,
and to hear her laugh
because we've been fooled into thinking
it is truly a watermelon.

No, in truth, I don't want a watermelon bowl.

If I could hear her laugh, I would
settle for seeds.

LD

If Thanksgiving was awful, Christmas was worse. We had
long-established traditions that never varied, and Kait was

part of all of them. It was Kait's self-appointed job to decorate the tree, and Kait who baked the pies for Christmas
dinner. It was Kait who set the table with her grandmother's wedding china; Kait who dished the cranberry
sauce into bowls; Kait who filled the celery sticks with
cream cheese and arranged them on a relish tray.

This year it was Donnie who put up the tree, tossing
ornaments on so haphazardly that by Christmas Eve half of
them were on the floor. We didn't bother with a relish tray;
the cranberry sauce made its way around the table virtually
untouched; and I bought pies at a bakery.

Our out-of-town children always came for the holidays.
This Christmas they made the trip reluctantly, and Kerry
almost backed out. Not only was she worried about the
effect their young aunt's absence might have on her children, she was afraid for their lives.

"What if this maniac decides to shoot more of us?" she
agonized. "Maybe it's a vendetta and he's out to kill us all!"

The "season to be jolly" was an emotional disaster. Kerry
and Ken did come with Erin and Brittany, but the visit was
soured by paranoia, and they insisted we keep the doors
locked and the curtains drawn even in the daytime. When I
walked down the hall, I could hear people sobbing in the
bedrooms, and we all took turns running back and forth to
the cemetery.

Kerry and her family left on the twenty-sixth, and on the
following day Brett loaded up his Chevrolet van and took
off for the East Coast. During the weeks preceding the
holidays he had become increasingly bitter and despondent,
furious at APD for their tepid investigation, and disgusted
with Don and me for giving credence to a psychic. When
the day finally came that he announced, "I'm bailing out of
this nightmare," I was filled with conflicting emotions of

sorrow and envy. I would miss my son, but I wished I could "bail out" too.

Robin stayed on a couple of days longer to help circulate the flyers. We concentrated most of our efforts on the section of town referred to locally as "Little Vietnam." As we drove down streets we had never had occasion to use before, we discovered a ghetto area that we hadn't known existed, only blocks away from upper-middle-class neighborhoods. The sidewalks and buildings were covered with Oriental gang graffiti and messages in English read, *Fuck the police! Die, Round-Eyes, Die!* and *Kill! Kill! Kill!*

With two of us working together we were able to accomplish a lot in a comparatively short time. I drove the car, and Robin jumped in and out with the tape and the staple gun. We decided a good way to give the flyers maximum exposure would be to tape them on the sides of Dumpsters behind low-rent apartment complexes. My first indication that we were putting ourselves in danger came as Robin was opening her door to hop out with a flyer, and I noticed two Oriental men in a dented green Plymouth parked across from the Dumpster.

Something about the way they were staring at us made me nervous.

"Let's skip this bin and get the one at the end," I suggested.

Robin followed my gaze and nodded hasty agreement. I drove on down to the other end of the parking lot, and she got out of the car and taped the flyer to a trash bin. In a matter of seconds the men had pulled up beside us and were rolling down their windows.

Robin leapt back into the car, yelling, "Go, Mother, go!"

My reactions were slower than hers, and by the time I took in the fact that the men were cutting us off, the Plymouth was blocking the driveway and the man on the passenger's side was getting out of the car. I hit the button to activate the automatic door locks and slammed my foot down on the accelerator, pressing it to the floor. The man made a grab for the door handle on Robin's side, but couldn't maintain a grip on it as our car jumped the curb and landed on the road with a jarring thud.

I drove down the street at top speed and then stopped at a stop sign.

"*What* are you *doing*!" Robin shrieked at me.

Glancing in the rearview window, I saw to my horror that the Plymouth was barreling down on us. Once again, I stomped on the gas pedal, and we hurtled through the intersection and took a sharp left onto Ridgecrest, a north-south street that ran through a residential neighborhood.

"Are they still there?" I gasped as we sped toward Central Avenue, the traffic-laden street that bisects downtown Albuquerque.

"They've dropped back," Robin said with relief. "*Why in God's name did you switch on your turn signal?*"

"I did it without thinking," I said. "I always use the turn signal."

"Daddy's right, you shouldn't be doing this," said Robin. "You don't have any street smarts. Promise you won't put up any more flyers in that neighborhood!"

"I can't promise that," I said reasonably. "That's where I want them."

"At least, don't do it alone! Take somebody with you! And don't go between buildings or into single-entrance parking lots where you can get trapped. Did you see the look on their faces? Those men could have killed us!"

"That's ridiculous," I said. "They're just creeps who like to scare women."

"That's probably exactly what Kait thought," Robin said. " '*She did not think this could be as bad as it was,*' and she '*felt no sense of any need to avoid or evade.*'"

"She *was* trying to 'evade' the Camaro. That truck driver reported a high-speed chase."

"You told me you accepted Betty's reading!"

"I do, but it has to be interpreted," I said. "It's like doing a puzzle—the lesson for us is in learning how to put it together."

"Where did you come up with *that* nugget of wisdom?"

"I don't remember." I had a strong feeling that I had made the statement before, but I had no recollection of when or where it had been.

After Robin returned to Florida, I continued to put up flyers, but I never again risked entering closed-in areas and was careful to pay attention to what was going on around me.

On New Year's Eve I managed to stay awake past what had become my usual bedtime, and, at ten P.M. our time, I sat with Don in front of the television set and watched the golden ball descend into Times Square to mark the end of the most horrendous year of our lives.

"I was sure they would have arrested somebody by this time," Don said with a sigh.

"They're not going to make any arrests."

"The case is still open," he reminded me.

"That doesn't mean it's active."

We sat there, staring at the screen like a couple of zombies, making no move to touch each other, while the crowds in New York screamed and kissed and blew horns in frenzied celebration.

A commonplace occurrence proved to be the catalyst that jerked me out of my lethargy. On January 4 the band on my

Timex broke. I went out and bought a new band, and when I got back with it, the watch had mysteriously vanished.

I'm one of those people who always have to know what time it is, and I owned two other watches—a dress watch that had been my mother's and a funky hologram watch I'd bought at a magic store. They were both keeping perfect time at the bottom of my jewelry box, but when I put them on, they immediately stopped working.

I was trying to decide whether or not to invest in a new Timex when I remembered the watch of Kait's that I'd taken to Betty Muench. I got out Kait's purse and emptied it onto my bed, and the watch tumbled out of a side pocket. As I was strapping it onto my wrist, I noticed that among the other contents of the purse there was a Weekly Planner with a page for phone numbers. Kait's regular phone directory had been in her desk, and I had handed it over to the police along with her correspondence, so I hadn't had access to the numbers of any of her friends. Now, as I scanned the list of phone numbers, I began to feel excited. There were people here who might know things about Kait that we didn't. For six long months we'd left everything up to the police. Maybe it was time to do some investigating on our own.

The first person I attempted to call was Susan Smith, but the number Kait had for her was disconnected. I recalled Kait's saying that Susan sold snow cones in front of Pier One Imports, so I checked with the people there to see if they had seen her. The manager told me that, soon after Kait's death, Susan applied for a job there, worked for several weeks, and abruptly stopped coming in. They couldn't get hold of her, because her phone was no longer in service, and when one of her co-workers drove over to the house on Nineteenth Street to check to make sure she was all right, she found it deserted. As luck would have it, however, Susan's boyfriend had recently returned some merchandise and, in the course of applying for a refund, had given his address.

I wrote to Susan and addressed the letter in care of the boyfriend. Several days later she phoned me and agreed to come over.

Susan was an open-faced girl with a touching air of vulnerability, and it was obvious she had been deeply affected by Kait's death. She apologized for not having attended the funeral, and displayed a scar on her arm, explaining that at the time of the service she had been at the hospital being treated for a dog bite.

"I'll never forget that night as long as I live," she said. "That's why I moved, I couldn't stand the memories in that house. Kait was planning to spend the night with me, and then changed her mind. I keep asking myself if there was any way I could have kept her there. If I'd done that she might be alive today."

"Why did she decide to leave?" I asked.

"She told me she had to study, but that wasn't the real reason. She was worried about where Dung was and what he was doing. She kept making me call the apartment to see if he was home yet."

"Did she tell you what she was so worried about?"

"She just said they'd had a big fight. That wasn't anything new, because they fought all the time, but I'd never seen Kait in the state she was in that night. She kept bursting into tears for no reason, and there at the end she was having me call the apartment every five minutes."

"Why didn't she call herself?" I asked.

"She didn't want to talk to Dung. She just wanted to

know where he was. She said if he answered I should act like I'd gotten a wrong number."

"When was the last time you called?"

"It was right before she left."

"You mean like ten-forty?"

"Yes, somewhere around that time."

"And you still didn't get any answer?"

Susan shook her head.

"That seems odd," I commented. "The friends Dung was out with that night supposedly dropped him back at the apartment at ten. Did he know where you lived?"

"He might have if he saw my map."

I'd forgotten the hand-drawn map that had been found in Kait's car.

"Do you think you could make me a copy of that map?" I asked her.

"Sure," Susan said obligingly.

I got her a pencil and some paper, and she outlined a route going west on Lomas, with a Wendy's hamburger restaurant shown as a landmark for a right turn north onto Nineteenth Street. The location of Susan's house was marked with an X.

I took the map and studied it a moment.

"So when Kait left your house, she had to go back the way she came. She didn't have a choice, because the end of your street was blocked off."

"Actually, she did try to get out that way," said Susan. "I wondered at the time why she did that. She turned north instead of south on Nineteenth and then realized she couldn't get through, so she had to turn around and go back the other way."

"Did you give her the map that morning?"

"No, it was early in the week," Susan said. "We'd been

planning to get together then for dinner and a movie, but Kait had to work overtime, so that blew our plans. We finally decided she'd just stop over for a while on Sunday."

When she got up to leave, she thanked me for asking her over.

"It's good to know somebody is finally doing something," she told me.

The next of Kait's friends I called was Laura, the girl Kait had planned to room with after Dung moved out.

"Kait got really pissed at Dung on Saturday," Laura remembered. "She'd invited my boyfriend and me to come over to watch videos, but as soon as we got there, Dung took off. He didn't come back all evening, and Kait was furious. She said he was always doing that. He'd leave around ten or eleven and he wouldn't come back till dawn."

"Where did he go?"

"Kait didn't know," Laura said. "All he'd say was he was going out to see friends. At first she was worried that he might be playing around, but I told her if he'd wanted to do that he wouldn't have moved in with her."

"Was there anything else that hit you as strange?" I asked her.

"Well," Laura said hesitantly, "there was this really weird thing about some car wrecks."

"I know about those," I said.

"You do?" She seemed relieved. "I hated to be the one to tell you when all those articles in the newspapers made Kait out to be so perfect. She *was* clean-cut—she wouldn't even smoke a cigarette—but she was really into excitement, and she wanted to know all about how the wrecks were set up. By the time they got back from L.A., she knew everything about them. She'd even met the Vietnamese lawyer who arranged them."

"Did she explain how the insurance scam worked?"

"She didn't name names, but the bottom line was that this lawyer would hire people to rent cars and take out a lot of insurance on them. Then they'd use the rented cars to intentionally run into other cars, and the people in those cars would sue the rental companies for all kinds of fake injuries."

"I can't picture Kait wrecking a car," I said.

"She didn't." Laura was obviously surprised by the suggestion. "Dung was the one who wrecked the cars."

"I know Dung staged one wreck—"

"I understand that Dung staged all of them," Laura said.

"But Detective Gallegos told Don he had an accident report that showed Kait was driving!"

"Then maybe they switched seats after the wreck," Laura suggested. "That would have kept Dung from having so many accidents on his record. As far as I know, though, all Kait did was let Dung use her credit card. That's how he talked her into going to California with him; he couldn't rent a car without showing a major credit card."

"Were Dung's friends doing this too?"

"I think An Le was. Kait told me he went to Orange County every week. She said that he'd fly there and stay just one day and come back."

"He was there in March when Kait and Dung went out there," I said. "Don made the plane reservations for all three of them through Sandia's travel agent. But when I picked them up at the airport, An wasn't with them. Kait said he turned in his ticket and drove back instead." As I thought back on that conversation, something else occurred to me. "One of Dung's other friends, Tuan, was out there too. Kait was surprised when he turned up. She told me he flew first class and went back the next morning. She thought that was crazy. She said, 'He didn't even stay long enough to go to Disneyland!' "

After Laura left, I remained seated at the kitchen table, staring at the pad on which I'd been jotting down notes, trying to sort out the many odd pieces of information. The thing that had made it seem impossible for Kait's killing to have been premeditated was that we had thought we were the only ones who knew where she was that night. Now, though, it seemed that a map had been around for days, available to anyone who looked in her purse. And Kait's actions that night seemed peculiar. Why had she been so frantic to know where Dung was? One possible answer was that she regretted their fight, but if that were the case, why hadn't she wanted to talk to him?

There was a second possibility that made more sense to me. Kait might have been worried that Dung was out searching for her. Betty's reading had said: "She will have known that night of one who will be looking for her, and that one will have others looking for her. There's a suggestion of a kind of setup." If Kait had been afraid that Dung and his friends would intercept her on Lomas, it would explain why she had attempted to leave by another route.

And what did Dung do every night between ten P.M. and dawn? I was struggling to come up with an answer to that when Robin called.

"Those are prime hours for prostitution," she suggested.

That struck me as absurd.

"Why would any man go to a prostitute when he's living with his girlfriend?"

"That's not what I meant," said Robin. "I meant maybe Dung *is* one. How was he able to live for seven months without working? He was getting money somewhere, and we know now that it wasn't from a sister in California. He's small and cute, a type perverts seem to be attracted to. If Dung was working as a prostitute and Kait found out about it, she would have been horrified. And she wouldn't have confided in anybody, she'd have been too ashamed."

I found the idea revolting, but I agreed to look into it.

For years I had taught for the journalism department at the University of New Mexico. Many of my former students now worked for local newspapers, and one, Mike Gallagher, was an investigative reporter for the *Albuquerque Journal* and had just completed a series of articles on prostitution.

I called Mike and asked him if Dung's name had come up in the course of his investigation.

"Not in connection with prostitution," he told me. "I have heard from several sources that the guy is a drug dealer."

When Don got home, I filled him in on my discoveries. He was shocked, not only by the news of Dung's alleged drug dealing, but by the fact that the police either weren't aware of it or didn't consider it important enough to tell us about.

"They're not playing straight with us about those phone numbers either," I said. "No matter what Steve Gallegos says, I don't think he's bothered to check them out. Sergeant Lowe didn't even know they existed, and every time I call down there to inquire about them I'm given the runaround."

"I'll go down to the police station tomorrow and demand some answers," Don said. "And I want them to show me that accident report on Kait."

But by the following morning that confrontation seemed unnecessary, for somewhere between midnight and dawn, we were awakened by a phone call.

It was Sergeant Lowe, and her voice was charged with excitement.

"We've just arrested three men from Martineztown for your daughter's murder," she said. "I'm very proud of Steve! He's found the Camaro, and we have an eyewitness to the shooting. Mrs. Arquette, I think we've got an airtight case!"

10

On January 18 Bernalillo County District Attorney Robert Schwartz held an afternoon press conference and distributed copies of the affidavit for the arrest warrant to the press.

It resulted in banner headlines and front-page news stories:

Albuquerque Journal, January 19, 1990:

TEEN SHOT AT YOUNG WOMAN ON A DARE, OFFICERS SAY

Kaitlyn Arquette was killed at random, the apparent victim of a dare, Albuquerque police said Thursday.

The dare allegedly was accepted by 18-year-old Miguel Garcia of 318 Rosemont NE, police said. Officers arrested him Wednesday night along with two other men in connection with the July 16 slaying. The others arrested were Dennis (Marty) Martinez, 18, and Juvenal Escobedo, 21, also known as Jose Hernandez.

All three were being held without bond after being arraigned on open charges of murder Thursday. . . .

The arrests were made after a fourth man turned

them in, according to an arrest warrant affidavit. The informant, Robert Garcia (no relation to Miguel Garcia), was questioned by police based on a Crime Stoppers tip that he knew the individuals involved.

Robert Garcia told police he was with the three suspects on a joyride when Arquette was shot. He has not been charged.

Bernalillo County District Attorney Robert Schwartz said investigators will review the circumstances and decide whether to bring charges against Robert Garcia. [Schwartz] said his office probably won't seek the death penalty, because the facts of the case don't appear to meet the criteria for a capital crime under New Mexico law.

The death penalty can be imposed in New Mexico for the murder of an on-duty law officer; for murders committed during a kidnapping or rape; or during an escape attempt from a jail or prison; in murder-for-hire cases, or for the murder of a witness to a crime.

Police found two .22-caliber pistols and a .22-caliber rifle along with ammunition at Miguel Garcia's home. A Chevrolet Camaro believed to have been used in the shooting also was seized.

Robert Garcia told police investigators the carload of armed men . . . spotted Arquette traveling east on Lomas . . . and pulled up alongside her at a red light. . . . Escobedo, who was driving, dared Miguel Garcia "to shoot at the female driver." Miguel Garcia "then pointed a dark-colored revolver at the blond female driver through his passenger side window and fired several shots." [They] sped away without knowing the shots had struck Arquette, and Miguel Garcia allegedly told everyone in the car "to keep quiet and not tell anyone what occurred."

The Arquette family distributed about 10,000 flyers

asking anyone with information on the case to call
Crime Stoppers.

Our initial reaction was overwhelming relief that Kait's
killers had been apprehended. Later, however, when Don
and I read the arrest affidavit, we found it confusing. There
appeared to be inconsistencies in the stories of the witnesses. The truck driver, Eugene Linquist, had reported
seeing Kait's *westbound* car chased by men in a Camaro,
while Robert Garcia made no mention of a chase and said
when they first spotted Kait she was driving *east*. He also
said they shot Kait while she was stopped at a red light. Not
only was this inconsistent with Linquist's story, it was inconsistent with the fact that the Ford Tempo had reportedly
been traveling at a high rate of speed.

"And none of this meshes with Betty's reading," I said.
"She told me there were three men in the car, not four."

"She seems to have been wrong," Don said.

"But she's been right about other things! She said Kait
was crying that night, and Susan confirmed that. She said
the car was a low rider, and it was. And Sergeant Lowe told
me the Crime Stopper tips came from women. Betty predicted the informants would be 'the feminine aspect.' "

"So, she was right about certain things and not others,"
Don said. "What I'm concerned about is all the newspaper
coverage. I don't like our being named as the source of the
flyers."

"Nobody is going to pick up on that," I said.

That statement fell into the category of "famous last
words." The story that mentioned the flyers was published
on Thursday, and we got the death threats on Saturday.

I received the first one. I was using my office computer
when the phone rang, and when I picked up the receiver,

although I could tell the caller was a woman, she was drowned out by the clatter of my printer.

"I can't hear you," I said. "Can you wait just a minute, please?"

The caller continued to talk, but I couldn't understand her.

Finally the page was filled, and the printer fell silent.

"—die," the voice was saying. "You're going to die. We hate you—you're going to die—we're coming to kill you."

"Who are you?" I asked unsteadily. "Why do you hate us?"

"You got my brother in trouble," the woman said. "That girl was a bitch and deserved to die, and so do the rest of you. You're going to die! You're going to die! You're going to—"

I hung up the phone and went to find Don.

"We just had a death threat," I told him. "It was from a woman with a Mexican accent who says she's the sister of one of the men who were arrested."

"What exactly—" Don started to ask, when the phone rang again. He picked up the extension and listened in silence. Then he grimaced and set the receiver back on the hook.

"Who was it?" I asked, knowing the answer.

"It was her—that same woman."

"What did she say?"

"The same thing she said to you. She must be some kind of nut."

"A murderous nut," I said. "It probably runs in the family. She said they're coming to kill us, and she sounded like she meant it."

Donnie was over at a friend's house, and I called and told him to spend the night there. Don tried to call Gallegos, but he couldn't be reached, and two young patrolmen came over to fill out a report. They were sympathetic, but it was obvious they didn't take the threats seriously, and one suggested that we have our number changed to avoid further harassment.

I couldn't believe what I was hearing. I wasn't worried about being harassed, I was worried about being killed!

We finally convinced them to have the telephone company put a tracer on our line, but they told us there would have to be three additional death threats before they could take action.

"What sort of action can you take at that point?" Don asked them.

"We can tell them to stop harassing you," they said.

After the police officers left I found I couldn't stop shaking. We had planned to have dinner with friends, but the thought of coming home after dark and being shot when we got out of the car was terrifying to me. Almost as frightening was the prospect of staying at home. The windows of our corner house faced out onto two different streets and made us ideal targets for a drive-by shooting.

After weighing our options we did go to dinner at our friends' house, but by the end of the evening I had worked myself into a state of such irrational panic that I refused to go home. We ended up sleeping on the fold-down sofa in their living room, and the following day I insisted on renting an efficiency in an apartment complex with a security system. Sergeant Lowe told us that the only one of the suspects who had a sister was Miguel Garcia, so I dialed the Garcias' number to verify her identity. When what sounded like the same woman answered the phone, I quickly hung up. Sergeant Lowe suggested we start recording all our calls, so we hooked a recorder to the phone. We didn't get any more threats, but someone continued to phone us, sighing and moaning and occasionally muttering obscenities. The background noises never varied; there was always the sound of television and the high-pitched jabber of a very young child.

I went over to our house every day to feed the pets and to pick up our mail, but even in the daytime I felt uncomfortable there. One Sunday I stayed later than usual to run a load of laundry, and when I left around six P.M., I noticed a car parked on the side street next to our house. Two Hispanic men were seated in front, and a woman and child in back, and there was no apparent reason for their being there.

Would it be safer to race back to the house or make a dash for the car? The fact that I'd double-locked the front door decided me. I lunged for the car, yanked open the door, and hurled myself into the driver's seat. As I twisted the key in the ignition, I could hear the engine of the other car starting up also. I floored the accelerator and sped down the street toward Lomas where, without pausing to signal, I plunged out into traffic. Brakes shrieked and horns blared as furious drivers swerved to avoid a collision. A glance in the rearview window revealed nobody behind me, but I took a roundabout route back to the apartment, in case I was being followed and was too dumb to know it.

It was evident, even to me, that I was becoming a basket case. Paranoia was not the only symptom I was exhibiting; I was also experiencing depression. APD's "airtight" case had been rapidly disintegrating. First Marty Martinez, the eighteen-year-old in the backseat, was released from the Juvenile Detention Center for lack of evidence. Then it was disclosed that the state's "eyewitness" had been lying and Betty Muench had been right about the number of men in the low rider. Robert Garcia had not been with his friends on the night of the shooting, he had been incarcerated at the Youth Diagnostic Development Center. And the fingerprint on the empty Budweiser can found in the gutter next to Kait's car did not match up with those of any of the Hispanic suspects.

Day-by-day changes in the scenario were chronicled by headlines:

Albuquerque Tribune, January 22, 1990:
ARQUETTE INFORMER'S STORY IS PROBED

Albuquerque Journal, January 23, 1990:
WHEREABOUTS OF SHOOTING WITNESS STIRS QUESTIONS

Albuquerque Journal, January 24, 1990:
WITNESS SNAFU CASTS DOUBT ON CASE, ATTORNEYS SAY

Albuquerque Tribune, January 24, 1990:
ARQUETTE SLAYING WILL GO TO OPEN HEARING

Albuquerque Journal, January 25, 1990:
MURDER CHARGES FILED IN ARQUETTE SLAYING

Albuquerque Journal, January 28, 1990:
ARQUETTE SLAYING HEARING POSTPONED

Albuquerque Tribune, January 29, 1990:
ALL CHARGES DROPPED IN ARQUETTE DEATH

Albuquerque Journal, January 30, 1990:
DA DROPS MURDER CHARGES AGAINST 2 ARQUETTE SUSPECTS

The most disturbing article appeared in the *Albuquerque Journal* and was based on Mike Gallagher's interview with "the witness-who-wasn't-there." In it Robert Garcia said the police bullied him into making the false statement that he had been an eyewitness to the shooting, despite the fact that they knew he hadn't been.

TEEN SAYS HE LIED TO POLICE ABOUT SEEING ARQUETTE SHOOTING

Robert Garcia admits he lied to Albuquerque police when he told them he witnessed the shooting death of Kaitlyn Arquette, but he says the police pressured him to tell the story.

Garcia, 16, said in interviews with the *Journal* . . . that he was interviewed by police for more than nine hours. . . . [He] said he initially told officers the truth [that he was in the Diagnostic Center] . . . but then changed his story.

He said he lied to satisfy investigators, who he claims threatened him with arrest and prison.

"They started scaring me and stuff," Garcia said. "They just told me that I was there. . . . They said, 'We've been watching you, you can't lie to us.'"

Violent Crimes Unit supervisor Lt. Pat Dunworth and Sgt. Ruth Lowe, also of the unit, refused to comment.

In a desperate attempt to salvage what was left of their case, the police went through a complicated series of legal maneuvers. With their "eyewitness" now discredited, District Attorney Schwartz felt there was not sufficient evidence to take the case to the grand jury. Other informants were proving hard to find, because, according to Sergeant Lowe, one of Juve Escobedo's relatives was walking around Martineztown with a gun, threatening to kill anyone who talked to the police.

Because there was a limitation to the length of time the men could be held without being indicted, the police withdrew the murder charges, with the intention of reissuing them later when they had obtained more evidence. Then they filed unrelated charges of burglary against Miguel Garcia to keep him in jail. They released Juve Escobedo, a Mexican national, on his own recognizance, after securing an agreement from the Immigration and Naturalization Service that they would hold him as an illegal alien. It turned out they were mistaken about Juve's status. He was held for ninety minutes and then released, because he was an applicant for an alien amnesty program. Several days later he was arrested for vandalizing a high school and sentenced to eighteen months probation.

Were the Hispanic men guilty or weren't they? Despite his erroneous confession Robert Garcia had been able to direct the police to Juve's gold Camaro, which had been painted and sold, and Marty Martinez had made a confession that he had later recanted.

Yet, everything in me kept screaming, "Dung's friends are responsible!"

"You can't have it both ways," said Don, who by now was thoroughly fed up with me.

Then, something happened that made me believe I could.

The voice on the phone was a woman's.

"Your daughter's not the first person those guys have

killed," she said. "Garcia's shot people before. He does it for pay."

Suddenly, there it was, the answer I'd been looking for! *If the Hispanic suspects were the triggermen, as the police seemed certain they were, wasn't it possible that somebody else had hired them to shoot Kait?*

I phoned Sergeant Lowe and repeated what the tipster had told me.

"It was a random shooting," she insisted.

"Won't you even consider—"

"There is no other possibility."

Her voice was kind but firm and allowed for no argument.

When I hung up the phone I was ready to weep with frustration. It seemed to me that this tip was worth following up on. Murder-for-hire was a serious enough crime to warrant the death penalty, and there were so many reasons to think that Kait's death had been premeditated!

To be fair, Sergeant Lowe was undoubtedly inundated with murder cases and could not be expected to keep track of every aspect of every one of them. I decided to write a letter that would put things into perspective for her and explain why murder-for-hire was a legitimate possibility. In the letter I told her all the things we had learned about the insurance scam and about An Le's constant one-day trips back and forth to L.A., which seemed to indicate the possibility of drug running. I reminded her of the phone calls made from Kait's apartment, and suggested again that the police identify the numbers. I told her about Dung's statement that he was "deciding" whether to divulge the identity of Kait's killer, and about his insisting to Brett, "This is all my fault."

I ended by listing the phone numbers in Kait's directory,

including those for Tuan, the only Vietnamese man listed, and for Dung's Hispanic friend, Ray, and I gave her updated numbers for Susan and Laura, both of whom had moved since the start of the investigation.

I hand-delivered the letter to the police station and mailed a copy to the FBI in Orange County.

When a week went by and I hadn't heard from Sergeant Lowe, I phoned to make sure my letter had reached her.

"Steve says there's nothing in it he hasn't checked out," she said. "Mrs. Arquette, I know this is hard for you to accept, but you're simply going to have to face up to the fact that your daughter died because she was in the wrong place at the wrong time."

11

February 1990:
It snowed last night,
So this morning I went to the cemetery
To sweep the snow from her grave marker.
Ice had formed in the letters that spelled her name.
When I sat on the ice to melt it, she was mortified.
I heard her voice shriek with the sleek black crows—
"Nobody *else's* mother squats in a *graveyard!*"

LD

Sunset Memorial Cemetery is a quiet place in February. Holiday visitations are long since over, Christmas decorations have been removed from the graves, and seasonal mourners have resumed their everyday lives.

In February I had the grounds to myself. I spent a lot of time there, walking and thinking, trying to make some sense out of the botched investigation.

I stood at Kait's grave in the silent, winter-white cemetery, and asked her, "What do you want me to do now, baby?"

I got no answer. We evidently still needed our intermediary.

Betty was out when I called, but I left a message on her

answering machine telling her I wanted to make another appointment. Since the case was falling through because of a lack of witnesses, we needed advice about what we could do to help revitalize it.

Betty returned my call in a couple of hours.

"You don't need to come in," she said. "We've already opened the channel to Kait. I had some extra time this afternoon, so I went ahead and got a reading for you."

She proceded to read me the transcript over the telephone:

QUESTION: THE CASE AGAINST THE TWO SUSPECTS IN THE MURDER OF KAITLYN SEEMS TO BE DETERIORATING. WHAT MAY WE KNOW AT THIS TIME TO BRING THIS CASE TO A SATISFACTORY CONCLUSION, AND WHAT CAN BE DONE IN LIEU OF WITNESSES?

ANSWER: There is a sense of Kaitlyn impressing with the letters *R & J*. These seem to be repeated and repeated. There will be this that will seem to be written and it will be as if she will have this very much in her own mind.

"This is like a capital *R* and a capital *J*, and the curlicue symbol for *and*, whatever that's called," Betty said. "Kait presents this R & J visually, as if it's printed on the door of a white vehicle."

ANSWER: There will be this that will show that she will have had some kind of connection to these two suspects and that they know her. There is something about them which will cause her to recoil as if there will have been some kind of other encounter at another time. They will seem to have some way to fear that something is known about them by her and thus now by others. This will seem to put a fear into them and they will still be under the containment and control of the questioners and can be asked questions even if there is not fully known the meaning of the questions even by the questioner.

"I guess that means just to badger them," Betty said. "They're scared right now, and if they're pressured enough they can be broken."

ANSWER: It is as if Kaitlyn will accuse and she will know them and they must know that she will know them and the search for this common denominator will be the problem. This third one will not be a part of this R & J symbol.

"The kid in the backseat wasn't part of the conspiracy," Betty said.
"Then why did they drag him along?"
"It doesn't say."

ANSWER: There will be many who could come forward, not as eyewitnesses, but as ones who will have heard the boasts and confession. There will be this that would show that actual eyewitnesses will not be necessary, but that there will be other forms of witness to bear in this case. The sense is to apply the heat, to turn the tourniquet. There is not enough pressure being applied to these two, and they can be broken down if there is the heart to pursue this at this time. The sense of an intimidated police force will also enter into this and they will not have anyone who will seem to want to take this into their own life and apply the full skills that will be necessary. The due process must be challenged in this case.

Kait *insists* on R & J!

"She's adamant about this R & J," Betty said. "I looked in the phone book and there are three local businesses operating under those initials. Why don't you check and see if they have white delivery vehicles?"

"Dung has a Hispanic friend named Ray," I said. "I wonder if his last name starts with *J*."

"That doesn't feel right," Betty said. "There wouldn't be any 'and' symbol."

"Could you ask another question for me?"

"Sure," Betty said.

"Would it be the right thing for me to turn all my information over to Mike Gallagher, an investigative reporter at the *Journal*?"

"I'll be back with you pretty quick on that," Betty said.

Ten minutes later she called back.

"This is strange," she said. "I've got these real funny images."

QUESTION: WOULD IT BE THE RIGHT THING TO TURN ALL THE INFORMATION OVER TO MIKE GALLAGHER, INVESTIGATIVE REPORTER?

ANSWER: There is an image of a flatbed with a great bomb on it. It will be that this will be for show and that there will be many other weapons that will be available in this. There will be this which will show that by putting this into the hands of the media it will not be allowed to become buried and intimidated. It will show that there will be this bomb, which will be this Mike, and it would be that this would appear at first to be overkill in all this, but the mere presence in this case of Mike would seem to cause some kind of intimidation in itself. It will be that intimidation is the game at hand and there will be this which will show that this will also cause a great headache.

"I was feeling a physical headache as I typed this," Betty said.

ANSWER: Yet there is a need to end this ordeal and to come to the kind of conclusion which will permit stability and peace in the community. There is a feeling that this will be simple to resolve and yet it will take this kind of intimidation to solve it. There is no need to drop this case for it will have some very important meanings in the overview in this community.

There will be in this then the knowing that the image of the great bomb will be Mike, but that there can be other avenues just the same. The media shows which will appeal from the national level will be one way, and Mike can be instrumental in getting this into that view. There is however a risk that Mike will be taking, and he will know that he would be very vulnerable and that he will need to share much of his information with someone who will be able to keep this going when Mike would *seem* to quit. This is for his own protection and another way for him to play the game the way he will choose. On the condition that Mike will keep many avenues open and share this information with another, then he can be the one to do this without harm to himself. There is no sense of any karmic connection to Mike alone, and it would be all his own choice at this time. He can figure ways to keep the heat on, and he can be one to have a personal stake in all this, and thus from this then Lois can seem to award him with this responsibility at this time.

He wants it.

"Mike isn't karmically involved with either you or Kait, so he can go at this in an academic, intellectual way," Betty explained. "He can pull up some very important things by keeping an exposed view of himself, and on the other hand having some secret help in the background. The bomb is symbolic of Mike's energy—it comes on like overkill—but in this situation it's necessary. If the police were pursuing this case in the proper way, it would practically be solved by now."

"It's hard to picture Mike on national television," I said. "Investigative reporters try to keep a low profile."

"All I know is it says that he'll do it," Betty said. "There are two references here to creating stability in the community. Maybe this case will get us a better police force. I hope either you or Mike will follow up on those R & J's in the phone book. Kait's very insistent about the importance of that symbol."

She said she would mail me the printouts of the two readings.

As before, she refused to let me pay her.

The next day I ran off a copy of the same letter I'd sent Sergeant Lowe and the FBI and mailed it to Mike at the *Journal* office. Then I drove around town, checking out R & J businesses. Because they were located in different areas of the city, it took most of the morning to visit all of them. None seemed in the least suspicious, and none had any sort of white vehicle.

In bed that night I told Kait I was tired of her game-playing.

"Let's cut out the middleman," I said. "We don't have time for this. If this R & J symbol is as important as you've made it out to be, you have to find some way to let me know what it means."

That night I dreamed that Don and I were in a car, parked on the side of a dark road. We dozed off, and when I opened my eyes I discovered that while I had been sleeping somebody had stuck a business card under the windshield wiper. It said "R & J Car Rental."

The dream was so vivid, I remembered it clearly in the morning and described it to Don at breakfast.

"You've already checked out all the R & J's in the phone book," he reminded me.

"Maybe it's a new business and doesn't have a listing yet."

Directory Assistance could come up with no R & J Car Rental.

Betty's printouts arrived in the mail, and I studied them carefully. The reading on Mike showed a crude thumbnail sketch of a bed with a bomb on it, and in the margin next to the word *headache*, Betty had scribbled, "the price of your suit." I hoped this didn't mean that media exposure would cost us the case against the hitmen, but if it did, it was too late to do anything about it.

That afternoon I went out to run errands, and as I was driving back to the apartment I passed a small branch library. It was fifteen minutes till closing time, but on impulse I circled the block and parked and went in. A shelf against the back wall held a collection of phone directories

1112 Dakota, NE.
87110

1/29/90 Lois Arquette

Would it be the right thing for me to turn allthe
information over to Mike Gallagher, investigative
reporter?

thereis an image of a flat bed with a great bomb onit, it
willbe that this will be for show and that there willbe many
other weapons that will be available in this. there will
be this which willshow that by putting this intoit the hands
of the media there willbe this which willnot be allowed to
become buried and intimated. itw illshow that there will
be this bomb which will be this mike and it will be that
this would appear at first to be overkill in allthis at this
time,but theme re presence in this caso of mike would seem
to cause some kindof intimidation in itself. it willbe
that intimidation is the game at hand and that there willbe
this which willshow that this willalso cause a great headache — *the game*
andyet there is a need to end this ordeal and to come to   *of ument*
the kindof conclusionwhich will parmit stability and peace
in the community. there willbe this energy which will be
simple to resolve and yet it will take this kindof intimidation, there is no need to drop this case for it willhave
some very important meanings intheir overview in this community-
there willbe inthis then the knowing that the image of the
great bomb will be mike but that there can be other avenues
just the same. the media shows which will appeal from the
national level willbe one way and that mike can be instrumental
in getting this into that view. there is however a risk that
mike willbe taking and he will know that he would be very vulnerable and that he willneed to share much of his information
with someone who ill be able to keep this information going
even when he would "seem" to quit. this is for his own protection
and another way for him to play the game the way he will chose,
on the conditon that mike will keep many avenues open and
share this information with another then he can be the one
to do this without harm tohimself. there is no senseof any
hair not — karmic connection to mike alone and it would be all his own
compelled choice at thist ime, khe can figure ways to keep the heat
by any on anche can be one to have a personal stake in all this
deep and thus from this then lois can seem to awardhim with this
spirited responsibility at this time,
conusultmend.

friends insource *he must's it*

Psychic reading by Betty Muench, done by "automatic writing"

from various areas of the country. I got down the Los Angeles phone book and checked the car leasing services, but no R & J Car Rental was listed.

Had I really expected to find one? No, of course, I hadn't. I was playing this psychic detective game to keep myself sane, but in the logical part of my brain I knew nothing would come of it.

I returned the book to the shelf and was getting ready to leave when I remembered the alleged purpose of Kait's trip to California. Disneyland wasn't in L.A. proper, it was in Anaheim.

I didn't know if Orange County had its own phone directory, but since I was already at the library, I decided to find out. I discovered there *was* a separate book of yellow pages for Orange County, and when I looked up rental car agencies, I was stunned to discover an "R & J Car Leasing" in Costa Mesa.

I could tell the librarians were impatient for me to leave, but I was in such a state of shock that I wasn't about to go anywhere. I must have looked as if I was getting ready to keel over, because one of them came over to ask if I was ill.

"No," I said, "I just need to sit down for a minute."

"R & J"—it was just as Betty had described it—not "R and J," but two letters bracketing the "&" sign. While the librarians were occupied straightening chairs and picking up litter, I ripped the page with the R & J listing out of the phone book.

I didn't even feel guilty.

That night when Don came home, I was not cooking dinner; I was seated at the breakfast bar, downing a martini. When I told him about my day, he fixed one for himself, and we sat on adjacent stools, draining our glasses, too shaken to think about eating. After we'd given ourselves some time to calm down, we drove over to the house, got out our tax file, and dug out our MasterCard statement for March 1989. Kait's credit card had been part of our family account, and every month she had reimbursed us for the charges she made on it.

The statement for March of the previous year reflected all the charges Kait had made on the trip to California, including the rental of a car from a place called Snappy Car Rental.

"That has to be the car Dung used for the wreck," Don speculated. "That's odd in itself, because the car I reserved for them was from Avis. Dung must have had some reason for canceling the Avis car and renting a car from Snappy to have the wreck in. At any rate, R & J must have some other significance. Maybe it's a money-laundering outfit or a cover for the car-wreck operation."

The statement showed that on the nights of the twenty-seventh and twenty-eighth, Kait and Dung had stayed at a motel in Costa Mesa. After that there were no more charges in Costa Mesa until March 31.

"If R & J set this up, the wreck must have been on March twenty-eighth," Don said as he studied the statement. "Then Kait and Dung flitted around having fun for a while and came back to Costa Mesa before returning to Albuquerque so Dung could collect payment."

We contacted Kait's bank and got a copy of her April 1989 checking account statement. We were not surprised to find a deposit of $1,490 made early in the month. We decided that Dung must have held back $510 of the $2,000 he received for the wreck and given Kait the remainder to apply toward the damage deposit and the first and last month's rent for their apartment.

I phoned the number listed for R & J Car Leasing and

was told it was no longer in service. I then did something I should have done many months earlier and dialed the numbers in Santa Ana that had appeared on Kait's final phone bill.

Both had been disconnected.

12

Kait was still there! More meaningful to us than any other aspect of the whole R & J experience was that it seemed to be proof of Kait's continued existence. Despite my conscious acceptance of Betty's communication with her, the skeptical side of my nature was an ingrained part of me, and there were times when I doubted my own sanity. This new experience convinced me that, not only did Kait still exist, she had the ability, at least in some cases, to communicate directly.

Spurred by this new revelation, I reread *Many Lives, Many Masters*, less interested in the subject of reincarnation than in the "space between lifetimes." I was especially fascinated by the sections that told about people who had been through near-death experiences. Drawing upon the research of such renowned authorities as Dr. Elisabeth Kübler-Ross and Dr. Raymond Moody, who had conducted extensive and well-documented studies on death and dying, Dr. Weiss pointed out the striking similarities among the experiences of people who had "died" and then been medically resuscitated. Almost without exception they described the sensation of becoming painlessly detached from their bodies and rising to a vantage point from which they could look down and observe the resuscitation efforts. Then, after a period of time, they became aware of a brilliant light in the distance, seen in a number of cases at the end of a tunnel, and felt themselves magnetically drawn in its direction. Some of these people attempted to go to the light and were turned back, because their duties on earth were unfinished. Others chose on their own to return to their bodies.

In one section Dr. Weiss's patient, Catherine, addressed the subject of people in comas. She described such people as "resting." If they still had lessons to learn or to impart to others, they were kept in their bodies until those lessons were absorbed, but if their mission in that particular lifetime was completed, modern medicine notwithstanding, they could move to the next dimension. If that were true, I thought, then perhaps my decision, "I can do that," had made it unnecessary for Kait to remain in her body to teach me the lesson that people can do what they have to do.

In mid-February I had a call from Sergeant Lowe saying that she had changed her mind about my letter and was going to send an investigator to California.

"I feel sure we've arrested the right men, but I'm starting to question the motive," she told me. "Right now we're busy digging up evidence to get these guys indicted, but as soon as we get that done, I'll be assigning a new detective to the case. From now on we're going to be working this thing from both ends. Barbara Cantwell will go over Kait's credit-card statement with you, and you can help her follow a paper trail through Orange County."

My opinion of Sergeant Lowe went shooting to the ceiling, and the name Barbara Cantwell immediately became a mantra for me. At night when I couldn't sleep, I repeated it over and over in my mind and visualized Joan of Arc in a policewoman's uniform.

Mike Gallagher received my letter and called to say that

his editor had assigned him the story. This *did* seem a bit like overkill now that I knew Barbara Cantwell would be working with us, but I figured there was nothing to be lost by having Mike involved also.

"APD has ignored a lot of things that they should have checked into," he said. "Did Kait ever mention a skinhead named Adrian?"

"I don't think so," I said.

"This guy lived at their apartment complex and apparently he and Dung were pretty thick," Mike said. "Adrian told neighbors that a couple of days before the shooting, he and Dung were driving around, tailing Kait, because Dung was afraid she was being followed by a beige VW."

"The car that was spotted in the area of the shooting?"

"That's a possibility," Mike said. "When I was doing a series on drug pushers, I talked with two men who live at the Alvarado Apartments. They said Dung told them Kait was killed by a Vietnamese gang. I personally dragged the guys down to the station to tell APD about it, but the police didn't want to hear it. They'd already concocted their scenario and didn't want it muddied. Dung's told other people all kinds of things about the murder. A contact at the courthouse told me the police have received—and shrugged off— six different reports from people who claimed to have heard him admit to being involved in some way in the shooting."

He asked for a picture of Dung, and I sent him a snapshot that I'd taken on Kait's last Thanksgiving. Dung was seated at our dinner table, and Kait was standing behind him. They looked very happy.

I leafed through other snapshots taken on that occasion— I was leaning over Don's shoulder as he carved the turkey; Brett was clowning around, pretending to swallow a drumstick; Donnie, bright-eyed and laughing, was hugging his girlfriend. The family we were today was far less photogenic, for all of us were experiencing stress-induced health problems. Don had lost ten pounds and looked ten years older, and I had developed high blood pressure. Our daughters reported headaches, insomnia, and bouts of heavy bleeding between their menstrual periods. Donnie, who had rebelled against living in the efficiency, had been camping out on the sofas of a series of friends, going short of sleep and overdosing on fast food.

As for Brett, we didn't even know where he was. When he'd left he had broken off all communication with the family. I knew that when Brett was unhappy he needed his space, but I also knew that his judgment was impaired by stress. I had recurring nightmares about him careening down the highway with an open bottle of Jack Daniel's gripped between his knees.

When Miguel Garcia was arraigned, the judge announced that if the state did not indict him within two weeks she would release him to the custody of his mother. With the deadline pressing upon her Deputy District Attorney Susan Riedel again charged Escobedo and Garcia with first-degree murder and related crimes.

On Friday, February 23, Sergeant Lowe called to say they were now ready to take the case to the grand jury.

"Do you have enough evidence?" I asked her.

"There's plenty," she told me. "Even though we don't have any eyewitnesses, we've rounded up a lot of people who heard the men bragging."

"Do the suspects know when the grand jury is convening?"

"We're required by law to give them thirty-six hours notice."

"Are both of them currently in custody?"

"We're still holding Garcia on the burglary charges," Lowe said. "Once the men are indicted, we'll issue a bench warrant for Escobedo."

I found it hard to believe it could be that simple.

"Aren't you afraid he'll run?"

"He can't run," Sergeant Lowe assured me. "He's on probation. He can't leave town without the permission of his probation officer."

Sixteen witnesses testified at the investigation, including Steve Gallegos, two boys from the Juvenile Detention Center, two staff members from JDC, and an assortment of residents of the Martineztown neighborhood. We were not allowed to attend the hearing, but later I was able to acquire the transcript. A fourteen-year-old girl testified to overhearing Juve Escobedo boast about his involvement in Kait's murder; an eleven-year-old boy said Miguel Garcia had bragged about it to him; and the residents and staff at the Detention Center had heard the story from Marty Martinez, the third man in the car.

Two neighborhood witnesses also testified to having seen Juve's Camaro pull up in front of the Garcia house after the shooting, and seeing Miguel leap out and run to the kitchen window. "I heard him knock on the window," one of them said. "And then somebody opened it, and he told them he had something to pass them because he wanted them to hide it. So he ran back and he grabbed what looked like . . . a gun or rifle or something, and he got it, and he ran back. He passed it in and he told them, 'Hurry up and hide this. . . . I just killed somebody.' "

Another witness, an inmate at the Detention Center, described a conversation with Marty Martinez.

"[He told me] they was driving along and . . . one of the people, I'm not sure which one, said they was gonna shoot somebody, and he [Marty] said he didn't think that was a good idea," he said. "He thought they was just joking around, and he was sitting back in the backseat, and the next thing you know, he heard them shoot and shoot again, and then he said by the time he looked up the car with the girl in it had ran into a pole. . . . He kept asking, 'You think I can get in trouble for that?—because I didn't want them to shoot her, I didn't even know.' "

The DA attempted to follow up on this.

"And he didn't know this was going to happen?" she asked.

"He said they had said something about it, but he didn't think they was really gonna do it," the boy said.

Don and I found that statement supportive of our suspicion that the shooting had been planned in advance.

After hearing five hours of testimony and deliberating thirty minutes, the grand jury handed down an indictment on charges of "willful and deliberate" first-degree murder, conspiracy to commit murder, shooting at an occupied vehicle, conspiracy to commit that crime, evidence tampering, and conspiracy to tamper with evidence.

A bench warrant was then issued for Juve's arrest, but when the police went to get him, he was gone. His attorney, who had assured the court that Juve was no flight risk, told the press, "I can only speculate he's been frightened off by all the commotion."

Miguel Garcia was still in custody, however, and was arraigned on March 5, 1990. He pleaded innocent to all charges, and his bond was set at $100,000.

Meanwhile, Mike Gallagher was performing his own investigation. He spent most of one week following Dung around and was surprised by the company he was keeping.

"He gets picked up by Mexicans in Hertz cars who take

him to strip joints," he told me. "I don't mean just at night, but during the day when you'd expect him to be at work. The guys are the kind of thugs I wouldn't want to meet in a dark alley. They stand a head taller than Dung and look like they just broke out of the pen."

He had also checked into the insurance scams in Orange County.

"The car-wreck deal is primarily a Vietnamese scam and it goes on all the time out there," he told me. "Apparently the participants in a wreck get a couple of thousand, while the lawyer pockets fifty thousand and the doctors and pharmacists rake in hundreds of thousands of dollars. We are definitely talking the kind of money people get killed for.

"I'm not having too much luck getting background information on that R & J outfit, because it's not in business any longer. It folded last year, shortly after the Westminster Police Department and the Orange County District Attorney's office closed down two medical clinics in Westminster for multimillion-dollar insurance fraud. It's coming down to Vietnamese ownership, but it's pretty tangled as to exactly who owns it, because we're dealing with about fifteen limited partnerships."

By now Don and I had spent a month holed up in the efficiency and were climbing the walls. We decided to sell the house and rent a town house.

The move to a town house from a five-bedroom home with a den meant a great reduction in living and storage space, and we had to find homes for the pets and get rid of possessions. The hardest of those to part with were personal mementos—sports trophies, kindergarten artwork, jigsaw puzzles carefully assembled and glued onto cardboard backing, sheet music from band recitals, ceramic molds of tiny handprints, handmade ashtrays and spool holders we'd received as Christmas presents.

We took with us the dozens of double-size photograph albums, because the largest number of the pictures they held were of Kait. Despite the fact that my father, Joseph Steinmetz, had been an internationally known photographer, I had not developed an interest in photography until Kait was born, so our older children had been short-changed on baby pictures. Soon after Kait's birth I had taken a photography course which had led, not only to a hobby, but to a supplementary career. From babyhood on, Kait's face had appeared on magazine covers, and now, as I leafed through the albums, I found her on page after page—sniffing a flower, stroking a kitten, climbing a tree, wading in a stream, running through sprinklers—and always in evidence on her left cheekbone was "God's fingerprint."

The irony of that term wasn't lost on me now, as I loaded the albums into boxes to store in the garage. What a stupid name for a hole in her face, I thought bitterly.

The one positive thing that occurred during that transition period was that Brett resurfaced.

"I'm sorry I worried you," he said. "I just had to get my act together."

We were pleased to learn he no longer was working with rock bands and had become a member of the "establishment," living in Miami and working as a computer operator. And, like Kerry, who had changed careers from television newswoman to free-lance writer so she could be at home with her children, he had started writing articles and submitting them to magazines.

Among these was an essay called "Our Little Hell," which he read to me over the telephone:

"It was a warm Sunday night, and I had just gotten off work and was beginning my usual wind-down ritual of nodding off in front of the television, when a late, unexpected phone call changed my life forever. The caller informed me that my eighteen-year-old sister, Kait, had been shot twice in the head by unknown assailants and was in critical condition in the hospital.

Less than eighteen hours later my beautiful sister and friend passed away.

Kait had always been what I would call a good person. She was a loving, caring young woman who wanted to be a doctor. Why would anybody kill a person like that? What kind of world do we live in that such a thing can happen?

While struggling to answer that question I've come up with a horrible possibility. What if this seemingly wonderful planet of ours is actually Hell, a training ground for Evil? Perhaps we who live here were evil ourselves in a past life and, as punishment, were sentenced to be preyed upon in this current one. Here in Hell some of us are cursed with the fate of being "good" for the sole purpose of honing Evil's skills.

Let's imagine that our Hell is comprised of a large meadow in which we (the good) are a flock of Sheep who do nothing but graze. Protecting us are the Dogs (the police) whose job it is to keep a constant watch for Wolves (Evil), while the Shepherd (God) tends His flock.

The sole purpose of this flock in Hell is to give Evil something to practice its talents on. Our Mother Sheep always told us that if we were good little lambs and stayed in the middle of the flock, we could count on being safe. Only the foolish ones who tempted Evil by existing on the outer edges of the flock would meet disaster. What

Mother Sheep didn't understand was that those on the outside edge had practice escaping Evil's advances. They did so on a daily basis and knew how to take care of themselves.

One day the wolves came sneaking around—as they always did—looking for an easy target. Without warning they attacked! The sheep on the outside sensed the strike and fled, splitting the flock down the middle. The sheep in the center had never been exposed to this type of threat and hadn't noticed how close the wolves were. Before the naive sheep could react, the wolves killed a lamb and escaped into the night.

The Dogs had been drinking coffee at a Dunkin' Donuts, and the Shepherd was sleeping.

"What do you think?" Brett asked. "Is it a good analogy?"

"I have problems with it," I said. "The wolves didn't split the flock, our lamb went frolicking to meet them. And I can't accept that our world is a training ground for Evil. Isn't it possible it might be the other way around, that it's a place where Good can learn to stand up to Evil and defeat it?"

"So, where was the Shepherd?"

"I don't know," I admitted.

That night I had a troubling dream. I was back in our family home and was going into Kait's bedroom to kiss her good-night. She was lying, propped up on one elbow, but as I approached the bed, she suddenly rolled over on her back and playfully pulled up her knees to block my view of her face. Then she lowered her knees abruptly, and I found myself looking down at a boy of about seventeen. He had an interesting, foxlike face with a pointed chin, and was gazing up at me with Kait's insolent green eyes.

I knew I should know who he was, but I couldn't say his name. Once I had known him well, but I had somehow forgotten him.

"This isn't your time," I told him. "I want my daughter."

He was instantly gone, and it was Kait on the bed again.

I gathered her into my arms and hugged her so tightly that neither of us could breathe.

"I want you back inside me again," I whispered. "I want you back where I can keep you safe."

But I could not do in a dream what I had not done in life, and I could not blame the Dogs, and I could not blame the Shepherd. Raised by gentle, devoted parents, who had believed that all people were good, I had not taught any of my lambs how to recognize wolves.

13

The spring of 1990 was long and cruel and windy, and I hated it. Just as flowers were beginning to break through the earth, we were hit with a sudden cold snap that killed the unopened buds and littered the ground with hailstones. On Easter I took a hyacinth out to the cemetery, but when I went back later to water it, it had blown away, pot and all.

At home in the town house I told myself I had to start working again. Nine months had passed since Kait's death, and that was enough. It had taken me nine months to bring her into the world, and the same length of time to see her out of it, and I couldn't continue indulging myself in bereavement. I had one teenage mystery still due under a three-book contract, and I was expected to write four to six articles a year for *Woman's Day*. All my editors had been sympathetic and understanding and had exerted no pressure on me to fulfill my obligations, but I knew I couldn't continue to vegetate indefinitely. Besides, Don and I were used to a double income, and I had not earned a penny for three quarters of a year. Our house was up for sale, but we were continuing to make payments on it, while at the same time paying rent on the town house, and our financial situation was not looking good.

I couldn't dredge up enough energy to create fiction, but

I did write an article for *Woman's Day*, based upon personal experience, about how to help friends in crisis. It wasn't much fun to write, but my editor liked it, and I realized I hadn't lost my ability to put words on paper.

The day I mailed off the article, Mike called to tell me he had been able to track down one of the two phone numbers and thought that possibly the other was for a beeper. The unlisted number had belonged to someone named Van Hong Phuc, who lived in Santa Ana. Mike said that although Van Hong Phuc still lived at the same address, his (or her) number had been changed to another unlisted number immediately after Kait's death.

"Don't let APD or the defense attorneys get wind that I'm investigating this," he said. "If APD finds out, they'll close down my sources of information, and the defense will get their clients off by implicating Dung and making a better case against him than the DA can make against Garcia. As of now the defense attorneys think Dung is dead. Somebody told them his suicide attempt was successful."

"Why would anyone do that?"

"You figure it out," Mike said. "All I know is I overheard them talking about what a drag it is that Kait's boyfriend killed himself, because, if he was still around, they would sure like to talk to him. I'm expecting any time now to see motions for discovery."

"What's that?" I asked.

"Discovery is where the prosecution has to show the defense all the material they have," Mike explained. "Personally, I don't think the state's going to show the defense everything. One reason I say that is that normally in most homicide cases, once the case has gone to the grand jury and the suspects have been indicted, everything the police have is filed in the records division, which means you or I or anybody else could go down and pay a dollar a page and get the file. In this case that hasn't been done. They keep saying the case is still under investigation, despite the fact that the grand jury returned an indictment. My guess is that APD may be busy editing the file to get rid of anything that points to a Vietnamese connection."

"Because they don't want to have to explore any avenues other than 'random shooting'?"

"Right," Mike said. "Those suspects are easy marks. APD wants to keep the case real simple—'Here are the guys, it was a random shooting, let's get on to other business.' If they're doing that, it's something to be concerned about, because if they don't play it straight—if they withhold information from the defense—even if the Hispanics are the killers, they're going to walk. The defense is bound to find out about it eventually. Then they'll file an appeal, and the case will be thrown out. That's what happens when cops don't follow the rules."

If Miguel Garcia was truly the person who shot Kait, I certainly didn't want him back on the street where he could kill others. But I couldn't rid my mind of the call from the tipster. It would be atrocious to have the Hispanics prosecuted as mischievous, gun-toting drunks on a joyride, while men who might have been responsible for hiring them sat back and laughed.

Could a link be established between the Vietnamese and the Hispanics? In an effort to tie them together I again phoned Betty Muench. She did a new reading and gave it to me over the telephone:

QUESTION: WHAT MAY WE KNOW AT THIS TIME ABOUT ANY POSSIBLE LINK BETWEEN THE HISPANICS (ESPECIALLY THOSE ACCUSED OF KAITLYN'S MURDER) AND THE VIETNAMESE (ES-

PECIALLY DUNG NGOC NGUYEN AND HIS CLOSEST ASSOCI-
ATES)?

"This is a very strange reading," Betty told me. "The story seems to be taking a whole new direction. A lot of this makes no sense to me at all."

ANSWER: There is a sensation which will seem to fall down over the face, and there will be a smooth-as-glass feeling.

"In other words, we're talking about a smooth operation," Betty said.

ANSWER: There is an image formed of a kind of statuary which will be seen as if looking up at it, and there is a serpent's head which will be made of a kind of green metal, a kind of turquoise with a darker outline of turquoise. This would seem to be something made out of brass or bronze which is weathered, and this is large and one can look up at it. This will seem to be a symbol of some great clan or force, and this will have power and wealth, and there will be the hiring of what they consider lesser ones—the Hispanics. The image will have to do with a certain Vietnamese group which will hold this power, and they will simply use the Hispanics to do their work.

"It seems they just use them and throw them away," Betty said. "They feel superior to the Hispanics and consider them expendable."

ANSWER: There will be known that one of the suspects in this murder will have relatives very close to this place where this reptile head will be and that there will be under this head many meetings. These meetings will be inconspicuous, as it will indeed be a public place. With this one suspect's relatives involved already, there will be no problem to recruit from this locale those who will do their bidding. There will be in this image that which will show that the reptile is, in a sense, seen as valuable and that this is a symbol which will be used often, and even in this locale there is something which will denote the following of this reptile theme.

There will be in this then a connection, but the relationship of one of the suspects to ones who will have already worked in this connection with the Vietnamese will become even more clear and evident. There cannot be the linking in simple ways. It will have to do with finding other ways in which payment is made than in instruments that can be traced. There will be payment in some unusual ways, and favors will exist. There is in this code of this reptile that which will have them functioning in a mafialike fashion, and there will be a code which will have the Oriental label to it. This symbol of the reptile can be looked for and found in some unusual places. A name will link all this with certainty—a Hispanic name, as common in Los Angeles as in Albuquerque. The same first letter as Garcia, but not Garcia. This one, Garcia, sought this so-called "honor" and must now undergo the pressure, and this one is in jeopardy also at this time from the reptile.

"Miguel Garcia feels that he's being protected, but actually, he isn't," Betty said. "He's as expendable as the rest of them and can easily be eliminated, especially if the police pick up Juve and cut a deal with him."

Betty then mailed me the transcript, along with a note:

Dear Lois,

I hope there is something here which will help resolve this case. There is something very wrong in a system that serves to protect the wrongdoer. Be careful, but don't give up.

Love and blessings,
Betty

As usual, she would not accept payment.

It was Don's opinion that we should share this reading with Mike.

"We owe it to him to give him all the information we have," he said. "Maybe he can figure out the significance of the snake head."

I had asked both Mike and the police to check out R & J Car Leasing, and had told them I'd gotten the name from a telephone tipster. It hadn't seemed prudent to mention that the tipster was a psychic.

"He'd laugh in my face," I said. "He's a newspaper reporter."

"Give him a chance," Don said. "He might surprise you."

The next time I talked with Mike, I casually asked him how he felt about the use of psychics in criminal investigations.

"They're useless," he said. "All they're out for is money

and publicity. I've never known one to turn up anything of value." He changed the subject. "I've heard an odd story about Juve. The last time anybody talked to him, he was on the phone with his girlfriend after the warrant was issued, and he told her, 'Well, the police are outside now. The next time I talk to you, I guess it will be from jail.' At that point he just disappeared, and nobody's seen him since."

"Is his family worried?" I asked.

"Apparently so."

"Is it true the police were outside when he was making that call?"

"I can't find that out," Mike said. "APD won't answer questions, but his girlfriend seems to think that there was foul play involved."

If it hadn't been for Mike we wouldn't have known anything, since the police wouldn't answer our questions or share information with us. Betty's statement that there would be "a certain advantage in the media system" had certainly proven accurate, as had many of her other predictions. But though I now accepted the fact that it was possible for a medium to channel information from the dead, I couldn't imagine how anyone could foretell the future.

Don surprised me by saying he had no problem with that.

"In the context of eternity time doesn't exist," he said. "That means that, on a plane where things are not bracketed by beginnings and endings, it should be just as easy to look forward as it is to look backward." He saw my look of confusion and attempted to elaborate. "Think of it this way —you make a videotape of your child's birthday party, and the next day you play it back and watch her spill her ice cream. You don't find that strange, because you know that it happened; you're watching a rerun of something that's already taken place. Now, what if you're able to see that video ahead of time and watch your child spill her ice cream the day *before* the party? If the video was created in a realm where time, as we know it, doesn't exist, it would be just as easy to view it before the fact as after."

"But that would mean we have no free will!" I objected. "If our lives are all mapped out for us before we're born, then none of us is responsible for anything we do."

"Of course we're responsible," Don said. "If the child is careful with her ice cream, the video shows she keeps her dress clean. The video doesn't *make* things happen, it simply *records* them, and a psychic like Betty Muench, who has extrasensory abilities, can zero in on the tape before the events on it take place."

I tried to translate that concept into something more familiar. Our three oldest children had been involved in community theater, and I had spent many hours rehearsing them in their lines. Occasionally during a performance an actor would forget his lines and start to ad-lib, which would force the other actors to ad-lib also, and the scene would become so chaotic that the story line was lost. What if our years on earth were scripted ahead of time, but, because we did have free will, we could write our own scripts, based upon the lessons we needed to learn and the lessons we agreed to help others learn? Although we had no conscious memory of those commitments, each person's script would be imprinted on his or her soul. If we "forgot our lines" and didn't play the scene as it was scripted, we could blow the whole play, not only for ourselves, but for everybody.

That raised a possibility I found terrifying to contemplate. Might a person who was involved in a creative career —who drew, day after day, year after year, upon information stored in the depths of the subconscious—inadvertently pull up fragmented flashes of material from scenes that were in the script but had not been played out yet?

"This is going to sound crazy," I told Don, "and I feel silly even mentioning it, but some of the things in my books seem to have been prophetic."

"Like what?" he asked.

"Well, take *Ransom*, for example, about a group of students who were kidnapped by the driver of their school bus. I wrote that story when I lived in Livermore, California. Soon after the book was published, a school-bus driver in Livermore kidnapped a busload of students and held them for ransom. The crime was so similar to the one in my book that the parents of one of the children wanted to have me arrested.

"There are also disturbing things in *Don't Look Behind You*. I modeled my heroine, April, on Kait's personality, and in the story April was chased by a hitman in a Camaro. One month after the book was published, that happened to Kait. In the book April's family was forced into hiding because of death threats, and the same thing's happened to us."

"Life is filled with coincidences," Don said.

"That's what I've been telling myself."

Glad that he hadn't been eager to pursue the topic, I made an effort to focus my mind on more practical matters, such as how to find out if Miguel Garcia did, as Betty's reading seemed to indicate, have relatives in L.A. who might be performing as flunkies for the Vietnamese.

An idea occurred to me as I was standing in line at the post office, waiting to turn in a change-of-address card. I knew Miguel Garcia's address because it had been printed in the newspaper. What if I turned in a change-of-address card for the Garcia family, so, for a short time at least, we would get their mail? Of course, it wouldn't be long before

somebody caught on, but in the meantime a letter might
arrive from Uncle Gonzales or Gurule or Gutierrez out in
Orange County, wanting to know if a date had been set for
the trial. In fact, if I timed things right, I might even receive
the Garcias' phone bill and discover that they made fre-
quent long-distance calls to California.

I tossed the idea around all the while I was in line, and
even went so far as to pick up a second change-of-address
card. Then, I lost my nerve and didn't fill it out. To tamper
with the U.S. mails was a felony, and I knew I would probably get sentenced to more years in prison for reading the
Garcias' mail than Miguel Garcia could get if he were convicted of blowing my daughter's brains out.

14

At least we knew the whereabouts of Miguel Garcia; he was tucked away in jail, out of reach of "The Snake."

That was more than could be said for Juve Escobedo. Everybody took it for granted that Juve had fled back to his native Mexico, but what if he hadn't? What if Juve's last words to his girlfriend had been spoken in all honesty—he *did* hear people outside, and he thought they were policemen, and he did, in fact, believe that the next time he phoned her it would be from the jailhouse. He had been there before, and he knew he would be allowed to use the telephone.

But what if the men he had heard had not been who he thought they were?

My experience in creating fictional scenes made this one easy for me. The setting: the Escobedo home in the armpit of Martineztown.

Action: There is a knock at the door, and Juve hangs up the phone and goes to open it. To his surprise he finds Vietnamese on the doorstep. "We've come to save you!" they tell him. "We're going to take you across the border! You and Miguel did a wonderful job getting rid of that bothersome Arquette girl, and now we feel it's our duty to help you escape." "*Gracias!*" Juve cries gratefully, and leaps

into their car, without even stopping long enough to pack a
suitcase or to leave his family a note to say where he is
going. They take the highway south in the direction of El
Paso, and after a hundred or so miles, when they reach the
wide open spaces south of Socorro, they pull over to the
side of the road, and Juve becomes history. Now there is
one less suspect to break under pressure and give away the
fact that Kait's shooting was premeditated. No one will
question Juve Escobedo's disappearance, since everyone will
assume he's holed up in Mexico.

The more times I played this scenario out in my head, the
more convinced I became that it was exactly what had happened. I phoned Betty and told her, "I think Juve's dead,
but I need to have that verified. Do you think you can do
that?"

"Probably," she said. "I'll see what I can get for you."

While I waited for her to call back, I organized my game
plan, pleased that my day would be filled with purpose and
activity. I knew the police would have problems accepting
my theory, and in order to convince them I would have to
present them with Juve's body, which was bound to be buried somewhere between Albuquerque and El Paso. With
Betty as a guide it shouldn't be all that hard to locate, but
would the two of us be able to dig it up by ourselves? I
considered the question and decided that probably we
wouldn't. I'd never been very well muscled, even in my
younger days, and lately I'd lost a lot of weight and had
been getting no exercise. Betty was a few years younger and
was in better shape than I was, but since it wasn't her
daughter who was dead, I didn't feel I had the right to ask
her to do the brunt of the heavy work while I just stood
there and supervised. I decided that the best thing to do
would be just to drive south with her until she pointed out

the grave site, and then to drive back to Socorro and find someone to do the digging. Maybe one of those men who stood on street corners holding signs that said I WILL WORK FOR FOOD would be up for the job.

An hour passed, and Betty still didn't call back. To keep myself occupied I fixed a lunch to take with us and went out to the garage to see if I could find something to put it in. In one of the boxes Don had brought over from the house, I discovered a picnic basket. At first I couldn't figure out where it had come from, but when I opened the lid and saw the red checkered cloth inside, I remembered all too well. On Kait's last Halloween she had been invited to a party, and she and I had spent most of one Saturday dashing from store to store, assembling her costume—a basket from one place, red-and-white checkered napkins from another, a cape from a third, so she could go as Little Red Riding Hood.

I closed the basket and stuck it back in the box, knowing there was no way I could ever pack a lunch in it.

When I went back into the house, the phone was ringing. It was Betty, calling to tell me Juve was alive.

"Are you sure?" I couldn't have said if I was disappointed or relieved. "I'd been planning that you and I would go hunt for his body."

"Are you out of your mind?" exclaimed Betty. "There's no way I'd do that."

"I didn't expect you to do all the digging," I assured her.

"I told you before, I don't like to do crime," Betty said. "I can't think of anything more revolting than digging up dead bodies."

"What do you normally do if you 'don't do crime'?" I asked. "What other kinds of readings do people ask for?"

"A lot of them want to know what their purpose in life is

and what their true relationship is to other people." Betty paused. "Aren't you interested in hearing the stuff I got about Juve?"

"You told me he's alive," I said, "so I presume he's in Mexico."

"No, he's here in Albuquerque," Betty told me. "Hang on to your hat, because this is one weird reading":

QUESTION: WHAT MAY WE KNOW AT THIS TIME ABOUT THE PERSON JUVE ESCOBEDO . . . IS HE ALIVE OR DEAD . . . WHERE CAN HE BE FOUND . . . WILL HE AND CAN HE COME FORTH?

ANSWER: There is a desire to look to the point where Juve would communicate from the other side, but the head is pushed down and this is not possible, for he is in the body.

"If the spirit is not in the body, I will usually see a misty image to my left up by the ceiling," Betty said. "When I looked up there for Juve, I didn't find him."

ANSWER: There is this which will show that he is seemingly in a state however that would resemble a kind of dying. He will seem to be desperate, and it is as if he is trying to pull himself up out of something and that he is unable to be free. There will be in this then this energy which will show that he will be left alone and that he will be in some place which confines him and that he is not attended to. There is a sense that this confinement is not something to do with this case. It will be as if there is this which is felt like a kind of vendetta and that there will be this which he seemingly is not aware of, as if some revenge is being taken upon him but he does not know why. There will be in this then this energy which will show much confusion in him and he will be unable to explain any of this to anyone. It is beyond him.

"This feels like some sort of vigilante activity," Betty said.

ANSWER: There will be in this one Juve that which is not totally aware of his surroundings, but he even knows now that this situation in which he finds himself will not be right and normal even under forms of vendetta. There is a sense of some secret force at work here and that there will be those who want to hold him and he does not even himself know who they are or what they are doing. They do not talk to him, and this causes him great fear.

This is some force acting unofficially but somehow felt to be connected with some kind of official work. There is a great fear at being found out in all this, but there is seemingly a plan which can then be instigated which would diffuse any suspicion on them. Two others are felt in this, and thus then some kind of conspiracy. There is not felt any energy of the foreign in all this, and it is as if this force would seem to be the authorities themselves.

"I don't get a sense that he's being held by the Vietnamese," Betty said. "It sounds like somebody in authority is acting independently without the people he works with knowing what he's doing."

ANSWER: There is a sense of this being like an old garage, and there is a pit in the ground, and he is seemingly kept there. This would be in this city of Albuquerque. It is as if he will suddenly become rearrested and will come forth in due time with all manner of confession. This is a clean place and it is as if it only recently has been emptied.

"He's in a garage?" I asked doubtfully.

"It has that sort of feeling to it. It seems to be a place with something like a grease pit. He's very frightened, but I don't think he's going to die there, or else this wouldn't say he's going to be recaptured. If you're going to go out looking for him, count me out."

"I'm not going to do that," I said, but, of course, I was. The moment I was off the phone I had the directory out and was opening the yellow pages to "Automobile Repairing and Service."

There were twenty-six pages of listings under that category. The obvious way to find out which garages had been vacated was to phone them all and see which numbers had been disconnected. With just three of us living at home we didn't make many phone calls, so when we moved into the town house, Don had subscribed to an optional billing plan that charged for each call individually. In the normal course of things this was saving us money, but now I realized that if I called every number on over two dozen pages it would cost us a fortune. The only solution I could come up with was to make the calls at night when nobody would be at work to answer the telephone. Knowing that Don would attempt to discourage this endeavor, I waited until he was asleep before I slipped out of bed and got busy on the telephone. The businesses that had answering machines were an irritant, but luckily there weren't too many of them, and I ended up with a list of twenty-three defunct garages with phones that were no longer in service.

By the time I made my last call, the sky was paling in the east, and faint strips of color were beginning to bring life to the clouds. I went back to bed for an hour, got up when the alarm went off at six A.M., fixed breakfast, and packed Donnie's lunch with the sandwiches I had made to take on the search for Juve's body. Then, as soon as I had the house to myself, I got out a notepad captioned "Dumb Things I Have to Do Today"—a Mother's Day gift from Kait the previous spring—and started making a list.

Kait and I had always been the list-makers in the family—she, because she was organized, and I, because I wasn't. My list of chores for that day differed only slightly from my usual lists:

Buy groceries—eggs, tomatoes, chicken, Kleenex, milk,
    bread, Tylenol, and remember to take coupons
Take Don's pants to cleaners
Buy stamps
Stock up on fish food
Find Juve
Make appointment with chiropractor

I studied the list and decided to rearrange the items on it, giving top priority to the chiropractor appointment, since tension had caused my neck to freeze into place. I then elevated finding Juve to the second slot, because I had no idea how long that might take me, and if necessary, mundane chores like buying stamps and fish food could be shoved over to the following day.

The chiropractor's office wasn't open when I called, so I

left a message on their machine to set me up for a late-afternoon appointment. Then I went out to the car and sat for a while with my list of garages, arranging them in groups according to location. Two were situated in Little Vietnam, which was where instinct would have taken me first, but since Betty had felt so strongly that Juve's captors were not Oriental, I decided to begin my exploration on the west side of the city, which encompassed the original Albuquerque and the tourist-centered "Old Town" area near which Kait had been killed.

Starting close to the center of the downtown area, I drove systematically up and down streets, checking out addresses. Several of the vacated buildings appeared to have been taken over by other businesses and were sporting signs that identified them as print shops, tile and lighting companies, and plumbing supply stores. One vacant building stood next to a busy shopping center, which was the hub of so much traffic that it didn't seem possible Juve could have been smuggled into it without detection. Another was part of a complex of auto-related businesses, a risky place to try to stash a captive who might spit out his gag and start yelling for help.

Having completed my tour of garages in the urban area, I continued my search on the west side of the Rio Grande in a rural part of the county known as the Valley. Crossing the bridge that spanned the normally sluggish river, which was now churning white with the runoff from heavy spring rains, I drove along country roads bordered by cottonwoods just beginning to come into leaf. When the children were small, Don and I had driven these roads on numerous week-ends, loaded down with picnic lunches and camera equipment. I passed the spot where I had photographed Kait in a pumpkin patch; the farmer's market where I'd taken a picture of Donnie sorting apples; the field where Kerry had posed, feeding daisies to a horse. The fast-fading covers of magazines documented those memories of the All-American Family having fun in the country. It had never entered our heads that we were dwelling in Camelot and that "happily ever after" existed only in fairy tales.

A building that wasn't on my list loomed up ahead of me, and I was certain it was a vacated garage. There was no logical reason to think that, but I had abandoned all semblance of sanity and was playing it as it fell, so I slowed the car and pulled off the road into a parking area next to a clump of poplars. I turned the key in the ignition, killing the engine, and the stillness of the countryside dropped over me like a shroud. After a moment, however, small sounds began to rise to infiltrate the silence. Birds twittered and chirped among the pale leaves above me, and somewhere on down the road the high-pitched yap of a dog was as rhythmic as a heartbeat. An unseen rabbit or chipmunk rustled the bushes next to the front fender of my car, and the drone of an airplane came faintly from a distant cloud bank.

I sat without moving, my full attention on the building. It was obviously empty, but it could not have been that way for long, because the panes of the windows were clean, and there were tire tracks next to mine in the damp earth of the parking lot. Getting out of the car, I walked around to the front and experimentally twisted the doorknob. As I had expected, the door was locked, as was a second door that faced to the east. I slowly circled the building, peering in through the windows, trying to make out the rectangular hollow of a grease pit, but the interior was so dark that I couldn't see anything.

When I reached the back of the building, I was surprised to discover that one of the windows had been left open a

couple of inches as if to let in air. Sliding my fingers into the
crack, I jerked up on the window, but wasn't able to move it.
Bracing myself, I yanked harder, giving my neck a painful
jolt in the process, but I still couldn't budge it.

I put my mouth to the opening and called, "Juve, are you
in there?" I was certain that he was. When I pressed my ear
to the crack, I was almost sure I could hear his breathing
like the hyperventilation of a great big animal in a trap. The
man who was accused of chasing down my daughter was
right here in this building, only yards away from me, trussed
and gagged, but alive and aware I was calling to him. Perhaps he had already identified me as Kait's mother and
decided he would rather put up with his present discomfort
than respond with a groan or a thump that would bring me
in there.

"To hell with you!" I shouted. "You can't fool me!" I
hadn't come all this way to turn around and go home, just
because I wasn't strong enough to force open a window.

I went back to the station wagon and returned with the
tire iron. Gripping the bar with both hands, I swung it back
like a baseball bat and aimed it at the windowpane. I stood
there for a good thirty seconds, posing for the majors, and
then lowered my arms and let the bar drop to the ground.
What would I do with Juve if I went in and found him?
Dead, he might have been manageable, but, alive, he would
be impossible. From the picture I'd seen in the paper, the
man was a Neanderthal. There was no way I could haul him
out of a grease pit. I would have to untie him and let him
climb out on his own, and if I did that, he would probably
kill me.

I carried the iron back to the car and stuffed it into the
compartment with the spare tire. Then I climbed into the
front seat and began to pound my fists on the dashboard like

a woman gone crazy. Actually, I *was* such a woman, I could no longer deny that. Who did I think I was, a female version of Mike Gallagher? Jessica Fletcher? Miss Marple? The whole idea was ludicrous. I shouldn't be out driving around, I belonged in a hospital where I could have my nervous breakdown without bothering anybody.

I ceased my attack on the dashboard and burst into tears, weeping for what I had lost and for the person I'd become because of that loss, a person with no identity and no reason for living.

After the flood was over, I looked for some Kleenex, but of course, I couldn't find any; it was one of those things I'd been planning to buy at the grocery store. Wiping my nose on my sleeve, I started the car and drove slowly and carefully home, resisting a sudden urge to drive off the bridge. When I entered the house, the answering machine was blinking to indicate two messages. One was from the wife of the chiropractor, saying he was sick and would not be back in his office for the rest of the week. The second was an obscene phone call. I listened twice to the moaning and heavy breathing, because it was the most diverting thing I had heard for a while.

Was this what my life had become? Was this going to be *it* for me—an unreliable chiropractor and a masturbating pervert on my answering machine?

I've got to do something, I told myself, or I'm not going to make it.

Switching off the machine, I picked up the telephone receiver. The number I dialed was getting to be a familiar one.

"Betty?" I said. "This is Lois. I want to make an appointment for a personal reading. I need to find out if I still have a purpose in this lifetime."

Happy "all-American family" in 1973: Seated: Don with Donnie, 5; Lois with Kait, 3; Robin, 19. Standing: Kerry, 17; Brett, 14

15

I hadn't seen Betty in person since the first reading she did for me, but after so many phone conversations I felt as if she were an old friend. Which was good, because I wouldn't have wanted a stranger to be with me when I received the message I feared most: "Your only job in this lifetime was to protect your children! You've blown it, and there's nothing left for you now except to vegetate, make your husband miserable, and die."

Betty took her seat in front of the typewriter and asked me how many questions I was going to want answered.

I had come prepared with just one, but now I decided that I might as well go for broke.

"I'll take the works," I said. "How many do I get?"

"Four at a sitting is about my limit," Betty told me.

"The question that brought me here is 'What is my purpose in this lifetime, and have I achieved it yet?' What else do you suggest I ask?"

"I think we can reword that question to get more out of it," Betty said. "The other thing people usually want to know is what their true relationships are with the people who are important to them."

"I already know that," I said. "Robin thinks I'm naive, Kerry thinks I don't spend enough time with my grandchildren, and my sons think I'm stodgy and uncool. And at this point Don probably thinks he'd be better off without me."

"That's not what I meant," said Betty. "Your *true* relationships are the ones that go back to the times you were together before."

"You mean in previous lifetimes?"

"You'll probably just get one of them—the lifetime that provides the foundation for the one you're now living."

"Okay, let's do it," I said. I wasn't sure I was ready for it, but I knew that I was committed to whatever came out of this. So, we sat as we had before—Betty at the typewriter, and I in a chair across from her—and I asked my questions aloud, and she typed out the answers. Her fingers danced on the keyboard, and page after page leapt out of the typewriter. As I watched the history of my soul pile up on her desk, I knew, before I ever read it, that the story would be true.

QUESTION: WHAT IS MY TRUE PURPOSE IN THIS LIFETIME, AND HOW MAY I BEST FULFILL IT?

ANSWER: There will be this energy which will move over into the right side, that of the masculine intellect, and there will be this energy which will move down into the shoulder, and that will have to do with the role playing, and this will have had to do with Lois in another time in which she will have been this one to sit around a fountain and to then teach those others who will have come to her.

There will have been much relaxed energy in that, and it will have been in a very secretive way, and it will have been shared by only a few in that time. There will have been works which will have covered healing and works which will have covered many things which will have had to do with more secret teachings, and none could speak of what they learned, and this will have caused some difficulty in some of them. The swearing to secrecy will have been that which will have been the problem, for it will have been that the teachings in that time would have been considered heretical and that, then, the teacher would have been in danger.

The students were so pleased with their learning that they wanted to share this with many, and this will have been impossible unless they wanted to destroy the very source of their learning, the teacher. There will have been in that, then, that energy which will have had Lois then as a male energy pattern and very strong in the belief of her own knowing, which will have been outside of the normal teaching, and thus meta and very metaphysical.

There will have been for her this energy which will have been on guard, and sometimes there will have been a strong passion in all this, and she will have used much red energy in the enforcing of her secrecy dictum. There will have been an offering by her in *this* time to return and to make her knowing available to all in the time of the new age when the media will be the major teaching vehicle. There will be in this then some safeguards for her, and there will be in this new age and in this country this freedom which would permit this kind of speaking out and not fearing for the life.

There will be this which will show that Lois will have been a robed teacher and one who will have enjoyed the strong loyalty of a small group, and that was sufficient for her to think through all her teachings and

to know that in *this* time it will be necessary to give
them out.

QUESTION: WHAT IS MY TRUE RELATIONSHIP WITH MY
DAUGHTERS . . . ROBIN . . . KERRY . . . KAITLYN?

ANSWER: There will have been very strong-willed ones
in her group, and she will have encouraged that in *this*
time. The male that she *was* has to be the female that
she is *now*, and also in that then, the *males* who will
have been so strong willed in that time will now be the
daughters, and there will be this very close affinity, as if
Lois will know of what they must address in this time
in order to become the balanced beings that can truly
understand the teachings of before and apply them to
this lifetime, the female in this time, applying the masculine energy, and then seeking to come into this balance.

There will be this energy with these specific daughters:

There is energy which will show that Robin will
have been one in that time who will have been chomp-
ing at the bit to give out this information. She will have
wanted to do this in her own way and go to another
country in order to fulfill this, and so she did. She did
not suffer for that, and it will be that this will also seem
to be the case now. It will be that Robin can say and do
certain things, even into this time, without seeming
censorship. This will be her way, and she will always be
one to find the method.

There will be in this one Kerry this energy which
will have been the student who will have been cautious,
and this one will have taken on some of the paranoia of
this old teacher. In this time, too, there will be fears in

Kerry from time to time which are unfounded, and she will fear exploring certain ideas, and she will be the last to try things.

There will be that there will have been this rebellious one, which is Kaitlyn in this time, and this one will have come very near in this other time to a fate similar to her fate in this time. There will have been in that time this one who will have been very warriorlike and who will have responded to the passions of this teacher and who will have taken up arms often. It will be that in that time she will have made certain mistakes, and in this time she will have made similar mistakes, and it will have had to do with the inability to know whom to trust. There will have been this lesson for Kaitlyn all this lifetime, and it will show that she will now know how this would be for her. In this other time she will have been the cause of certain harm to her teacher, and in this time it is as if she will not have wanted that and took her lesson on to other dimensions to complete.

There will be in this then still the ability in Lois to teach all in this time and she will seek to know that she will continue to be their teacher in all realms.

QUESTION: WHAT IS MY TRUE RELATIONSHIP WITH MY SONS . . . BRETT AND DONNIE?

ANSWER: There will be this energy which will soften and fall into the throat center. It will be that there will have been in this other time of Lois as the teacher those who will have wanted to speak her word but knew they could not in that time. They will be stuck in the throat chakra levels, and these men, Brett and Donnie, will have a hard time saying what they will know. They will not often speak up giving deference to this teacher. This will put a burden on Lois in this time and she will be here now to encourage them to speak out and to try to give them both some manner of credence in their thought processes.

There will be this green energy in Brett, and it will have to do with a certain healing ability. This learning from this other time will be very strong in him, and he will have this clear pure green-yellow light all around him which will show that he is indeed a pure healer and would do well in those fields which would have to do with healing. There will be this special ability in this one, and he cannot hide it and keep it back. There is a fear in him to speak up in this time, and this has to be given attention. He must be encouraged to speak out his truth and his knowing of the healing processes will prove to be very valid in this time, but he does not think so. He does not seem to remember, but he will, and it is within him now.

There is in this one Donnie this energy which will hold much pure white light in the head level, and it will be that this one will have been one to have no fears but truly trusted in the teaching. The *teacher* could learn from this one, and it will be that this one will have a need for trust in this time and not have his life beset with doubts and mistrust of his fellowmen. There will come a situation in which he will need this trust, and this will have to do with certain works that he will do in the manner of speaking out in service. This will seem to take on certain political connotations. It will have to do with the giving out of pure truth facts, but still trust and not facts created out of empirical thinking. He will just *know*, and it will quickly be validated. This one has a special power that has to be given out, and it is his responsibility to find the forms of application in this time. This one Lois will have withheld in the forms of application in this past life out of fears for their lives in a time that was unkind to new thought. In this time there should be no fear, only the venturing forth in a very strong way.

QUESTION: WHAT IS MY TRUE RELATIONSHIP WITH MY HUSBAND DON?

ANSWER: It will be that in this other time, this very important time to Lois, there will have been this one who will have been intrigued by her thinking processes but who will have nevertheless been more fearful than intrigued, and thus then this Don will have been one who will have seemingly betrayed this one in this time. There will be in this then this energy of someone who will owe Lois and who will be very true to her in this time out of this past life experience, and it is as if he will be resigned in this time to going all the way with this and seeing it through. He will have been one in a position of some trust by Lois in this other time but will have betrayed her to some kind of other outside authority, and this will have caused Lois suffering. In this time Don will seemingly be very solicitous of her feelings and her well-being. He will be almost a nurse to her at times, and he will want to repay her for this seeming difficulty that he will have caused her and will be one to seek to have her be well in order to give out her truths, and thus then he will be someone who will want to be there when she will deliver her fullest knowing, her fullest truth in this time, and he will want this, and so he will have it.

> There will be in Don no secret ambitions of his own,
> then or now, only then there will have been misunder-
> standing of the truth, and in this time there will be the
> knowing that he is following his destiny with Lois.
> They will do much together, and she will share much
> with him in this time, but he will permit her to know
> her own rewards.

Betty made no attempt to discuss this reading with me.
There was no way she could help me interpret it, because
she knew nothing about my relationships with Don and my
children.

She allowed me to pay her because it was a "routine
reading."

Although I didn't like the idea that Don would "be almost a nurse" to me, I drove back to the town house filled
with a sense of tranquility that I had not experienced for a
very long time. It was comforting to realize that I did still
have a purpose in life and to know that I had been in training for centuries to achieve it. It was easy to imagine myself
as a robed teacher, since I'd spent so much of my present
lifetime teaching writing. I decided my previous experience
had probably been in Rome, either in 325 A.D., when Con-
stantine the Great deleted references to reincarnation from
the New Testament, or in 553 A.D., when the Second Coun-
cil of Constantinople declared the concept of reincarnation
a heresy because it weakened the power of the Church by
allowing people more time to seek salvation. It was also no
problem to picture myself as a "male energy figure." In my
autobiography, *Chapters: My Growth as a Writer*, I had written: "It's interesting to note that in every story I wrote
during my early years, the main character was a boy. I had
always wanted to be a boy. I dressed like a boy as often as

my mother would let me and almost pulled my arm out of the socket trying to kiss my elbow, which I'd heard was the magic formula for changing sex. Needless to say, I was unsuccessful. What I couldn't accomplish in real life, I *could* do on paper. All of my stories were written from a boy's viewpoint."

I had entered the world a precocious and unappealing child. The things I wrote about in my early years were not the kinds of subjects most children are drawn to, and I had spent those years filling lined composition books with poetry. I still had those books, but I hadn't read them in years. Now I was curious enough to go search them out and found them stored in a box in the garage.

I opened one notebook at random, and as I leafed through it, I came across a poem I had written when I was twelve:

THE SONG OF LIFE
by Lois Duncan Steinmetz
(October 7, 1946)

This is the song I am singing tonight
When the stars are pale and the sky is deep.
It's a song I have learned from all things bright,
When the weeping laugh and the laughing weep,
When the dying live, and the living die,
For something is singing that's stronger than I,
Like the sun or the rain or the earth or the sky,
While the sleeping wake and the waking sleep.

This is a song of forgotten things,
The flowers of summer, the hush of the snow,
The millions of glorious, golden springs
That blossomed and faded and died long ago.
It's a song that was made when the earth was begun

Of the dances we dance and the races we run,
Of the laughter and tears that will never be done
And the millions of things that we never will know.

Where did that come from? I asked myself in bewilderment. At the age of twelve I couldn't have understood such
concepts. Was it possible that they had seeped over from a
previous personality who had "thought through all her
teachings" and "been very strong in the belief of her own
knowing"? In his book Dr. Weiss had cited studies by Dr.
Ian Stevenson, professor of psychiatry at the University of
Virginia, who had collected over two thousand case histo-
ries of young children who displayed reincarnation-type
memories. A number of those children were able to speak
foreign languages to which they had never been exposed, an
ability Dr. Stevenson attributed to learning that had been
acquired in previous lifetimes.

Most of those past-life memories had faded before pu-
berty, as had the promise of genius I had shown as a child.
By the time I reached adolescence I was a typical teenage
girl with an unremarkable IQ, and an eye for good-looking
boys. The only two things that set me apart from my peers
were my driving desire to be published and the fact that I
knew with certainty that I would have five children.

"Betty's reading says that my purpose in this lifetime is to
give out my 'truths' through the media," I told Don that
evening. "I'm going to write a book about Kait's murder."

"I'm sure you will," he said.

"I'm going to start it now."

"How can you write it now? You don't have an ending."

"The ending will come," I said. "I'll just write until it
does."

That night as I lay in bed, willing morning to come

quickly so I could get up and start working, I thought about what the reading had said about my children. Their past-life personalities were clearly defined, yet all had the power to move beyond those identities. Even Kait could still grow, as she watched from another dimension and learned that the people to be trusted were the people who loved you.

My renegade baby—my student—my rebellious young warrior! I had no doubt now who the green-eyed boy in my dream had been.

16

When I got up the next morning I was pleased to find that I was sane again. How could I ever have considered driving off a bridge! As soon as Don and Donnie left for work, I rushed to the bedroom I used as an office, inserted a disc in my computer, and began to type: "Our daughter, Kaitlyn Arquette, was murdered in Albuquerque, New Mexico, on Sunday, July 16, 1989. They got her at night."

Although it was emotionally draining to set our story on paper, the writing itself was not difficult, because the chapters were already laid out for me. I had kept meticulous records of everything that had happened and by now had fifty-three pages of single-spaced notes. I also had dated copies of all Betty's readings, newspaper articles arranged in chronological order, and a drawerful of tapes of all our phone conversations since the death threats, including those we'd had with members of the Homicide Department. There was no way I could get any facts wrong or misquote anybody.

"Is it legal to record phone conversations without the other party knowing?" Don asked doubtfully.

"It must be," I said. "The police are the ones who told us to do it."

As I watched the story unfolding chapter by chapter, it

became increasingly apparent to me that the police were not following up on anything we'd told them. It had been three months since Sergeant Lowe had said Barbara Cantwell would be calling us, and we still hadn't heard from her. I wrote another letter to the FBI in Orange County, asking their help in investigating the car-wreck scam, and, as before, they didn't respond.

In May I took a break from my book to fly to Dallas to celebrate Erin's fifth birthday. While I was there, Kerry confided to me that for most of her life she had been having a recurring past-life death dream.

"I died in Auschwitz," she said. "In the dream I'm standing in the queue, waiting to be taken to the showers."

My second daughter had a tendency to be overdramatic.

"I think your imagination's working overtime," I said.

"I've always felt Jewish," she said. "Remember back in high school when I told you I wanted to convert to Judaism and you wouldn't let me?"

"Sixteen was too young for such a major decision," I said defensively. "You wanted to convert because you had so many Jewish friends, and you loved going over to their houses for all the celebrations. Chanukah lasted seven times longer than Christmas, and they got more presents than you did."

"It went deeper than that," Kerry insisted. "I kept choosing Jews for friends, because I felt so comfortable around them, and all their prayers and traditions felt so right and familiar. So, of course, I married a Jew."

"A fallen-away Jew. Ken doesn't even observe the High Holy Days."

"Things have changed," Kerry said. "He's attending services now, and we do Shabbat on Fridays. Wait until you hear the girls recite the shehecheyanu!"

That night I was introduced to the Jewish Sabbath. We ate at a table set with Ken and Kerry's good china and dined on kugel and home-baked challah, and I saw my son-in-law in a whole new light as he lit the Shabbat candles and led his family in prayer.

"Blessed is the Lord our God, Ruler of the Universe, for giving us life, for sustaining us," the children intoned in sweet, soft voices before lunging for the challah.

Before I left, Kerry told me she was converting to Judaism.

"For my Hebrew name I've chosen 'Keshes,' " she said. "That means 'rainbow.' I chose it because of the rainbow that appeared over our house the day of Kait's funeral."

"Won't your belief in reincarnation be a problem?" I asked her.

"I've discussed that with our rabbi, and she says there's no conflict," Kerry assured me. "Judaism doesn't promote a belief in reincarnation, but it doesn't reject it either. Our rabbi also told me she's had visitations from the dead, and she doesn't have any doubts about their validity."

When I got back to Albuquerque, Don told me that he had been trying without success to get back the correspondence from Kait's desk.

"First Sergeant Lowe said I could pick everything up," he said. "Then Gallegos said I couldn't. Then the sergeant said I could have everything back except some letters. Now Gallegos tells me that everything has been tagged as evidence, and we can't get any of it back until after the trial."

"If they're calling the shooting 'random,' how can Kait's things be evidence?"

"I have no idea," Don said. "It's been ten months now, and they haven't even looked at the stuff. I asked Gallegos if they've translated the Vietnamese letters, and he said, no, they don't see any reason for doing that."

"They must be holding those letters to keep us from having them," I said. "They know that if we get them we'll have them translated ourselves, and there might be something in them to implicate Dung and his friends."

Mike had given me the name of Mary Martinez, the head of the Crime Victims Alliance in New Mexico, as someone to call if we had questions about legal procedures. Now I phoned her and asked what our rights were in this situation.

"The law says you have a statutory right to have your daughter's possessions returned to you unless APD has a 'compelling' reason for keeping them," Mary told me. "The problem comes with interpreting the term *compelling*. The police can say, 'We need these things for the trial,' and they're not required to tell you what use they're going to make of them."

"A reporter friend has suggested they may be editing the file," I said.

"They could be," Mary said. "Everything the DA gets must be shared with the defense. The police would want to get every bit of information out of that file that might be used to work in favor of the suspects."

"But isn't that illegal?"

"Of course, but it's done every day. When the cops take notes, those notes are their personal property and they can pick and choose what they want to write up for the record. If something comes up in an interview that doesn't support their scenario, there's nothing to prevent them from leaving it out of the report. That way they can shape the case into anything they want it to be."

"What if my husband and I went directly to the DA?" I asked.

"That depends on which DA is handling your case."

"It's Susan Riedel."

"The little bit I've dealt with Riedel, I've found her to be ethical," Mary said, "so she probably would do what she's supposed to do and share everything you tell her with the defense. And even if that's the right thing, you may not want it, because chances are the result won't be what you're hoping for. The defense will grab on to this Vietnamese angle and run with it, and since the cops aren't willing to make the effort to try to prove murder-for-hire, the men who quite probably shot your daughter will walk."

"But all we want is the truth!"

"As far as the law is concerned, the truth just complicates things," Mary said. "It's the duty of the defense attorneys to get their clients off, and to do that all they need is to raise a 'reasonable doubt.' It's their job to take the truth and twist it around. It's amazing to see how tiny bits of information can be warped in front of a jury to make them think something entirely different happened."

"What if we hired a private detective?" I suggested. "Then we could play the same game as the police and give the DA only the information that points to murder-for-hire."

"That could backfire on you," Mary said. "The defense can subpoena the detective and bring out all the things you don't want divulged."

"So this is how the justice system works in America!"

"It's deplorable, and there isn't any way to fight it. If you try, you'll be labeled a mental case. 'Isn't it too bad about Lois Arquette! You know, that tragic experience has really affected her. Look how paranoid she is now. Look how negative she is toward the law-enforcement agencies. That poor, demented woman is so pathetic!' "

I was too depressed to discuss that subject any further.

"Do you think we will *ever* get Kait's things back?"

"You can give it a try," Mary said. "Put the request in writing. Write a formal letter saying that when there is no longer a 'compelling' reason for those things to be held, you want them returned to you. Send copies to everybody at APD. Send a copy to your lawyer. Address a copy to the evidence room, and specify that you want it to be attached to the evidence tag, so your daughter's things won't be 'inadvertently destroyed.'

"I wish I'd known enough to do that myself. When my teenage son was murdered, all his things that had been marked as evidence were thrown out—just dumped in the trash—between the trial and the appeal."

As if that wasn't enough, on May 29, Mike called to tell me that he still had not been able to turn up an accident report on Kait's car wreck. He did, however, have a copy of the report on Dung's wreck on August 15, 1988.

"The 'accident' took place in Santa Ana," Mike said. "It was an insurance scam from the word go. Dung rear-ended a vehicle filled with Vietnamese gang members, and all of them were taken to Humana Hospital complaining of neck injuries. Dung was driving a privately owned car, a Plymouth Sundance with California plates, registered in the name of An Le."

"An is Dung's alibi for the night Kait was shot!" I exclaimed. "He's also one of the two men who was with him when he stabbed himself!"

"And he's the cousin of Bao Tran, the paralegal who sets up the car wrecks," Mike told me. "Tran used to work for a lawyer named Minh Nguyen Duy at a law office in Garden Grove, but he apparently switched jobs right after Kait's murder. He's now vice-president of some sort of bedding

company. I'm trying to get his home address and phone
number. I'd like to see if they match up with what we have
for Van Hong Phuc, which would mean he's the person who
was called from Kait's apartment as soon as she was pronounced dead."

"How do you know he set up the wrecks?" I asked him.

"I got that from Ray, Dung's Hispanic friend," Mike
said. "Ray also claimed that An is a big-time cocaine dealer.
Dung fed Ray the same line he did Kait about having a
sister in L.A. who provided him with money. He also
bragged to Ray about the insurance scam. Ray told me that
a year ago August, Tran and two other Vietnamese men, all
decked out in three-piece suits, came to Albuquerque in a
big black car and drove Dung and An back to California to
stage wrecks."

"If you could get the accident report on Dung, why can't
you get the one on Kait?" I asked.

"I don't know," Mike said. "It just doesn't seem to be on
file anywhere. Since she rented the car with your credit
card, maybe you can find out about it. Why don't you call
the people at Snappy Cars and tell them you're having
problems getting insurance coverage for Kait? You could
say the company's boosting the rates, because they say she's
high risk, and you want to know if she had a wreck in their
car."

"Why do I have to lie? Can't I just play it straight with
them?"

"You do that, and you've blown it," Mike said. "You
know what their reaction would be—'If this is for real, why
haven't the police been in touch with us?' This will only
work if you play it really cool, Lois."

"I'll think about it," I said, but I knew I couldn't do it.
When the people at Snappy asked me the obvious question

—"Why don't you *ask* your daughter if she was involved in a wreck?"—I wouldn't be able to keep from bursting into tears.

The following day I flew to Las Vegas, Nevada, to meet Robin and help man her audiocassette booth at the national convention of the American Booksellers Association. When I checked into the hotel, I found a message that Robin had missed connections and wouldn't be able to get a flight in until morning. We had planned to have dinner and take in a show on the Strip that night, but I didn't feel up to an evening on the town by myself, so I ate in the hotel coffee shop and went to bed early.

Normally, I am a light sleeper, conscious of everything—rattling rainspouts, cat fights, the sound of Don's snoring—but that night, in a lumpy bed in a second-rate hotel, with roars of drunken hilarity floating up from the casino, I slept as though in a coma and woke up in the morning with Kait's distinctive voice ringing in my ears:

"THE CAR THEY TOOK SOUTH WAS THE WATCH CAR—THE BEIGE VW!"

The beige VW went south? That doesn't make sense!

It was true that a beige VW had been seen near the murder site, but Juve Escobedo's car had been a gold Camaro.

And the three Hispanics had apparently never left Albuquerque. For me that had been the stumbling block in Betty's second reading. She had said that the killers had spread themselves out in a triangle—one going south with the car, one going west, and the third—"the one with the least guilt in all this"—going northeast in the direction of Chicago. I had read that at first as a reference to Dung and his cronies, but in a later reading she had identified the Hispanics as the triggermen.

"THE CAR THEY TOOK SOUTH—"

My heart crashed into my ribs, as another piece of the puzzle tumbled into place. The reading had not been wrong; I had misinterpreted it! I had consolidated two sections that should have been viewed separately!

By the time I met Robin at the airport, I was so excited that I blurted everything out while we stood waiting for her luggage.

"I had this dream, but it wasn't a dream!" I found myself inadvertently using the same words that Donnie had when he phoned me at the Cape Cod Writers Conference. "In the dream Kait said there was a second car involved in the shooting! The Camaro may have been the hit car, but the VW was the *scout* car!"

"But the reading said—"

"I asked two different questions in that reading. First, 'What may I know about the circumstances of Kaitlyn's killing . . . about the car and any people involved?' The answer to that was a literal description of what Kait saw during the final moments of her life 'just before she will have departed.' A low rider pulling up next to her. Two heads in the front and one in the back. A rifle or long-barreled pistol 'like the handle of a plastic brush' protruding from the car window. That coincides exactly with what the police say happened.

"But my second question wasn't related to that first one. I asked, 'What may I know about the identity of the killer . . . specifically the person, location, and present situation of this being?' The answer to that was presented in a whole different paragraph, *and the people referred to in that answer weren't the ones in the hit car!* Kait considers her killers the people who hired the hitmen! That second section of the reading pertained to the *Vietnamese!*"

Robin caught on immediately.

"Of course!" she exclaimed. "Dung's relatives took him to recuperate in Kansas City, which is northeast in the direction of Chicago! An Le took off for the West Coast where his paralegal cousin lives; and the third man took the VW south to dispose of at the border."

"Everything fits if you think in terms of two cars," I said. "Kait must have seen the scout car before she became aware of the Camaro." I'd gone over the readings so often, I could quote them from memory. " 'There is this image which she gets so briefly that it is almost nonreal. There will be this which will seem to show some recognition in her, and it is as if she is not afraid—someone she will seem to recognize and know. . . . This car will seemingly turn off to her left as if to drive away.' And that's exactly what happened, the VW bug turned north! According to the police report the people who saw that car live two blocks north of Lomas on Arno. They heard the shots and got up to look out their window and saw the VW come racing up the street—"

"And the driver was someone Kait knew and wasn't afraid of! That's one reason she feels so betrayed!"

We were interrupting each other, completing each other's sentences, oblivious to the fact that the luggage from Robin's flight was long gone from the carousel and the last stray pieces had been carted off to the unclaimed baggage area.

The trade show proved so exhausting that any ideas about nights in the clubs fell quickly by the wayside. During our days in the booth 26,000 booksellers paraded through the exhibit hall, and by the time we got out in the evening, we were too worn out to do anything but grab a bite in the coffee shop and collapse on our beds. We would lie there, with our eyes tightly closed to shut out the kaleidoscope of lights that blinked outside our window, and talk until one or the other of us fell asleep.

I still was convinced that Dung hadn't wanted Kait killed and may even have made an ineffectual attempt to save her.

"He must have been worried that Kait was in danger," I said. "Dung's neighbors told Mike that Dung and a friend named Adrian were tailing Kait to see if a VW was following her days before the shooting took place. He probably didn't realize that outsiders would be hired. He thought the VW bug would be used for the hit."

"But his friends knew the truth," Robin said. "And they knew where Kait would be that night. They were at the apartment often enough to have seen Susan's map. On the night of the shooting Dung was probably out canvassing the town, searching for Kait in order to warn her that there was a contract out on her. Didn't Betty say there was 'one that night who was looking for her, and that one will have had others looking for her, and it will have had to do with some kind of message to be given to her'? That's why Dung wasn't home when Susan called the apartment. If he wasn't with An and Khanh, he was out with Adrian."

"That would have left An free to go out in the VW," I said.

"It would also explain why, right after Kait died, Dung told you he had no friends. He could have suspected his buddies of being the ones who killed her."

On our final night in Las Vegas, as we lay talking in the darkness, I repeated what Mary Martinez had told me about the danger of making information available to the defense attorneys that they could then use to divert suspicion from the Hispanics.

"It seems that we have to make a choice," I said. "Since the police won't consider anything but random shooting, we either go for the hitmen or for the people who hired them."

"Kait made that decision for us when she sent you that message," Robin said. "She wanted to focus our attention on the man in the VW. She was telling us to go for the gold."

"We don't have a chance without her accident report," I said. "Right now, we don't have proof she even knew about the car wrecks. Mike wants me to con Snappy Cars into getting the report for us, but I'm afraid I'll trip over my tongue or burst into tears."

"Kerry could do it," Robin said. "She's our 'Little Miss Television.' "

"I don't know," I said doubtfully. "You know how Kerry is about anything unpleasant."

"She's changed since Kait died," Robin said. "She's gotten a lot nervier. I'm going to stop over in Dallas on my way back to Florida, and I'll try to talk her into it.

"There's still one thing in that reading that I don't understand, though. It's that image of a boat going fast across water. It came in answer to your question 'Does Kait have a message for me?' "

" 'There is an image of a straight line which will seem to come down,' " I quoted. " 'There will be wakes out from either side of it as if to try to show motion. There will be this which seems to be moving through water very fast, and this would have something to do with the energy of one who is leaving, departing, and there is a far and urgency in this as if to leave and not return. A long trip across water is indicated in this image.' "

"That's the part I mean. Does it make any sense to you?"

"Of course. What she wants is to get those bastards deported."

17

When I got back to Albuquerque, I learned that Brett had been trying to reach me. Donnie, who had taken the message, had not written down the the phone number, and since Brett had recently moved, I didn't know how to get back to him.

Halfway through the week I came home from the store to be greeted by the shriek of the telephone and hurried to answer it.

The voice on the line wasn't Brett's, it was Kerry's.

"I have the information about the wreck!" she announced triumphantly.

"How in the world—" I began.

"I pretended I was you!" she said. "I called Snappy's national office and told the woman there that I was Lois Arquette and my husband was threatening to divorce me because he'd been going over last year's credit-card statements and discovered I'd paid a bill without checking out the charges. He was accusing me of paying Snappy for the rental of a car in California at a time when nobody in our family had been out there."

"The woman *bought* that?"

"She was lovely! It took her two days to locate the rental

agreement, and she had to go digging through piles of back records to find it. I think we should send her flowers!"

"*Was* there a wreck?"

"Oh, yes, there was a wreck all right. When were Kait and Dung in the same town as R & J Car Leasing?"

"March 28, 1989."

"That was the date of the wreck! And do you know why Mike couldn't find the report on it? It's because it was in *Dung's* name—*he's* the one who was driving!"

"They probably switched seats—" I began.

"No, they didn't," Kerry said. "Not only did they not switch seats, *Kait wasn't even in the car!*"

"But Detective Gallegos told us—"

"What he said wasn't true, Mother. Dung was alone in the rental car, and he rear-ended a personal vehicle driven by a man named Bob Manh Bui. There were two passengers in the second car, Kim Bui and Dung Bui. Police report #89-3303 was filed in Westminster by Officer J. M. Waller, badge #56313. Nobody reported any injuries at the scene."

"Then the accident could have been legitimate?"

"That's how it seemed on the surface, but not when I called the head of Snappy's liability department. She told me that, after the fact, all three of the Buis made large personal injury claims for cervical strains and soft tissue injuries. They were covered one hundred percent by liability insurance from a high-risk company called Progressive Insurance."

"How in the world did you get all this?" I asked incredulously.

"I just went with the flow," Kerry said. "It was like that time when I took the kids to Wet and Wild and was going down the water slide with Brittany on my lap. We came zipping around a curve, and there in front of us was this big fat man who was *stuck on the slide*! I thought, Oh, no! Disaster time! But when we were right at the point of slamming into him, the water just swept us up and whooshed us around him. It was like that with those phone calls. Every time I was sure I was headed for a crash, I was swept around the blockage and got just what I needed!"

She laughed, and I suddenly realized how long it had been since I'd heard Kerry laugh.

"We'd better sign off so I can give Mike a call," I told her.

"I've already called him," she said. "When I couldn't reach you, I phoned Mike at the *Journal*. He sounds like a hunk."

"You're happily married," I reminded her.

"Mother, *really*! I was thinking about Robin."

"Mike's spoken for," I said. "Besides, Robin already has more hunks than she knows what to do with."

"Oh, well, it was just an idea." She laughed again. "The people at Snappy are going to mail you the accident report, and I promised Mike you'd give him a copy. He says the defense has a husband-wife team of private detectives named Hicks who are digging up stuff on the Vietnamese, and maybe he can find some way of using that to help us."

That night Brett called, and I was relieved to learn there was no crisis in his life. What he wanted to tell me was that he'd had a dream about Kait.

"I think she may be getting ready to reincarnate," he said. "I've never had a dream as vivid as this one, and I think she was trying to get a message across to me. In the dream I was on a train filled with Russians, and it was pulling into a station. I was getting ready to get off, and there was Kait, sitting in the seat right next to the door. I said, 'Kait, is that you?' because she didn't look much like she used to, but she gave me that funny little smile, and then I was sure. I sat down next to her and said, 'Kait! It's so great to see you! Now that you're here, you can live with us again!' She said, 'No, I can't. I'm going to have new parents, and they already love me.' I said, 'That means you can't come back?' And she said, 'No, I can't come back. I have a new life now.' It blew me away! She's getting ready to run out on us!"

"She won't do that until her murder is solved," I said. "And even then, you know we're going to catch up with her."

"I think the message was 'put up or shut up,' " Brett said. "Kait's getting antsy. She wants us to get a move on."

Betty had said that the "game at hand" was intimidation. Now we decided the time had come to reveal that we had a "bomb." Mike was not enthusiastic about being detonated, but reluctantly agreed to allow us to tell APD he was investigating the case provided we didn't disclose his sources of information. Don thought the best person to talk to would be Sergeant Lowe, and I agreed with him. I felt that Lowe was honest and well intentioned and that, if we ever had the chance to meet with her in person, we might be able to make a breakthrough. Don tried to call her and was told that she was out sick and would not be back in the office until the end of the month. He tried phoning Steve Gallegos, but couldn't get through to him. I finally called Barbara Cantwell, the detective we had been told would be "following a paper trail through Orange County."

"I don't know what you're talking about," Cantwell said, when I got her on the line. "I've never had anything to do with your daughter's case."

"Sergeant Lowe said you'd be investigating R & J Car Leasing."

"That was four whole months ago!" exclaimed Cantwell.

"Did you do it?" I asked.

"There is no such business in Orange County."

"Mike Gallagher was able to get information about it."

When Cantwell spoke again there was an edge to her voice. "Why is Gallagher checking out things in California?"

"He's taken a personal interest in the case," I told her. "It's my impression he's going to do an in-depth story on it."

The next day, Mike was called to the police station for a two-and-a-half-hour interview with Gallegos and Lieutenant Patrick Dunworth, head of the APD Violent Crimes Unit. Sergeant Lowe had not been included.

After the meeting, Mike called me.

"They made it clear they do *not* want me to write a story," he said. "They refuse to consider any possibility other than that Kait was the victim of a drive-by shooting by a bunch of drunk Martineztown kids. 'This is our case—this is the way it's going to be,' they said. They wanted to get my cooperation in calming you down. They think you're a woman who didn't relate well to her daughter and is feeling guilty now that she's dead. They can't understand why you can't just accept the situation at face value and are trying to complicate things by inventing a dramatic conspiracy. I tried to explain that people who are not used to being mixed up in crimes tend to have a lot of questions about what's going on. They're going to set up an appointment and try to pacify you."

That appointment was scheduled for seven thirty A.M. on June 18.

Our meeting with Steve Gallegos and Barbara Cantwell started off pleasantly enough. Gallegos apologized for the fact that Sergeant Lowe had an important meeting and couldn't be with us, which was a surprise to us, since Don had been told he couldn't speak with her because she was ill and wouldn't be back at work until the beginning of July. I found myself wondering if we were deliberately being prevented from talking with her and, if so, why.

The file on Kait's murder had now been completed and released to the DA, which meant that the public had legal access to it. It was over a thousand pages long, and since it cost a dollar a page to have it reproduced at the courthouse, Gallegos agreed for us to borrow his copy and get it photocopied.

With this settled I asked if their case was as weak as we'd been led to believe by the media. This was not a wise question. Both detectives were quick to inform me that "if our case falls through and your daughter's killers go free, it will be all your doing." Cantwell seemed especially angry and accused me of "trying to sabotage this case by talking to everybody—the press, the FBI, the attorney general, and the defense attorneys."

I told her in all honesty that I'd had no contact with either the attorney general or the defense attorneys.

"You don't have to talk to them *personally* to wreck things!" she told me. "When you force information on *us*, you make it available to the *defense*!"

In an effort to yank me out of the fire by changing the subject, Don asked if there was any way we could be certain that Kait's things would not be destroyed when the trial was over. Gallegos assured him we had no cause for worry.

"I would have to give signed permission for that to happen," he said. "It can't occur inadvertently."

"It happened to Mary Martinez," I interjected. "All her son's things 'disappeared' between the trial and the appeal."

"Who's Mary Martinez?" Gallegos and Cantwell asked in unison.

"The head of the Crime Victims Alliance in New Mexico."

"I've never heard of such an organization," they chorused.

By now things were so bad that I didn't see how they could get worse, so I asked about the status of the investigation in Orange County.

From then on the dialogue sounded as though it had been written for *Night Court*:

CANTWELL: "Nothing in California needs to be investigated. Nobody there had reason to want to harm your daughter."

LOIS: "What if she was getting ready to blow the whistle on the car-wreck scam!"

CANTWELL: "Those are common in the L.A. area. Everybody does them."

LOIS: "Why does the fact that they're common make them unimportant? I'd think it would be just the opposite. Kait was getting ready to explode a scam worth hundreds of thousands of dollars!"

CANTWELL: "If her boyfriend made that much money, he'd be living in luxury."

LOIS: "I didn't say *Dung* got that much! The people who are raking it in are the Vietnamese lawyers, doctors, pharmacists, and clinics!"

GALLEGOS: "What makes you think Kait was going to blow the scam? Why would she do something to incriminate herself and hurt her boyfriend?"

LOIS: "She realized she'd made a mistake and was prepared to take the consequences. When she left our house that night she said she was breaking up with Dung."

GALLEGOS: "She was always telling people that, but she didn't mean it. She left a note on the counter that night saying she was sorry about their fight and signed it 'love.'"

DON: "Was the note signed?"

GALLEGOS: "No."

DON: "Then how do you know Kait wrote it?"

GALLEGOS: "It had to be from her. It was right there on the counter."

CANTWELL: "I've read the transcript of the statement by that truck driver. It's totally convincing."

LOIS: "Sergeant Lowe told me she thought you had the right men, but she was no longer sure about the motive."

GALLEGOS: "I don't know why she'd say that. You must have misunderstood her."

LOIS: "She said Barbara Cantwell was going to check out R & J Car Leasing. R & J *did* exist. It went out of business after Kait died, at the same time two Vietnamese clinics in the same area were closed down for insurance fraud."

CANTWELL: "Where did that information come from?"

LOIS: "I'm not at liberty to say, but I think you ought to check up on it."

CANTWELL: "You expect us to waste our time phoning out to Orange County for information you already have?"

LOIS: "I do expect you to verify information. You're the police—that's your job."

Cantwell got up and stalked out of the room in fury.
Alone with Gallegos the atmosphere was less venomous,

for he was a likable man and could be very charming. He was certain that he had convinced Mike that the Hispanics were guilty and couldn't understand why he couldn't convince us also. When we were finally able to get across to him the fact that we weren't challenging that aspect of the case, he seemed greatly relieved.

"That makes me feel better," he said. "I'm sorry I was so cold to you. I thought you were trying to say I didn't arrest the right guys."

We again explained that, assuming the suspects were guilty, we thought that they had to be hitmen, because the bullets in Kait's head had been too well placed to have been fired by a drunk during a high-speed chase.

"Actually, she wasn't going all that fast," Gallegos said. "When her car hit that pole, it didn't cause much damage. She might even have been stopped completely, and when she was shot and fell forward, her foot bumped into the accelerator and started the car coasting."

"But didn't the truck driver say she was driving at top speed?"

"She might have stopped at a light," Gallegos suggested.

"If Kait was running for her life, she wouldn't have *stopped*!"

"You think your daughter would actually have *run a red light?*" he asked incredulously.

"Considering the circumstances, I think that she might have."

The interview ended amicably, with Gallegos once again promising to get the Vietnamese letters translated and to send us copies of both the originals and the translations. He also agreed to get copies of the Garcia phone bills for the months of the murder and of the arrest to see if they had made any calls to the L.A. area.

When we got up to leave, he handed Don the huge file.

"This is everything we have on your daughter's case," he said. "Every letter we received, every interview we had with anybody, is required by law to be in here."

When we read the report we discovered it did *not* contain everything. A number of things were either omitted or incorrect. There was no mention of the evening we had summoned the police to our home to tell them about the car wrecks. My letter to Sergeant Lowe, outlining the reasons we suspected Vietnamese involvement, was not in the report. Nor was Dung's admission to me that he knew who killed Kait and was "deciding" if he loved her enough to tell. I was misquoted as saying Kait ate dinner at our house on the night she was shot and went to Susan's house later in the evening, when, in truth, she left for Susan's at six-fifteen. There were identically worded incorrect statements from Gallegos and Cantwell, attributed to the manager of the Alvarado Apartments, that "the same key opened the apartment door after Kaitlyn was murdered. The Arquette family changed the apartment-door key after that." The implication was that Kait's cold-hearted family had evicted her grief-stricken boyfriend from his home. The truth, of course, was that the *manager* had thrown Dung out and had the locks changed, because Dung and his friends were prone to violence.

It was evident also that, although the Hispanics had been grilled relentlessly, blatantly false statements by the Vietnamese had gone unchallenged.

We copied the file, and Don returned the original to Gallegos with a letter:

June 24, 1990

Dear Detective Gallegos:

Thank you for allowing us to borrow and copy the report APD has filed on our daughter's murder. I am returning the original herewith.

You told us to get back to you if we had questions or problems with it. We do have several of these.

For one thing, all the Vietnamese seem to have been lying during their interviews with APD, as though frantically trying to cover up their L.A. connections. This makes us wonder if there is validity to any of their statements.

An example of this is the APD interview with Dung on Thursday, February 15, 1990. Dung's account of the car wreck in Westminster in March 1989 does not mesh in any way with the accident report. Dung said Kait was in the car at the time; the report shows he was alone in the car. Dung said they were hit from behind; the report shows he rear-ended a car. Dung said no one was hurt; the Snappy Car Rental people say there were large personal injury claims, covered 100% by their liability insurance. When questioned about the calls made from their apartment the night Kait died, Dung stated he was lying on his bed and overheard Khanh Pham make the call to a personal friend named Bao Tran. That call was made at 9:10 P.M., when Dung was at the hospital with us. He then went home with us and spent the night at our house. He could not possibly have heard Pham make the call.

The fact that Dung blurted out this unnecessary lie seems to indicate that the mention of those calls threw him into such a panic, he couldn't think rationally. It also seems odd that the call lasted only two minutes—just time enough for a quick report that the mission was accomplished. If the call had been made to impart tragic news to a caring friend, you would think that it would have taken longer than two minutes.

Detective Barbara Cantwell said the medical insurance scams are so common in Orange County that nobody could possibly consider them important enough to kill for. Yet Bao Tran . . . had his phone and beeper numbers changed as soon as he was told Kait was dead. And . . . he quickly took on a new identity as vice-president of a company called San Diego Dream Life Corporation. That company must have come into existence very suddenly, as it's not listed in the 1989–90 phone book. It would be interesting to know if it exists as a functioning business. It would also be interesting to know if Bao Tran had any connection with R & J Car Leasing. (Attached is a copy of the R & J listing from the 1987–88 Orange County phone book, which proves that it did at one time exist.)

According to your report, in his phone conversation with Barbara Cantwell on February 23, 1990, Detective Frank, of the Westminster Police Department, said the staged accident scam is a multimillion-dollar business. That sounds to us like a profitable enough operation to make it worth hiring a hitman to wipe out someone who threatens to blow the whistle on it. Detective Frank sounds knowledgeable. Perhaps he could be of help to you in investigating Bao Tran and R & J Car Rental.

Upon a quick first reading there seem to be several things missing from the file on Kait's murder that ought to be in there. However, the report is so voluminous, we may have missed them. I will be out of town this week, but will reread the report more carefully upon my return.

Sincerely,
Don Arquette

As an afterthought he attached a stick-on note saying, "We still have not received the promised translations of the Vietamese letters."

In keeping with my usual practice I mailed a copy of the
letter to the FBI in Orange County. In keeping with their
usual practice they did not acknowledge receiving it.

The police never spoke to us again.

We did find a couple of interesting things in the report.
Dung had produced a business card with Bao Tran's address
and phone number, which were the same as the ones Mike
had for "Van Hong Phuc." There was also a copy of a note,
possibly written by the tipster who had phoned me, accusing Miguel Garcia of being a professional killer.

Mike gave me a call after reading his own copy of the
police file.

"This case is worse than I expected," he said. "I've been
doing some chronology, and the times don't fit. In fact,
they're so far off that when that truck driver, Lindquist, first
went down to the station with his story, an 'unidentified
officer' told him to go home. Susan said Kait left her place
at ten forty-five. Kait was found shot in the car at eleven
P.M. That gives us a fifteen-minute time frame for the shooting to take place in. Lindquist said he saw the chase on
Lomas between nine-thirty and ten P.M. That's not possible
—Kait was still at Susan's house! Plus, the Ford Tempo he
reported seeing was 'dark blue,' the driver had 'long black
hair,' and the car was traveling west, not east the way Kait
would have gone.

"But the problems go beyond that, Lois. We're into
something serious here. APD's representation of the conversation between Miguel and Juve when they were left
together in the holding cell could cost them the case. The
police planted a recorder in the cell that the suspects didn't
know about. In their report one of the suspects is quoted as
saying, 'We'll back up each other. Just don't rat me out, and
I won't rat you out.' If you go to the transcript of the tape,

you get something very different. What the suspect actually said was, '*If we would have done it, I'd be telling you right now,* "Shut it up. Just don't fuckin' rat me out and I won't rat you out." *But . . . we didn't do shit!*' Using part of that quote out of context reverses the meaning."

"So, what are you saying? Do you think the men are innocent?"

"I'm leaning in that direction," Mike said. "You're not going to like this, but here's my theory—Dung and Kait have this big fight on Saturday night, and she threatens to squeal on the car wrecks. She sleeps on the couch and runs out on Dung in the morning. He spends the day with his buddies, complaining about Kait. That night they get drunk and decide to 'take care of the bitch.' "

"Dung wouldn't do that," I said.

"I'm not saying Dung pulled the trigger, but my guess is he was there when it happened. Then guilt set in, and he told his buddies he was going to the police. That's probably the point when one of them stabbed him."

"You don't believe he attempted suicide?"

"I think it's doubtful. Stabbing yourself in the liver is not a nice way to go. Besides, when the ambulance came, that dorm room was a shambles, like there'd been a big fight and Dung had been trying to defend himself. So—on with my theory—the guys told Dung that if he wanted to live he'd have to promise to keep his mouth shut. He agreed, and they called an ambulance. Khanh refused to talk to the cops unless he had a lawyer present. Is that a normal concern when you've saved a suicide victim?"

"No," I admitted. "It isn't." I hadn't known about the lawyer. "Are you going to write your story now?"

"You'll be seeing it soon," Mike said.

I hung up the phone and hurried to get the police file to

ALBUQUERQUE POLICE DEPARTMENT
SUPPLEMENTARY
OFFENSE REPORT*

OFFENSE ___HOMICIDE___ CASE NO. ___89-___

OFFENSE LOCATION ___ARNO & LOMAS NE___

VICTIM ___KAITLYN ARQUETTE___

PAGE 43

time surrounding the homicide he was working for PNM Maintenance. (Refer to transcribed statement from Juvenal Escobedo.)

Detective R. Foley was assigned the responsibility of going to David Quintana's residence at 10014 4th Street NW, and locate the Camaro. Detective Foley was in possession of a search warrant and the vehicle was to be sealed and towed. Also assigned to assist Detective Foley was Field Investigator C. Romero. At approximately 2159 hours, officers located the Camaro at 10014 4th Street NW. Detective Foley attempted to contact David Quintana, but found he was not at home. Officer Romero sealed and photographed the vehicle. The vehicle was then towed to 4512 2nd Street NW, by A&E Towing Company and stored in an indoor storage area. Detective Foley taped a copy of the search warrant and the tow-in report on the front door of Mr. Quintana's trailer. Also present were Bernalillo County Sheriff's Department Deputy Rohlfs and Sergeant Dennis. Detective Foley and Detective Romero then returned to the main police station Investigations Bureau.

After all interviews were concluded, Michael Garcia and Juvenal Escobedo were placed in an interview room together by Detective Foley. A tape recorder was also placed inside the interview room and recorded the two talking to each other. During their conversation, the two said, "We'll back up each other. Just don't rat me out and I won't rat you out." (Refer to transcribed conversation by Michael Garcia and Juvenal Escobedo.)

2ND MALE:	(INAUDIBLE) July (INAUDIBLE) I was with Tina. I was with Tina, you know that.
2ND MALE:	If I...if we would have done it I'd be telling you right now, "Shut it up. Just don't fuckin' rat me out and I won't rat you out", but...
BOTH:	We didn't do shit.
1ST MALE:	This is (INAUDIBLE). But if I get to do time I'm gonna be more pissed (INAUDIBLE) fuck, you watch.

check the statement attributed to the suspects in the holding cell. I compared it with the transcript, and it was just as Mike had told me—the statement had been altered so its meaning was reversed.

That night I turned on the television set and was greeted by a rerun of one of my own stories. *Summer of Fear* had been made into an NBC Movie of the Week, retitled *Stranger in Our House.* It had now gone into syndication and kept popping up on the screen at odd times and on odd channels.

I watched for a moment before turning to something more stimulating and heard actress Linda Blair, who was playing the part of my heroine, introduce her boyfriend to a visiting cousin.

I had written sixteen books since *Summer of Fear*, and I could barely remember the plot. It was like reviewing a story that had been written by a stranger.

A stranger whose mind had been touched by a memory of the future.

The name I had chosen for my heroine's boyfriend was "Mike Gallagher."

18

Albuquerque Journal, July 8, 1990:

KAITLYN ARQUETTE'S DEATH SNARLED IN CONTRADICTIONS

by Mike Gallagher—*Journal* Investigative Reporter

It began to rain shortly after Kaitlyn Arquette was shot on a midsummer night in 1989, but not hard enough to wash away the bloodstains on the street. For days kids from the Martineztown neighborhood walked down to Lomas and Arno NE to look at the stains on the pavement. Adults recalled the sirens and the streets being blocked by police cars that night.

At the Summerfest in Civic Plaza several blocks away, teenagers talked about the killing. Some "bad dudes" bragged about drive-by shootings they had committed. Rumors started to circulate that the killers were kids from the Martineztown neighborhood.

Six months later, when the weather finally had washed the street clean, police returned to the neighborhood and rounded up four suspects. A year after Arquette's death, one of the suspects is in jail awaiting trial; another is a fugitive. Charges against the other two have been dropped.

The slaying initially was described by police as a random shooting. And it was presumably solved as a random shooting: a few drunken young men in a car firing a pistol on a dare. But police reports reviewed by the *Journal* indicate the case against the two men now charged with the shooting might be shaky. The reports show witnesses who have given contradictory information, statements since recanted, and little in the way of physical evidence.

The reports also disclose other theories have been offered about Arquette's killing.

Defense attorneys Michael Davis and Joseph Riggs are critical of police efforts.

"We've been on this case for six months, and we're absolutely astounded at the poor quality of the police investigation," Riggs said. Davis and Riggs, who represent defendant Miguel Garcia, said it has taken five months to obtain police investigatory reports and that they believe officers still haven't turned over all the information. . . .

Mike's front-page article ran under a banner headline and continued on to fill another full page in Section A of the Sunday paper. He summarized the steps of the investigation, pointed out blunders the police had made, and, in a lengthy side bar, illustrated by a five-by-eight blow-up of the snapshot I had given him of Kait and Dung at Thanksgiving, described their participation in the insurance scam.

The first paragraph of the second story was particularly explosive:

POLICE CLEAR BOYFRIEND, BUT RUMORS PERSIST

The postcard was sent from Albuquerque to the state attorney general's office on February 9, 1990. It read: "Did it ever occur to you that Kait Arquette was murdered as the result of a 'hit' order by the Vietnamese mafia? APD refuses to do anything!"

I now understood why Barbara Cantwell had accused me of contacting the attorney general—she suspected me of having written that postcard.

I hadn't done so, but now I wished that I had.

In his article Mike also reprinted the text of the affectionate note the police had found in Kait's apartment the night of the shooting: *Hon, where are you? I know you're still mad. . . . I'm so sorry, ok! I miss you today. I went to mom's house to return these books. I'll see ya. Love.* The police report said the note had been found on the dining room table and "Dung Nguyen said the message was written by the victim, who must have come home sometime during the day when he was out."

The wording of the note didn't sound like Kait to us, and Don checked to see if there was a copy of it in the police file. There was, and the contents were not precisely as they appeared in the report. The note was written in pidgin English and the word *return* was misspelled: *Hon, Where are you? . . . I know you still mad. . . . I'm so sorry OK! I miss you today. I went to Nam house to retune there Books. Ill see ya!* Love.

More important, *the note was not in Kait's handwriting.*

The flamboyant script was so different from Kait's meticulously rounded lettering that it seemed impossible that the police had not noticed the difference when they had numer-

Kaitlyn Arquette

The term "schizophrenia", meaning a "splitting
of the person's thinking," was originated in 1911 by
Eugen Bleuler. This large group of disorders is
defined as manifested by characteristic disturbance
of thinking, mood and behavior. Disturbances
in thinking are marked by changes of idea
formation which may lead to delusions and

Dung,
where are you...
I know you still
mad... I'm so sorry
ok! I miss you
today.. I went to
Nam's house to
return there books
I'll see ya!
Love

A specimen of Kait Arquette's handwriting taken from a school
notebook

The note police say Kait left for Dung on the night of her death

ous samples of her handwriting marked as evidence. The
note appeared to have been written by Dung. If he had
planted it on the table that would seem to imply that he had
known the police would be coming.

Don came up with a more palatable explanation.

"He could have left the note for Kait while she was at our
place. It doesn't say, 'I went to Mom's house,' it says, 'I
went to *Nam* house.' Perhaps he went out that night to do
something he didn't want Kait to know about and left the
note so she'd think he was over at a friend's house."

"But the police report says Dung told them that Kait left
the note for him!"

"The report says whatever the police *want* it to say," Don
said shortly.

He wrote another letter to Steve Gallegos, pointing out
the fact that the note was not in Kait's handwriting and
enclosing some copies of her handwriting so comparisons
could be made without the inconvenience of going to the
evidence room.

When a week went by and Gallegos didn't respond, we
mailed copies of the handwriting samples to Mike.

The day Mike's story came out, we were braced for
phone calls, but we didn't get any. Our friends were evidently so horrified, they didn't know what to say to us.
Since the arrest of the Hispanic suspects back in January,
the feeling in Albuquerque had been one of relief that the
mystery had been solved and justice was being served. The
suggestion that APD had blown the investigation—that the
wrong men may have been indicted—that the Arquettes'
"golden girl" might have been involved in illegal activities,
was not a pleasant thing to read over Sunday morning
breakfast. What do you say to parents about such exposure

—"I was sorry to learn that your daughter was involved with the Vietnamese mafia"?

After the article came out, I spoke briefly with Mike. He told me he had received phone calls from residents of Martineztown who told him Juve was back and was staying at his girlfriend's house. Nobody knew where he'd been during the time he had been gone. ("Nobody but me," I amended silently, picturing Juve in the grease pit.) Juve's neighbors told Mike they had phoned the police several times to inform them of his whereabouts, but no one had ever arrived to pick him up.

On July 15 Don and I flew to Chautauqua, New York, where I taught for a week at the Highlights for Children writer's conference. On the anniversary of Kait's death we sat on a paddlewheel boat in the middle of Lake Chautauqua, eating a picnic supper and sipping New York wine, and promised each other we would try to put our grief behind us.

When we got back we found that Donnie had made some decisions also. He told us he'd had his fill of sleeping on our sofa and was moving out to share an apartment with friends. This seemed like a healthy transition and was actually a relief. Having had one child leave for the evening, never to return, I was continually braced to lose the next one. When Donnie was out at a party, I would lie in bed, hyperventilating, as I waited for another soul-shattering call from the emergency room. The times he slept over at his girlfriend's were particularly frightening, for dawn would come and I still would not have heard the front door open and close to announce his return. At the same time, how can you force a lusty twenty-two-year-old to check in with his mother every time he does what lusty twenty-two-year-olds are noted for? You can't—or you *shouldn't*—but I tried—and there was a lot of resentment on both sides. It was good for all of us to have that problem disposed of.

When Donnie moved out, I stripped the sheets from the sofa and tried to decide what to do in my empty nest. I had brought my book up to date, the police would no longer communicate with us, and Mike seemed either to be playing his hand close to his chest or to have lost interest in the case. Betty Muench had predicted that there would come a time when Mike "would *seem* to quit," but would "share his information with another" who would carry on the investigation undercover. I decided that, since he was firmly convinced that the Vietnamese had shot Kait, he probably had felt morally obligated to share his information with the defense attorneys.

Since I was still unable to generate enough energy to write fiction, I decided to do some reading. I had deliberately been steering clear of books about psychic phenomena, because I had wanted a chance to think things through on my own. By now, however, I had found some beliefs that felt right to me and was curious to find out if there were others who were on the same wavelength.

Skeptical about anything that could not be backed up by documented research, I chose books by doctors and psychiatrists. Among these authorities were Dr. Kenneth Ring, author of *Life at Death* and *Heading Toward Omega*; Dr. Raymond A. Moody, Jr., author of *Life After Life*, *Reflections on Life After Life*, and *The Light Beyond*; Dr. Roger Woolger, author of *Other Lives*, *Other Selves*; and Drs. Bruce Greyson and Charles Flynn, coeditors of *The Near-Death Experience*.

Of particular interest to me was *Full Circle*, a book by a woman named Barbara Harris, who described her own dramatic near-death experience following an accident when, paralyzed and comatose in her hospital bed, she had felt herself leave her body to float near the ceiling and gaze into the tunnel of death. She did return to her body and recover from her injuries, but this powerful experience had transformed her life and led her into years of research on near-death pheonomena.

In her book Barbara described her mentor, Dr. William Roll, project director for the Psychical Research Foundation, a parapsychology institute that served as a scientific and educational research center to investigate the possibility of continuation of consciousness after the death of the physical body. Her story inspired me to write Dr. Roll myself, telling him about the communication we felt we'd had with Kait and about the foreshadowing of future events that had appeared in my books. I told him I was interested in learning more about such things and would appreciate any guidance he could give me as to where to find it.

The more I thought about the subject, the more I wondered how many other people there were out there who had the same sort of abilities Betty Muench did. The easiest way to find such people would be to research an article on the subject, and since I owed *Woman's Day* another story, I queried them to see if they would be interested in an article about psychic detectives. My editor gave me a go-ahead on condition that the accomplishments of the psychics were documented and that they had used their abilities to be of service to others.

Wanting to be sure that the subjects of my article were reputable, I phoned the American Society for Psychical Research in New York. They suggested I get in touch with a parapsychologist at the Department of Sociology at Eastern Michigan University, who had coauthored *The Blue Sense*, the definitive book on the application of psychic detective techniques in modern crime detection.

"Dr. Marcello Truzzi is a skeptic about people who claim psychic abilities," they told me. "Anybody he refers you to is bound to be good."

"Marcello Truzzi!" I exclaimed. "I went to school with a boy with that name!"

"I think he grew up in Florida—"

"It was in Sarasota, back in the days when it was winter quarters for Ringling Brothers Circus! My father did the photography for the circus, and Marcello's father was the juggler!"

I wrote to Marcello—*Hello across the years and miles! I have a favor to ask you*—and crossed my fingers that he would remember me and respond.

That night I went to bed early, as I usually did in those days of emotional fatigue, but was so worn out, I had trouble falling asleep.

"Can't you just *solve* this thing?" I asked Kait wearily. "Damn it, you got us into this mess, so get us *out* of it!"

My anger dissolved and was immediately replaced by pain, as raw and overwhelming as on the night of the shooting.

"I didn't mean that," I whispered. "I'm sorry, honey, I didn't mean it. All I want is to hold my baby in my arms again."

I buried my face in my pillow and cried myself to sleep. I don't know how long I slept, but I awoke in the night and found that Don had come to bed and was sleeping so heavily, he must have been there for hours.

"I want to hold my baby," I whispered, and something wonderful happened. I lifted my arms and felt them close around the chubby body of a three-year-old. The child was positioned as though I had her on my lap facing outward with her back pressed against my chest. Although I knew that I had to be dreaming, I wasn't asleep; I was keenly aware of every aspect of my physical surroundings. The shifting current of air from the fan on the window ledge. The warmth radiating from Don's body. The radio of a car in the street beneath our window, spouting country-western music.

I gingerly pulled up the child's pajama top and felt the smooth, damp skin of her chest, rhythmically rising and falling beneath the palm of my hand. I lowered my hand and slid it under the elastic waistband, gently caressing the familiar round belly. I was under no illusion that the body was physical; Kait was dead, and her corpse lay rotting in the cemetery. Yet this was the gift I had asked for; in sensation, if not actuality, I was holding my baby.

After a while I said, "Thank you," and released her to God.

It was an experience that was never to happen again.

At the end of August, Mike mailed us a copy of an interview the police had conducted with Dung on July 9, 1990, the day after Mike's exposé of the investigation had appeared in the *Albuquerque Journal*.

He enclosed a note that said, *I've been trying to run down the rumor that Dung was stabbed as a warning to keep his mouth shut. Apparently it began with An Le, who told a girl named MaryBeth, who split to California earlier this year. I've got several other assignments to work on now, but I'll try to keep track of the case and pass on anything I get. Take care!*

When Don and I read the transcript of Dung's interrogation, it was hardly the sharply focused interview we had come to expect from scenes in the movies:

INTERVIEW WITH DETECTIVE S. GALLEGOS AND DUNG NGUYEN
07-09-90

[This transcript has been slightly condensed in the interest of space. The first page and a half were devoted to obtaining Dung's name, address, birth date, and place of employment, which was information that was already in the police report. Then:]

GALLEGOS: Now, the reason why I'm talking to you is I want to ask you some questions about some things that have happened such as traffic accidents and some people in California, okay?

NGUYEN: Okay.

GALLEGOS: Now, first of all, were you involved in any traffic accidents in California?

NGUYEN: Yes. [Since Dung had previously denied any knowledge of the car-wreck scam, there had obviously been an unrecorded conversation during which he was confronted with the accident reports.]

GALLEGOS: How many?

NGUYEN: Two.

GALLEGOS: Okay. Was Kaitlyn Arquette with you during any of these accidents?

NGUYEN: No.

GALLEGOS: Was she in the car with you?

NGUYEN: No.

GALLEGOS: Okay. The two of you, you and Kaitlyn, went to California together some time ago. Is that correct? On a vacation? To Disneyland and that sort of thing?

NGUYEN: Yes.

GALLEGOS: Okay. Was that when you got into one of the accidents?

NGUYEN: Yes.

GALLEGOS: Okay. Was she with you then in the car?

NGUYEN: No.

GALLEGOS: Who was with you when you got into this accident?

NGUYEN: Myself.

GALLEGOS: Just by yourself?

NGUYEN: Yeah.

GALLEGOS: Are you sure about that?

NGUYEN: Yes.

GALLEGOS: Did you receive any money from that accident?

NGUYEN: Yes.

GALLEGOS: How much?

NGUYEN: One thousand five hundred.

GALLEGOS: One thousand five hundred. Was that for that accident?

NGUYEN: Yes.

GALLEGOS: Were you paid in cash or check or how were you paid?

NGUYEN: When I go with Kait they write me a check, and we deposit it in her bank account.

GALLEGOS: Tell me about these accidents. Were they staged accidents? Were they something that was planned?

NGUYEN: Yes.

GALLEGOS: Okay. Who planned these accidents?

NGUYEN: This guy.

GALLEGOS: Okay, you gave me a card some time ago from a guy. He was a paralegal out in California—Westminster Avenue, California—and the business card is a Bao

Tran. Is this the individual who planned these accidents?

NGUYEN: Yes.

GALLEGOS: Okay, and it says "Law Office of Minh Nguyen Duy." Who's that?

NGUYEN: I don't know.

GALLEGOS: Do you know who that is?

NGUYEN: No.

GALLEGOS: Okay, so Bao Tran is the person who staged these accidents?

NGUYEN: Yes.

GALLEGOS: Both accidents?

NGUYEN: Yeah, um . . . yes.

GALLEGOS: Okay. Tell me about the first accident. Uh, you went out to California and you got into this accident?

NGUYEN: We got there and we rent a car.

GALLEGOS: You and who?

NGUYEN: Me and An Le.

[This line of interview continued for two more pages with no new information surfacing as Gallegos asked questions to which he already had the answers.]

GALLEGOS: Was anyone hurt during this [the first] accident?

NGUYEN: No.

GALLEGOS: So, let's get to the second accident, then. The second accident is when you were out there in California with Kait. Was she with you in the car when you got into this accident?

NGUYEN: No.

GALLEGOS: Who was with you?

NGUYEN: By myself.

GALLEGOS: Okay. Did Bao Tran set this accident up also?

NGUYEN: Yes.

GALLEGOS: Okay. How much money did you receive for this accident?

NGUYEN: One thousand five hundred.

GALLEGOS: One thousand five hundred. Okay, Bao Tran wrote you a check, is that correct?

NGUYEN: Yeah.

GALLEGOS: Okay, where was Kaitlyn Arquette at the time that this accident happened?

NGUYEN: She in a motel that we rented.

GALLEGOS: Okay. Did Kaitlyn know that you were going to get into this accident?

NGUYEN: Yes.

GALLEGOS: What did she say because of this?

NGUYEN: She told me she gets nervous, but just so I'm not hurt. After I wreck and I come back I told her everything is fine now.

GALLEGOS: Okay, when did you receive the money? Did you receive the money right after the accident? . . . Did he mail you a check?

NGUYEN: No, because the first thing, we wreck the car and we spend a whole week in California, visit a long time, and just, he gave us some extra cash that we borrowed him and we go to Disneyland, we go to Newport Beach. . . . And when we get back, we get back to rest, we write out the check.

GALLEGOS: Did you ever introduce Kaitlyn to Bao Tran?

NGUYEN: Yes.

GALLEGOS: Was there any problems between the two of them?

NGUYEN: No.

GALLEGOS: Okay. Once you told Kaitlyn about these acci-

dents, did she mention it anymore after that when you
guys got back to Albuquerque? When the two of you
argued or got into any kind of argument, did she ever
threaten to tell on you about these accidents to the
police?

NGUYEN: No, we totally forgot about it.

GALLEGOS: Did you tell Bao Tran up in California that you
told Kaitlyn Arquette about the accidents? Did he
know that she had knowledge of these accidents and
how they were planned?

NGUYEN: Does he know?

GALLEGOS: Yeah, did he know?

NGUYEN: He didn't ask. I don't know.

GALLEGOS: Did he ask if she knew?

NGUYEN: Um-um.

GALLEGOS: Did you tell him that she knew?

NGUYEN: No, but I think he knew that I told her.

GALLEGOS: You think he knew that you told her?

NGUYEN: Yes.

GALLEGOS: Did he know this after the accidents or before?

NGUYEN: He, I mean he told her too.

GALLEGOS: He told her also?

NGUYEN: Yes.

GALLEGOS: So Bao Tran told Kaitlyn also?

NGUYEN: Yes.

GALLEGOS: Okay, was there any problem with that? Did
Bao Tran ever mention to you that he did not trust
Kaitlyn? Did he ever tell you that he felt that Kaitlyn
was going to tell anybody because of what was going on
with these accidents?

NGUYEN: No.

GALLEGOS: How about An Le, did he know that Kaitlyn
knew?

NGUYEN: Yes.

GALLEGOS: How did he feel about that?

NGUYEN: He didn't say anything about it. I think he's fine.

[The next section of the interview consisted of a series of questions about how the car was rented, how long they kept it, and—again—whether Kait was in the car at the time of the wreck. Finally, another subject was raised.]

GALLEGOS: To your knowledge, did Bao Tran or anybody else in California who stages these accidents, do they know that Kaitlyn Arquette was killed?

NGUYEN: In California?

GALLEGOS: Yes.

NGUYEN: By the time Kait and [inaudible] after that we went home and Khanh and An were staying around my apartment.

GALLEGOS: This was the night she was shot?

NGUYEN: Yes. And I heard An make a phone call when I go upstair.

GALLEGOS: You heard *Khanh*?

NGUYEN: An.

GALLEGOS: *An?*

NGUYEN: To make phone call to the guy Bao Tran.

GALLEGOS: Bao Tran? What exactly did he say while he was on the phone with Bao Tran?

NGUYEN: He told him he can't go over California, and he told Bao Tran what happened to Kait. He say Kait got shot, but we don't know who it is and he stay, I mean, he can't go now, he had to stay with us, with me around with me.

GALLEGOS: Do you know when this phone call was made?

NGUYEN: When he called, like that time I heard?

GALLEGOS: Yeah. Was it the next day, day after, two days after, do you remember?

NGUYEN: I really don't know but . . .

GALLEGOS: Was it night?

NGUYEN: The day.

GALLEGOS: It was during the daytime?

NGUYEN: Yes.

GALLEGOS: Morning, afternoon?

NGUYEN: Afternoon, during the afternoon or night. I really don't remember.

GALLEGOS: So it was at night or in the afternoon?

NGUYEN: Night.

GALLEGOS: Nighttime. You don't remember the time, do you?

NGUYEN: I'm not very sure on that.

[We wondered if that was what was meant by "leading a witness." The summary in the file might legitimately have read: "Although unsure about the time, Nguyen told investigator he heard An Le make the phone call at night."

The interview terminated with Gallegos asking Dung if Kait had ever threatened to go to the authorities and whether he thought his friends in California were responsible for her death. Dung answered no to both questions.]

GALLEGOS: Why do you think Mrs. Arquette thinks that the Vietnamese have something to do with her death?

[*Good Lord!* I thought. *This is setting me up for the next bullet!*]

NGUYEN: Because, um . . . she think we did something like that [inaudible] I mean what happened to Kait that we deserve [sic] from car wreck.

GALLEGOS: She thinks because of what you guys did in the wreck that Kaitlyn was killed?

NGUYEN: Yes.

GALLEGOS: Um, to your knowledge, there's nothing that would say that anyone in California's responsible for Kaitlyn's death?

NGUYEN: No.

GALLEGOS: Are you sure?

NGUYEN: Yes.

GALLEGOS: Since Kaitlyn's death, have you been back to California?

NGUYEN: No.

GALLEGOS: Have you talked to Bao Tran?

NGUYEN: No.

GALLEGOS: Is he a close friend of yours?

NGUYEN: He's like An's cousin. I just know him, but he's really a nice guy.

GALLEGOS: Is this pretty common in California? These types of accidents? Does this happen quite often that you know of?

NGUYEN: No.

GALLEGOS: Has Bao Tran ever done this before with other people that you know of besides you and An?

NGUYEN: I don't know.

GALLEGOS: So the two times that you were in California Bao Tran set up the accidents? These are the only accidents you know of?

NGUYEN: Yeah.

GALLEGOS: Are those the only accidents that you know of that Bao Tran set up?

NGUYEN: Yes.

GALLEGOS: Okay. I'll ask you one more time. To your knowledge do the accidents or the Vietnamese or Bao Tran in California have anything to do with Kaitlyn's death?

NGUYEN: No.

GALLEGOS: This statement will conclude. The time is eleven thirty-five A.M.

END OF INTERVIEW

In the district attorney's office, seven months later, when Dung was quizzed about the content of this interview, he stated to Miguel Garcia's defense attorneys, Joe Riggs and Michael Davis, and to Deputy District Attorney Susan Riedel, that he knew of up to twenty people from Albuquerque who had been imported by Bao Tran to stage wrecks in California.

He also said once the tape recorder was turned off, that, Gallegos had advised him to sue me for "saying bad things" about him.

A photocopy of the check signed by Bao Tran, given to Dung to pay for his car wreck in March 1989. Kait filled in her name and deposited it in her account.

19

The interrogation raised questions we found impossible to answer. For one thing, why did Gallegos conduct the interview by himself? Where was the man on the force who was fluent in Vietnamese? Wouldn't it have been reasonable to have had him there as interpreter? Around us Dung's English had been awkward, but adequate for everyday conversation, yet in this interview he sounded as if he were fresh off the boat.

And why had obviously inconsistent statements gone unchallenged? In a previous interview Dung had identified Khanh Pham as the person who had put through the call to California. He seemed now to have spaced out the fact that he had made that statement and this time had insisted the call was made by An Le, despite Gallegos's attempt to steer him back on track. Why hadn't Gallegos confronted him with the fact that he could not have overheard *anybody* make the call because he was at the hospital at the time that it was made?

And what about Dung's statement that he had been paid for the wreck with a personal check? Wasn't that significant enough to follow up on? We hadn't considered the possibility of payment by check, because we'd been told that the car wreck participants received $2,000. If the payment was

$1,500, it was a wholly different story; in that case the $1,490 deposit in Kait's checking account might have been part of a $1,500 check, with $10 cash withheld for spending money.

I called Kait's bank and asked the form of the deposit. They said it had been a check, and I asked them to mail me a photocopy.

When the check arrived, we found it was signed by Bao Tran.

Betty Muench had told Robin, "There is . . . evidence of something which was not done right and in which there will have been the instigating energy in all this." Tran had made a miscalculation. When he'd written the check he had left the space for the name of the recipient blank, so that Dung, who didn't have a bank account, could have it cashed by a friend. What he couldn't have expected was that Kait would fill in her own name and deposit the check in her account. Could this piece of concrete evidence against the financier of the car wrecks have put the seal on her death warrant?

If so, we had that death warrant in our hands now, but we didn't know what to do with it. The police could easily get it themselves if they wanted it, but obviously they didn't, for Gallegos hadn't even bothered to ask Dung where Kait's account was. I did mail a copy of the check to the FBI, along with the interview in which Dung confessed to the wrecks and identified Tran as the person who arranged them. I hoped this evidence of a felony crossing state lines would cause the federal authorities to start taking us seriously.

They didn't respond.

Since Dung had said that An Le had also staged wrecks, we checked back through the police file to see if An's accident reports were in it.

The file contained two of them.

An's first recorded "accident" was in Westminster at ten forty-four A.M. on January 11, 1989. His driver's license number was A4437875. He was driving a silver Dodge Colt with a New Mexico license plate and told the investigating officer he lived at Bao Tran's address. Nam Pham, a friend from Albuquerque—(*I went to Nam house to retune there books*)—was a passenger in the car when it rear-ended a vehicle driven by a man named Delmar Bardsley. Bardsley was covered by insurance from National General.

An's second "accident," in June 1989, was bizarre. In this case his car was struck by a stolen vehicle that was fleeing the scene of a robbery. An's driver's license number was listed this time as C5410018; his address was 8081 21st #8, Westminister; and he gave police new phone numbers for both a home and a business. He was covered by Farmers Insurance, and all six occupants of his vehicle were taken by ambulance to Humana Hospital, complaining of leg, neck, and head pain.

By now we knew a few things about Bao Tran. A friend who worked for a credit bureau had pulled up his file on the computer, and from this we had obtained his Social Security number; two addresses for him in Santa Ana, one on South Townsend and one on South Fairview; his credit background; and what make car he was making payments on. We also had a copy of his new business card showing that he was currently vice-president of Japan Life Sleeping Systems at 14541 Brookhurst Ave. in Westminster. The address of a branch office, also known as San Diego Dream Life Corporation, was given as 7520 Mesa College Drive in San Diego.

But Tran's previous business card showed that at the time of Kait's death he had been working at the law office of Minh Nguyen Duy at 10240 Westminster Ave. in Garden

Grove. Since Tran had changed his phone numbers after Kait's murder, I wondered if Duy had done so also, so I dialed the number on the card to see if it was still in service.

The woman who answered said, "Law offices," in a voice without an accent, but I could hear male voices speaking Vietnamese in the background.

"I'm sorry, I must have dialed the wrong number," I said hastily.

The fact that the number could have served more than one law office was interesting. In an effort to find out who practiced there, I spent most of one day at the library checking the number on Tran's business card against the numbers of all the lawyers in the Orange County phone book. The result was not what I had expected. Not only were there no other attorneys with that phone number, but Minh Duy himself wasn't listed. The address and phone number on the card that read "Law Offices of Minh Nguyen Duy" were those of a firm called "Business Management Services."

I didn't want to alert the receptionist by calling twice, so I asked Kerry to see what she could find out about this company.

She phoned them and called me back.

"A man with a Vietnamese accent answered," she said. "It didn't sound like a business, because he just said, 'Hello.' I told him I was trying to locate an attorney I had done business with, but I couldn't remember his name. I said, 'He gave me this number. This *is* Business Management Services, isn't it?' The man didn't answer. So I asked him, 'Which lawyers are in practice there? I'm sure I'll recognize his name if I hear it.' The silence went on so long I was starting to wonder if he'd walked away from the phone. Finally he said, 'Lawyers?' There was another long pause, and then he said, 'I need to talk to somebody,' and put me

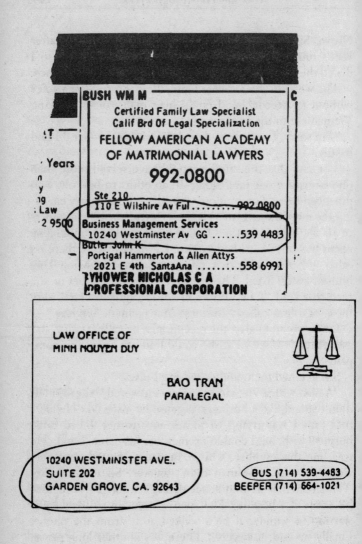

BUSH WM M

Certified Family Law Specialist
Calif Brd Of Legal Specialization

FELLOW AMERICAN ACADEMY OF MATRIMONIAL LAWYERS

992-0800

Ste 210
110 E Wilshire Av Ful 992 0800

Business Management Services
10240 Westminster Av GG 539 4483

Butler John K
Portigal Hammerton & Allen Attys
2021 E 4th SantaAna 558 6991

**YHOWER NICHOLAS C A
PROFESSIONAL CORPORATION**

LAW OFFICE OF
MINH NGUYEN DUY

BAO TRAN
PARALEGAL

10240 WESTMINSTER AVE..
SUITE 202
GARDEN GROVE. CA. 92643

BUS (714) 539-4483
BEEPER (714) 664-1021

on hold. I sat there holding the receiver for what seemed like hours, and finally I got so jittery, I hung up."

When our frustration over our inability to obtain information became unbearable, Don and I had occasionally discussed the possibility of hiring a private investigator. Our problem was that we didn't know how to go about it. Anybody could put an ad in the yellow pages, and I'd heard some frightening stories about unethical investigators. A private detective that we picked at random out of the phone book might sell our names to the people we wanted to have investigated.

The idea now occurred to me that we might be able to work through an intermediary, and I opened the Albuquerque phone book to the listings for attorneys.

"Paul!" I exclaimed. "I'd forgotten that he's in private practice now!"

Paul Becht and I had dated for two of the four years between my marriages, when he was a purchasing agent for Sandia Laboratories. Since then he'd graduated from law school, established a practice in business law, and served three terms in the New Mexico State Senate.

I made an appointment for a consultation.

It had been twenty-five years since we'd seen each other, but Paul was amazingly unchanged, except that he now wore glasses and his thick brown hair had turned a distinguished silver.

"This is the information we need," I told him, as I handed him a list of questions about people in California. "And this is the reason we need it," and I gave him a typed synopsis of everything we'd learned since the time of Kait's murder.

"Bao Tran, Van Hong Phuc, Minh Nguyen Duy—all Vietnamese names?" He laid aside the list and reviewed the

case history, frowning as he did so, and running his fingers
through his hair in a way that brought back memories.
When he had finished he lowered the sheaf of papers and
gave a long, low whistle.

"My God!" he exclaimed. "Was your little girl involved
in all that?"

"Yes," I said.

"And the police aren't following up on it?"

"They don't think it's applicable."

"Not applicable!" Paul exploded. "With a copy of that
check, she was a threat to everybody involved in this, including, in all probability, a lot of doctors and pharmacists.
What you need is a private investigator in the L.A. area."

"We're afraid we might get one who would sell us out," I
said.

"I'll act as the middleman," Paul said. "The person we
hire won't even know what your name is. I think the best
tactic is not to reveal this is a murder case, since most PI's
don't want to dirty their hands with murders. Instead, I'll
say I'm looking at potential litigation on a civil RICO action."

"A RICO action?" I repeated blankly.

"RICO—Racketeer - Influenced Corrupt Organizations.
There's a federal statute that permits individuals to file suit
and get triple damages from organizations and companies
that may be controlled by the Mafia or involved in organized crime. The federal government has been using it to
shut down and take the assets away from front organizations, money-laundering companies, and so on, but they
also allow civil action, so it will make a good cover story for
us."

"How much of a retainer do you want?" I asked, reaching
for my checkbook.

"First let me find a good guy, and then we'll see what his rates are."

"I mean, for yourself—"

"Don't worry about that, we go back a long way," Paul said. "I've been keeping track of your family over the years. Your oldest daughter was the cocktail-hour singer at the Hilton."

"She's produced her own series of recordings for children," I told him.

"And the other daughter had a television show."

"That was Kerry."

"She interviewed me once when I was running for office. She was gorgeous! I couldn't get over it, she was all grown up! The last time I saw her, she couldn't have been more than seven."

"She's married now and has two little girls," I said.

"I kept looking at her and thinking, Boy, what a knockout!" He paused and then added gently, "I could see a lot of you in her."

I got up from my seat and went around the desk to hug him.

"I can't believe you have so little gray in your hair," he commented, gazing down at the top of my head. I was grateful he was wearing bifocals and couldn't see the roots.

As I exited through the reception area, the woman at the desk said, "Ms. Duncan, I just want you to know you're my very favorite author!"

All in all it was a better-than-average day.

Paul moved ahead quickly. In less than a week he called to say he'd found an investigator based in San Diego.

"He's with an attorney services outfit," he said. "He does a lot of 'skip tracing'—that's finding people who don't want to be found—and he's very familiar with the Vietnamese and their automobile scams."

I suddenly found myself panic-stricken.

"You do think this is safe?"

"There's no way this man will know who he's working for," Paul assured me. "I'll need to sign a security agreement, so when he goes to the state authorities to get secured information, there's an affidavit that shows that he's doing it for a reasonable purpose, but only my name will be on that. And I'm setting up a trust fund, so I can make payments for you and you won't have to sign the checks."

"Do you know what this is going to cost?"

"He wants to start off with a two-hundred-dollar retainer. After that he'll send regular billings for whatever he's doing. My feeling is that the first thing we ought to have him check out is R & J Car Leasing. Who were the principals in it? Who owned the limited partnerships? Have any of those people been sued in any civil fraud claims? If so, we'll get the names of the plaintiffs' attorneys and see if they're willing to make their research available to us."

"I want information about the lawyer, Minh Nguyen Duy," I said. "Duy may or may not have been involved in the insurance scam, but we know that Tran was employed by him. I want to know what Duy's connection is with Business Management Services, and I want the names of the other attorneys who are in practice there. Once we have those, we can ask the insurance companies which, if any, of those lawyers were involved in lawsuits against them."

I told Robin I had hired a PI, expecting her to be pleased, but instead she was discouraging.

"You're wasting your money," she said. "You know APD won't accept information from us, no matter how we get it."

"We'll go over their heads and take it to the district attorney."

"She won't take it either," Robin said.

"We can't know that. I've been told that Susan Riedel is ethical."

"I don't care how ethical she is, she's bound by the rules. I had a date with a criminal defense lawyer the other night, and I asked him what our rights are. He told me we have no rights unless it's a civil suit. This is the state's case, not ours. The way this lawyer explained it, there are two factions involved in prosecution—there's the information-gathering team, who are the police, and the go-to-court-trial team, who are the district attorneys. The two are totally separate. The police are the sole information-gathering group and the prosecuting attorneys are only allowed to use information the police hand over to them."

"You mean even if we handed them concrete evidence against the people in Orange County, they wouldn't be able to use it?"

"Not unless they could get the police to follow up on it and present it as part of their own investigation. What this boils down to, Mother, is that this pitiful stab at investigative work APD did is the only representation we have. When this guy told me that, I was just horrified. I went home and cried all night. We have *no rights* at all, absolutely *none*! Do you know that in some states they won't even allow the family of the victim to attend the trial, because the sight of their grief might influence the jury?"

"That's not how it is in New Mexico," I said. "We're going to be allowed in the courtroom."

"Don't count on it," Robin said. "All either side has to do to keep you out is to put your names on their witness list.

They don't even have to use you. Just putting your name on the list will get you banned from the courtroom."

"Then I'll wear a disguise," I said. "I'm going to be there."

"Somebody is sure to spot you, and you'll cause a mistrial. Then we won't get the Vietnamese or the hitmen either."

I had been concentrating so hard on the activities in California that, Betty's reading to the contrary, I was starting to wonder if Mike might be right in his belief that one of the Vietnamese was the triggerman and the Hispanic suspects were innocent. When I went back through the police file, however, I did find several entries that seemed to support the case against Miguel Garcia and Juve Escobedo.

These entries centered upon Marty Martinez, the alleged third occupant of the Camaro, the one Betty Muench had said was "not part of the R & J symbol." Statements made to the police by people who knew Marty portrayed him as a young man with multiple problems. Not only had he grown up with a physical deformity—a harelip that had only recently been improved by cosmetic surgery—but, according to neighbors, he also had a severe drinking problem.

According to the police file, after his arrest, Marty had talked a lot about the shooting to both inmates and employees at the Juvenile Detention Center and had even told one fellow inmate that "his friend [Miguel Garcia] had killed somebody [in addition to Kait] and didn't get caught for it."

The most convincing of these statements came from Chris Mares, an employee at the center, who had been working there during the time that Marty was incarcerated. Mares came across as a kind and caring man of the type that troubled boys might turn to with their problems, and apparently Marty had felt the need to confide in him.

Marty's statements to Mares constituted an unsolicited confession.

What follows are selected statements from a lengthy transcript:

GALLEGOS: During the time Martinez was incarcerated and you were working, how many separate times do you remember talking to him?

MARES: I'd say maybe three or four conversations.

GALLEGOS: So, basically what [Marty] was saying was that he didn't do the shooting, he was just a passenger in the vehicle?

MARES: He definitely said he didn't do the shooting.

GALLEGOS: Mike Garcia did the shooting?

MARES: That's correct.

GALLEGOS: But he was in the vehicle at the time of the shooting?

MARES: On one occasion he indicated that he was asleep in the vehicle at the time of the shooting, and another occasion, he seemed to have firsthand information as to what was going on during the shooting.

GALLEGOS: What were his exact words at that time?

MARES: Basically, they were gonna drop him off at his house and right about the time they were approaching the area to drop him off, they spotted the Arquette vehicle, at which time, I guess they began to pursue the Arquette vehicle.

GALLEGOS: Did they say where they were pursuing her?

MARES: Not specifically, but if I remember correctly, it was into that Lomas area off of the Edith area, and apparently [when they were] catching up with the vehicle [it] accelerated, trying to get away from them. Michael Garcia had . . . a .22 caliber revolver, and rolled

down the window, taking aim and shooting at Ms. Arquette.

GALLEGOS: Did he describe the vehicle they were in?

MARES: He mentioned it was a Camaro.

GALLEGOS: Did he describe the vehicle that Michael shot
at?

MARES: He said it was a smaller vehicle but didn't have
much power . . . I'm trying to remember if he said
red, but I'm not sure . . . but he did say it was a small
vehicle and was trying to accelerate away from the
Camaro, but the Camaro had more power and over-
took it.

GALLEGOS: At the time of the shooting, did he indicate
whether the vehicles were at a stop or moving?

MARES: I got the impression they were moving.

GALLEGOS: Any words exchanged between anybody in the
vehicles?

MARES: Not that I can remember. It was more like she sort
of ignored them and all of a sudden, it was in Michael's
hands, [Marty] felt he was gonna shoot this girl.

GALLEGOS: Did he describe the girl at all?

MARES: He mentioned that . . . she was a pretty girl, or,
you know, she was a cute girl.

GALLEGOS: Did he say anything about Michael carrying
the weapon on a usual basis?

MARES: No. The thing I remember asking was if they felt
any sort of remorse, and he says that Michael didn't
seem to feel any remorse in this matter. And I got the
impression that [Marty] may in fact feel some degree of
remorse and maybe fear.

GALLEGOS: Did [Marty] say anything about what happened
after the shooting?

MARES: At one point during the stories, the variations of

stories he gave me, he indicated that Ms. Arquette apparently had gone to the side of the road, hit the curbside, jumped the curbside, hit a pole or struck some sort of an obstacle or something.

LOWE: Did he seem to have a bond with Michael Garcia and Juve Escobedo? I mean, did he say he always hung around with them?

MARES: I assumed that he must have had a bond, or else he had some sort of a fearical reaction toward them, because he definitely said he wouldn't snitch them off. I remember asking him why he didn't go to the authorities, and he said, "I'm not a snitch."

GALLEGOS: During your conversation with Martinez, did he ever indicate to you that Michael Garcia was familiar with weapons?

MARES: Yes, he did. I remember asking the question, "Did Michael have trouble shooting from a moving vehicle?" And he indicated that Michael had expertise with guns, because his dad had had guns, and he had been around guns since he was a little kid, and so he had no difficulty in shooting that weapon.

GALLEGOS: Did Martinez at any time sound like he was bragging about this?

MARES: No, never. He sounded concerned about the situation legally. I got the impression from him that he also had some degree of remorse.

LOWE: Is there anything else you can remember that he said to you?

MARES: What I remember most about him is he's a very good kid, a very cooperative kid, and I have a feeling if he were approached by the right people he would give a lot more information. I'm sure he knows a lot more than what he's talking about.

A statement from a neighbor of Marty's supported this image of a good but weak-willed young man who had a "fearical" relationship with Garcia and Escobedo.

According to this witness, the two men "always carried a gun . . . they both used it. . . . [Marty's] a good kid. He really is. He's not bad. It's just that he's afraid of Juve, and he's afraid of Michael. . . . He's always been scared of them."

How scared? I wondered. Scared enough to allow himself to be pressured into riding with them to carry a back-up gun that he didn't fire? Or perhaps he did fire but deliberately aimed to miss, which would account for the misplaced bullet in the side of Kait's car.

The calls that Don and I had received from Miguel Garcia's sister were also damning to his case. Her announcement that she and her relatives were planning to kill us seemed proof that the Garcia family was capable of murder, and her statement "The girl was a bitch and deserved to die" implied that she was aware of a motive behind Kait's murder.

And for anyone who accepted the concept of precognition, there was an additional, soul-chilling indication that Miguel Garcia was the triggerman. It appeared in an interview held by Detective A. V. Romero with Robert Garcia, the "witness-who-wasn't-there."

The question Romero asked concerned Garcia's name:

ROMERO: Do you know if Mike Garcia was his last name . . . ?
ROBERT: Mike Garcia?
ROMERO: Yeah.

ROBERT: I don't know. Well, his nickname was vampires or something. They always called him "Vamp."

In *Don't Look Behind You* my hitman was named "Mike Vamp."

Statement in police report giving Miguel (Mike) Garcia's nickname as "Vamp."

ROMERO: Do you know if Mike Garcia was his last name, wasn't it?

GARCIA: Mike Garcia?

ROMERO: Yeah.

GARCIA: I don't know. Well his nick name was vampires or something, they always called him vamp.

INTERVIEW: DETECTIVES S. GALLEGOS & A.V. ROMERO, ROBERT GARCIA
PAGE #13

ROMERO: Do you know if Mike Garcia was his last name, wasn't it?

GARCIA: Mike Garcia?

ROMERO: Yeah.

GARCIA: I don't know. Well his nick name was vampires or something,
            they always called him vamp.

DON'T LOOK BEHIND YOU   51

moved to a different part of the country and given new identities so nobody can trace them."

"I don't want to move!" cried Bram. "Then I can't play with Chris!"

"And what about Steve!" I exclaimed. "I won't leave Steve!"

"I know this is tough," said Dad. "I'd give the world if I hadn't gotten us into it, but the fact of it is, we *are* in it, and there's no pulling out. You know about the letters that I've been getting. After what happened today, we have to take them seriously."

"The person who wrote those letters could be bluffing," I said. There was no way I was going to agree to leave Norwood! "That man who tried to shove his way into our hotel room might only have been planning to put a scare into us. There's no way we can be sure he intended to hurt us."

"Mike Vamp doesn't play pattycake, April," said Max. "He's one of the most notorious hitmen in the country. It's not just because of his name that he's known as 'the Vampire.' He follows the scent of blood as though he's got a hunger for it."

I closed my ears to that statement. "I won't leave Steve!"

"I'm afraid you're not going to have much choice," said Max. "There's something I haven't told you. We *did* find Jim tonight."

"I don't understand," began Mother. "Then why did we have to—"

"The reason I was in such a rush to get you out of the Mayflower was because I knew it was due to be invaded by police." Max paused and then continued. "Jim was shot in the head. His body was crammed in a linen closet at the end of the hall. He was carrying a gun, but he never got to use it. Apparently he wasn't able to get it out of his holster."

For a moment we were all too stunned to react.

"His hands," I finally whispered. "He had arthritis in his fingers."

"Mike Vamp" as described in *Don't Look Behind You*

20

I was hopeful that I would hear from my old high-school friend Marcello Truzzi, but was taken by surprise when, in early October, I received a phone call from Dr. Roll, the director of the Psychical Research Foundation.

"I found your letter about your precognitive experiences very interesting," he told me in a gentle voice with a rich Scandinavian accent. "The tragedy you have experienced in the loss of your daughter has created openings for you on a number of levels. You've started to realize the potential of the human mind and to recognize and accept your ability to see into the future."

"That's something you can accept?"

"Of course," Dr. Roll said easily. "Precognition is quite well established and creative individuals seem to have more of this ability than others. There are some notable instances in literature involving precognition. One, for example, involved the sinking of the *Titanic*. Several years before that event took place, a story was published about a Titan ship hitting an iceberg. Most of the details, including the tonnage, the lack of lifeboats, the number of people on board, and the number of fatalities were duplicated in the actual sinking."

"I never realized I had this ability," I said.

"We all do to some degree, particularly when it involves violence to people we're close to," Dr. Roll told me. "It seems that our family and close friends become tightly united with us, as though we are parts of a single organism, and we sense the pain that will affect other members of that body. ESP impressions about those we are close to often relate to injury or death. Your antenna was extended toward Kait from the time of her birth, and this sensitivity got woven into your creativity. Creative individuals seem to have the capability to tap into the same universal source that people tap into when they experience ESP. A colleague of mine did a series of ESP experiments with music students from Juilliard, and they did much better than the ordinary run of subjects. Of course, to people whose minds are closed to these possibilities, it all seems like nonsense, the way it undoubtedly did to you before you opened up to it."

"Why would I suddenly become aware of this now?" I wondered.

"You've been jolted into it," Dr. Roll said. "There aren't many times in our lives when someone we're close to dies violently, and when this happens to a mother, it's a shattering experience. A mother has a multiple identity, because her Self includes her children. In losing your child, you have, in effect, lost a part of your Self, and a shock of that magnitude can have a strong effect on the psyche."

"Do you believe in life after death?" I asked.

"As a possibility?"

"As a fact."

"The image of a mind attached for a time to a body has been the guiding hypothesis for research into that question," Dr. Roll said. "Being of a different substance from the body, the mind would not be subject to the mechanical laws governing that body, so when the bodily machine winds down, the mind would still continue. It's my own belief that the psychical detaches from the physical, and in that way, the soul transcends death."

"I don't understand—"

"To put it simply, there are several different levels of the soul. First there is the small soul, an 'everyday' soul, if you will. This is the soul that emerges from the body in times of stress. Have you ever had an out-of-body experience?"

"No, but I wrote about it in *Stranger with My Face.*"

"Such experiences aren't all that unusual. I've had a number of them; in fact, that's what led me into this type of research. They most often occur at times of physical or psychological distress, when the body image becomes momentarily detached from the body. As an example, in a near-death experience, a woman may be projected out of her body on the operating table. She moves up toward the ceiling and then down the hallway to the waiting area, where she sees her family, and notices her daughter is wearing mismatched clothes, because the maid, in a hurry, picked up whatever was on top of the laundry pile. That will upset the mother, who is reacting with her *little* soul with the same sort of orientation she would have in daily life. Why isn't her daughter dressed right? She'll try to communicate with her daughter—why are you dressed like this? She'll get angry with her husband for not overseeing things. She still has the small concerns about everyday matters.

"At the other extreme is the soul at its most advanced level. That's when the ego merges with something that is experienced as a universal being of light and love. That doesn't happen to people during near-death experiences. Those who progress to that level don't return to earthly circumstances."

"But what about Kait? Do you feel she is really communicating with us?"

"That's very interesting, the specifics about R & J and all. The way such communication takes place is through the 'family soul' or 'tribal soul.' People throughout the centuries have had varying names for it. The Iroquois Indians refer to it as 'the Long Body,' while Christians call it 'the Body of Christ.' It's at that level that the soul has the ability to identify with people, places, and physical objects that it's close to. There are several references to it in the New Testament."

A passage leapt to my mind.

" 'Inasmuch as ye have done it unto one of the least of these my brethren, ye have done it unto me'?"

"There's a more specific reference in Corinthians: 'For as the body is one, and hath many members, and all the members of that one body, being many, are one body: so also is Christ. . . . And whether one member suffer, all the members suffer with it; or one member be honored, all the members rejoice with it.' "

"Kait, in her current situation, is still an individual? She hasn't become a part of that universal light yet?"

"In the space in which she now resides, Kait does still seem to be Kait, as she was in her relationship to you. The closest way I can explain this is to compare it to my body. My kidneys are quite different from my lungs, my heart from my liver, my right hand from my left hand, so each has a separate identity; at the same time, all are a part of my body. Your soul and Kait's, and perhaps the souls of certain other members of your family, are a part of one 'tribal body.' Kait still retains that relationship, and that's how she reaches you. You have interiorized Kait, she is an abiding presence within you. She can transmit the energy of her intelligence, because she's still a part of you."

"You also referred to 'places and physical objects'—"

"The Long Body is characterized by features that are simultaneously mental and material. Any embodied existence takes place in a *place*, and the places experienced by the soul in physical form may also be a part of the Long Body. When you take a look at reports of apparitions or 'ghosts,' they nearly always appear in areas the deceased person occupied when alive. These are most frequently seen at the time of death and then decrease rapidly during the following days and weeks, although images of persons who died suddenly or violently may persist longer. It is this tendency of the dead to be seen in their physical or social environment that has led to the legend of hauntings."

"What about objects?"

"The same principle applies. That's what makes the practice of psychometry possible."

"I'm not familiar with that term," I said.

"Psychometry is the means by which a person with psychic abilities may connect with others through contact with objects they have touched. The majority of mediums work this way. The concept is that a person's memories may persist after death in the objects with which the person was connected when living."

"A psychic here in Albuquerque did that," I said. "When she held Kait's lipstick, she told me Kait had been crying, and when she held Kait's watch, she said Kait had kept checking the time on the evening she was shot. The girl who was with her that night verified both things."

"She sounds like a talented psychic, but there are some who are charlatans. When you start consulting psychics, you need to be cautious."

"Do you know of a person named Marcello Truzzi?" I asked him.

"Yes, he's quite well known."

"How do you feel about him?"

"The man has a role to play, and he does a good job of it. There is a group of people who are highly skeptical about things of this nature and are trying to get rid of all types of parapsychology. They're almost religiously fanatical about destroying the field. Truzzi is an open-minded man who acts as a mediator between such people and those who do research in this field."

"It's a lot to take in," I said.

"Indeed it is. But I want to do everything I can to encourage you to persevere in your efforts to continue learning and growing in this area."

"In the area of the paranormal?"

"This is *not* 'paranormal,' " Dr. Roll said emphatically. "Our psychic relationships are very normal and natural. The only thing that makes them supernormal is that they don't fit with the most plebeian concept of reality. But if you accept the concept that your mind is connected to others—that all of us are placed on this earth to relate to each other—then 'psychic phenomena' no longer seems phenomenal. We then see these things, not as spooky and supernatural, but simply as manifestations of the way we are."

Before he rang off, Dr. Roll asked me to write a paper about my precognitive experiences for *Theta*, the journal published by the Psychical Research Foundation.

Several days later I had a phone call from Marcello Truzzi. I was pleased to discover that he remembered me from high-school days and was willing to give me the names of some psychic detectives.

"Noreen Renier, in Maitland, Florida, has had some remarkable hits," Marcello said. "She's been featured in a couple of criminology textbooks, and she lectures to law-enforcement agencies. In fact, it was during a lecture at the FBI Academy that she predicted the shooting of President Reagan two months before it took place.

"Nancy Czetli, in Greensburg, Pennsylvania, has an impressive track record also. She gets most of her information through telepathy, by viewing photographs of crime scenes.

"Then there's Greta Alexander in Delavan, Illinois. She's had some striking successes. One of her big hits was when she found a body where the police had already looked—she made them look again—and she gave twenty-two accurate predictions about the situation, including the fact that the person who would find the body would have a deformed hand. That woman's sort of neat in some other ways too. She runs a kind of Ronald McDonald House for sick children, and most of the money from her fees goes to support that charity."

"Have you ever had any psychic experiences yourself?" I asked.

"Nothing in any way conclusive," Marcello said. "Certainly, I've had lots of experiences that might be interpreted that way, just like everyone else, but I'm basically a skeptic."

"Then what led you into this line of work?"

"I'm intrigued by anything strange and unusual," Marcello said. "Always was, if you remember, even as a teenager. People report all kinds of fantastic things, and I find them interesting. I keep thinking there must be some fire behind so much smoke. There certainly are things I've explored that I don't understand, and I've been very impressed by the qualitative character of some evidence presented by psychics. When somebody describes something at a distance, and you look at the photograph, and it looks exactly like what they described, it's very impressive. At the same time, I have enough sense to know, it could be coincidence."

I wrote letters to Noreen Renier, Greta Alexander, and Nancy Czetli, telling them I was a contributing editor for *Woman's Day* and asking for bios and tear sheets about cases they'd worked on. I ended each letter with the statement that I was personally interested in the subject because my youngest daughter had been murdered.

The first to respond to my letter was Noreen Renier, who seemed more interested in our personal tragedy than in being featured in a magazine.

"My speciality is homicide work," she told me. "I've worked with police from all over the United States and as far away as Japan. If I'm sent an object that was on the body of the victim, I can usually describe the victim and recreate the murder scene. Once that's confirmed, I switch the channel to the killer. I go into a trance and describe the killer to a police artist, who draws the face. Some faces are better than others, but they're usually pretty close. So far, I've never had anyone come back and say, 'We arrested a black man, and you described a white man,' or anything like that."

"That's unbelievable!" I exclaimed.

"It's my craft," she said. "There's no hocus-pocus, I come at it from a scientific background. Do you have any of the things from your daughter's body?"

"Her earrings and a watch."

"If you'd like to send them to me, I'll see what I can get. I charge the police for my work, but I'll do this for you for free. The artist who does the composite will expect to be paid, though."

"Does the artist have psychic abilities?"

"No, he just does what I tell him. He's a policeman. He's used to victims saying, 'This is who raped me—this is who mugged me—' and drawing a picture from their description. Do you want to take a shot at it?"

"Yes," I said immediately.

"Okay. No guarantees, but we'll give it a try."

"How long does a person's energy stay in the object? Kait's been dead over a year now."

"I worked last week on two crimes—one was four years old, and one was five years old—with good results," Noreen said. "I don't know how it works, so don't ask me to explain it. Just send me the things from her body. It works best if they're metal."

"I've been wearing the watch myself."

"Then I'll pick up on you as well as your daughter. You said there were earrings?"

"They weren't metal."

"Plastic? I don't do well with plastic."

"They were seashells, but they have gold rims."

"Send me the seashells and the watch—send me as much stuff as you have, and I'll just keep touching everything and see what I get. Please, don't include information about the murder. I don't want to be told about the girl or about the case. When I'm done, I'll send you the tape and the artist's composite."

"The *tape*?"

"I'll audiotape everything. I work with an assistant who asks me questions when I'm in a trance, and you'll hear those as well as my answers. Actually, if you want, we can do a phone hookup; you can be right there on the line at the time it's done. I don't usually do it that way with the victim's family, but you seem levelheaded enough to be able to handle it."

As soon as I was off the phone, I packed Kait's purse, wallet, earrings, lipstick, and sunglasses in a mailer to send to Noreen. It was frustrating that so few of those objects were metal. Then I remembered the cross Kait had been wearing. I knew that it had been meaningful to her because it had been her grandfather's, so I'd given it to her favorite cousin, Heidi.

Heidi was away at college, and I didn't know how to reach her, but I called my brother and asked him to get in touch with her and to ask her to mail the necklace directly to Noreen.

I felt sure that if Kait's energy remained anywhere, it would be in the cross.

21

Halloween had always been one of Kait's favorite holidays, because she loved to dress up, and long after she was too old for the practice herself, she had taken the neighborhood children trick-or-treating. This year I took a jack-o'-lantern to the cemetery and felt she was pleased with it. Other graves sported mundane bouquets of autumn flowers, but only Kait had a pumpkin.

I stayed for a little while, enjoying the warmth of the Indian summer sunshine as it slipped between the branches of the trees to make patterns of light and shadow on the grass. Then I went back to the town house to spend the rest of the day in the makeshift darkroom Don had set up for me in the laundry room. The renewal of my friendship with Marcello had brought back memories of his father juggling balls and plates while my father took pictures of the performance, and I'd queried my publishers about the possibility of doing a children's book about Ringling Brothers Circus. They had greeted the idea with enthusiasm, and now I was making proofs of my father's fifty-year-old black-and-white negatives of dancing elephants, grimacing gorillas, and such legendary personalities as "The Great Karl Wallenda" teaching his five-year-old daughter to walk a backyard high wire.

Proofing up hundreds of negatives was a lengthy procedure. I was still at it five days later and was in the process of printing a picture of the tramp clown, Emmett Kelly, taking a bubble bath, when the phone rang. Dropping the print into the fixer bath, I hurried to answer it.

The call was from Gwen Spoon, Noreen Renier's assistant.

"Noreen's ready to roll," she said. "The police artist is on his way over to her place, and they're going to do a composite sketch of your daughter's killer. If you want to sit in, you can put through a conference call and get on the line with us."

"You're not there with her?" I asked in surprise.

"No, I'm calling from work. I'll be using my lunch hour to do this. Do you want to listen in?"

"I certainly do!"

"Then, set up the call, and when we're all on the line, Noreen will see if she can home in on Kait's personality. She'll be asking you for feedback to see if she's on the right wavelength."

I dialed the long-distance operator and set up the conference call. A few minutes later the three of us were on the line together.

"Did my niece send you Kait's cross?" I asked Noreen.

"Yes, and she enclosed a letter saying she hasn't worn it yet," Noreen said. "That's good, because it means your daughter's energy hasn't been defused by her cousin's. I'm going to see if I can describe her emotionally and mentally. Gwen, will you say her name, please?"

"Her name is Kait."

"I want to be Kait," Noreen said. "Kait—I want to be Kait. . . . Was Kait just in the process of a move or planning to move, or had she just moved recently? I see a move around her at about the time this happened."

"That's correct," I said. "She'd just recently gotten her own apartment."

"Kait . . . I want to be Kait. I feel a little school around me. Not a lot, just a little. I don't know if she didn't go that much or what, but it's just a little school."

"She was taking two summer-school classes at the university."

"I want to be Kait. . . . I want to be Kait. I want to go into her emotionally. I want to go into her mentally. I want to be Kait. . . . Everything looked good to Kait. Everything sounded good. She wanted to try everything a couple of times. She was interested in many, many areas, and she had a low threshhold of boredom. Kait, let me just see you. . . . She wasn't always thoughtful. She might be late for an appointment, because she had so many things going, but people liked her—her peers liked her—she was popular— she liked people. She was the type of person with her vitality that she liked a lot of people—she might have changed men in her life—maybe there was someone on the fringes, a past relationship or someone who maybe never really entered into her life.

"Kait—I want to go into your body. . . . I feel like she's always had bad cramping. I feel stomach problems—a stomachache with her. I am Kait, and my stomach seems to hurt me a great deal. Lois, will you verify?"

"Her intestines were damaged by celiac disease when she was a baby," I said. "She suffered a lot of abdominal pain all her life."

"What night was she killed?"

"It was Sunday night, July 16, 1989."

"July 16, 1989. I see myself in a car—I feel I am driving,

so it must be *my* car. I want to see what happens to me that night. . . . There were people around me. I wasn't alone before this happened. . . . I feel there was a knife. I was threatened by a knife."

"That's not what happened," I said, startled.

"Then it's not right. That's okay, it's not always right, I sometimes get sidetracked. Still, I feel a knife so strongly. Why do I feel a knife?"

"She wasn't killed with a knife," I said. "She was shot."

"Still, I just see a *knife*! I keep seeing a *knife*! I am *scared* of the *knife*!"

"Maybe that was another occasion we're not familiar with," Gwen suggested.

"I wasn't shot," Noreen said. "I don't *think* I was shot—"

"She was shot in the head while she was driving," I said.

"Oh, then she *was* driving? Good! I felt so sure of that. But the gun just isn't that clear to me. I don't think she got a good look at it. What we ought to have is the bullet or the projectile. Then I could pick up who put the bullet in the gun. Would the police release that to you?"

"No way," I said.

"Too bad. It would help so much. Kait . . . what were you doing? I want to be Kait—before I'm killed—I want to be alive. . . . Kait—go to that night. . . .

"I feel like there are hills, strong inclines around me. I see city lights, but I don't feel I'm exactly in the city at this time as I'm driving. I feel that I'm entering into it—is that accurate, Lois?"

"Albuquerque's surrounded by mountains, but she wasn't on a hill when she was shot. She was driving through a downtown area."

"That's not what I'm seeing. I have this feeling I'm entering into the city. The city is below me. . . . I see the lights." She paused. "Lois, I'm afraid I can't go on with you on the line. I know you have preconceived ideas, and whether they're right or wrong, I seem to be resisting into entering into what *you* think, because it won't do us any good for me to echo it back to you."

"You mean I can send you visions out of my mind?"

"You can do that very easily, and I seem to be bracing against it. I don't want to see what *you* see or what you want *me* to see; I have to make sure it's really what *I* see on my own. So let's cut off this call, and I'll work with the artist and see if we can get a face. Then I'll call you back and fill you in on what's happened."

For the next two hours I sat in a chair by the telephone, trying to communicate with Kait.

Take advantage of this opportunity to get a message through to us, I told her silently. *Send us more than a picture of Miguel Garcia. We'll probably never have a chance to do this again, so, if you possibly can, try to tell us why you were killed.*

Finally, Noreen called back.

"We're finished," she said. "The artist just left, and we've got two pictures. One is the man I feel did the actual shooting, and the other is the person who is responsible for the murder."

"What race are they?"

"Well, we've got them both looking sort of white, but I'm not certain about their nationalities. There may be some Mexican or Italian or other stuff in there."

"Could the man responsible for her murder be Oriental?"

"I can't really say, because that picture's not as detailed as the other one. He has a square face and very straight, dark hair with highlights in it. The pictures aren't going to be one-hundred-percent accurate, because this artist tends to get people looking too pretty, but they're close to who I saw in my mind.

"I'll send you the sketches and an audiotape of what you missed. Look over the pictures and listen to the tape. Then you can see if there are other questions you want answered, and we'll set up a second session to fill in the gaps."

Three days later I received the sketches of Kait's killers.

The first was of a face that looked vaguely familiar, as if I'd seen a photograph of it in the newspaper, but it was the second picture that caused my knees to buckle.

The triggerman was "Mike Vamp."

The hitman in *Don't Look Behind You* appeared in the police artist's sketch exactly as he was portrayed on the jacket of the British edition of that book. That picture wasn't on the cover of the American edition, so people in the United States hadn't seen it, but the British edition showed my heroine talking on the telephone while the face of the hitman peered in through a window behind her.

Somehow I managed to drive myself home from the post office and maneuver the house key into the door lock. Then I headed straight for the bookcase that held the foreign editions of my novels. When I held the sketch next to the jacket of *Don't Look Behind You*, the resemblance was even more startling than I'd thought. Every detail of Mike Vamp's face appeared in the sketch—the hollows in the cheeks; the deep-set black eyes; the bulbous nose; the large, pointed ears; and even a scar that ran horizontally between the eyebrows. It was as if Noreen's artist had copied the book jacket.

Noreen had sent the audiocassette with the pictures, and I inserted it in our tape player and sat huddled on the sofa, shivering as if I were freezing, as I listened to the continuation of the phone conversation.

Gwen Spoon's side of the dialogue had not been re-corded, but from Noreen's responses I could follow the line of questioning.

"It wasn't working with the mother on the line," Noreen said. "She was too emotional. Now, let me see if I can get back into Kait.

"What can I get about the killer? Why did he murder the girl? What was the motive? . . . Oh, my God, it was a *setup*! . . . He killed her because she knew too much. . . . I think she *accidentally* knew too much. She got involved in something way over her head before she knew she was over her head. I think they overestimated what she knew. She was someplace when something happened and saw too much and saw too many people.

"There were several people involved in this thing she found out about. One was a man who *owned* stuff. I don't know if he's one of the men in the sketches or not, but he was around there. Did he work at or was he maybe part owner of a club? Maybe some sort of disco or nightclub? That's very strong around me, a nightclub or disco. . . . Did Kait work for him in some way or work at the place in some way? I feel *work*—that she worked for him in some way—*how* she worked for him I don't know at this time.

"Now, let me see if I can figure where all this took place. There's this man who's thinking—'Because I'm just here to set up this organization, I don't necessarily have to *buy* a home, I can rent.' I almost want to call it sort of a villa, because it has stucco in it, a low roof, a Spanish- or Mexi-can-style roof. There's a strong backdrop of a mountain right behind it.

"I think Kait was leaving this place, going back into town. I don't know if she was followed by them or not, but when I first tuned into her, the city was in front of me and I was coming down the mountain into a valley where I saw the lights of the town. This man lived on the outskirts of town, and definitely east, maybe a bit northeast. If we were put where Kait was found and we drew a clock around her, I would put his villa maybe at two or two-thirty. It was maybe twelve miles or a little over twelve miles away. There's a twelve involved in it. And I see a five. That has something to do with a time frame. I don't know how long ago the girl was killed, but I see a five. I don't know what it means, but I see a five."

The tape ran out, and I went to the phone and dialed Noreen.

"Something crazy happened with one of the pictures," I told her. "Your artist drew a character from one of my books."

"Which picture?"

"The one with the tight curly hair. The triggerman."

"He came out of a *book*?"

"I wrote a book called *Don't Look Behind You* and modeled my heroine on Kait. In that story my heroine was chased by a hitman in a Camaro. The book came out in June 1989. In July 1989 Kait was chased down and shot to death by a hitman in a Camaro. Your artist drew my hitman."

"That's impossible!" Noreen said. "I *told* the artist what to draw."

"But the face you described was of a fictitious character! This isn't the person who shot Kait, it's a person I *invented*!"

"I couldn't have pulled him out of your mind," Noreen said. "You weren't on the line at the time. We'd severed connections."

"But it's him!" I insisted. "It's Mike Vamp! You got the

picture *somehow*! In my book Mike Vamp was a hitman hired by interstate drug dealers."

"Did Kait ever see a picture of this character?" Noreen asked me.

"She's one of only a few people in this country who has. The proof for the artwork arrived a few days before her death, and I asked her opinion about how it compared with the American jacket. She said she thought it was much scarier."

"That's the answer, then," Noreen said. "The picture is symbolic. The message Kait was trying to send us is that a hitman was hired to kill her because she was going to expose illegal activities."

"You said she saw something that night that led to her death," I said. "There wasn't any time for that. She went straight from our house to her girlfriend's house that evening and was shot right after she left there."

"Maybe I'm wrong, but that's not what I got," Noreen said. "I got she went somewhere that night and was threatened with a knife."

"Can you go back into a trance and dig deeper into this?"

"Yes, but I've got a heavy schedule this week. I'll try to get it done within the next ten days or so. Then we'll give all the stuff to the police and let them run with it."

"The Albuquerque police wouldn't touch this with a stick," I said.

"They will when they look at my credentials," Noreen said confidently.

"They won't look at your credentials. The police here won't look at anything. They're so furious with us right now, they won't even talk to us."

"So, go federal," Noreen said. "What about the FBI? If

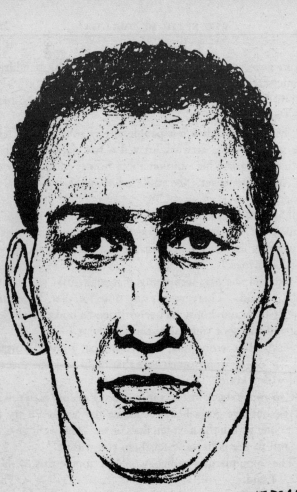

MIKE DEAL
5 NOV 90

The composite sketch of the triggerman drawn by police artist
Mike Deal, working from the description given by psychic
Noreen Renier

Drug runner hitman "Mike Vamp" peers through the window on the jacket of the British edition of *Don't Look Behind You*

this is interstate trafficking, you ought to be able to get the feds involved."

"We've tried," I said. "The FBI won't answer our letters."

"Why not?"

"I don't know."

"So, where do we go from here?" Noreen was clearly irritated. "All this work isn't going to be worth a hill of beans if nobody will follow up on it."

"Please, let's keep trying to put the pieces together," I said. "If we get it worked out so everything fits and makes sense, then maybe we can force APD to investigate it."

"If what you're after are concrete facts, you won't get them from me," Noreen said. "That's not how this works. If I could come up with names and addresses, hell, I'd be charging millions and living in style. Psychic detective work is based on impressions. The case is a jigsaw puzzle—you get a lot of pieces and you know they'll make a picture—but putting it all together is a job for the police."

22

When we moved to the town house, we had asked for an unlisted phone number. The telephone company got careless, however, and in November, when the new phone directories came out, our new number appeared in it.

At once we began to receive more calls from tipsters. Most were obvious weirdos, but one knocked the breath out of me.

"The night your daughter got killed, she went snooping and saw some big shot buy coke," he said.

"Who did she see?" I asked, trying to remain calm.

"The guy I heard talking about it didn't give a name."

"Tell the police," I said. "They won't listen to us."

"They record their calls. I don't want my voice on tape."

"Then call Mike Gallagher at the *Journal*. I'll get you his number."

My own recorder was hooked to the phone in my office, but, as luck would have it, I had taken this call in the kitchen. Now, I raced to the other extension, punched the record button, and snatched up the receiver, to be greeted by the dial tone.

The man had hung up.

I was shaken by that phone call, not only because the man had sounded so sure of himself, but because what he told me seemed to confirm what Noreen had said about Kait's activities on the night she was shot. Betty, also, had told us, "There will be this which [Kait] will have done *just that night* . . ." and, in another reading, "There will be this that is felt as an occurrence *that evening*, a visit incomplete and information incompleted, a clue she was looking for missing and no cooperation."

Still, I could see no way that Kait could have gone "snooping" anywhere that night. Every minute of her time appeared to be accounted for.

I dragged out the well-worn police file and began to re-read it. In an interview Gallegos had conducted with Susan Smith, I found a piece of information that had previously slipped past me:

Smith said . . . the victim went to her parents' house for dinner. . . . [Kait] came to [Smith's] home at about 2130 hours and they sat around her home talking for a while.

I wasn't used to thinking in terms of military time, and the number 2130 had made no impression on me. Now I realized it translated into "nine-thirty P.M." Kait had lied when she told us she was eating at Susan's, and she had lied to Susan when she told her she had eaten at our house! She had set herself up with an overlapping, two-sided alibi to give herself three secret hours in which to do something she didn't want any of us to know about.

I turned back to an earlier section of the report that contained a statement that had been incorrectly attributed to me by Gallegos: "Mrs. Arquette said her daughter had eaten dinner at her home earlier in the evening and then left, saying she was going to visit a friend." I had discounted that inaccuracy as a careless but innocent misquote and had not considered it important enough to take issue with, but now I could see that it camouflaged a three-hour time gap.

I wrote to Noreen and asked her to concentrate her next session on finding out where Kait had been during those three missing hours. I also told her that Kait had been an organ donor and gave her the name and address of the man who had her heart and lungs. We couldn't very well ask him to fly to Florida so Noreen could do her next reading with her hand on his chest, but perhaps she had the ability to zero in long distance and draw some residue of Kait's energy from her hand-me-down organs.

I wasn't aware that Noreen had done her second reading until it was over and I received the recording in the mail:

NOREEN: This is Gwen and Noreen. It's November 27, 1990—in the evening. I want to work on the case for Lois Duncan involving Kait. Her heart's still here and her lungs. Her heart . . . her lungs . . . her heart . . .

I'm still alive!

Gwen, take me to where you want me to go.

GWEN: We're interested in the night you were killed. You left home saying you were going to Susan's house. We need to know what happened between the time you left home and the time you got to Susan's.

NOREEN: I went up the hill toward the north to that big place up there—walls of some sort around parts of it— not all of it, because there's a lot of land up there. I go up there. There's a man. . . .

GWEN: Are you alone?

NOREEN: I'm alone when I'm driving.

GWEN: Are you driving your car?

NOREEN: I'm driving my car. No, wait a minute—*am* I driving my car? I am at first, but I'm meeting somebody. I'm meeting somebody at a shopping center with a C in it. I park my car and get into his. His has got a four-wheel drive.

GWEN: Was he expecting you?

NOREEN: We had plans to meet to go to this—I want to call it the Desert Castle.

GWEN: How well do you know this person you are with?

NOREEN: We've been friends—or maybe more.

GWEN: Tell us more about this person.

NOREEN: He's sort of . . . Mother wouldn't like him.

GWEN: Does she know him?

NOREEN: She's met him maybe once or twice. But I could see her disapproval.

GWEN: Did you have a romantic relationship with this person?

NOREEN: Yes.

GWEN: Does it continue?

NOREEN: Without her knowing, yes.

GWEN: And so it was prearranged to meet at this spot?

NOREEN: Yes.

GWEN: And you had an appointment at the Desert Castle?

NOREEN: Yes.

GWEN: Upon your arrival at the Castle, how are you greeted?

NOREEN: There seem to be a lot of other cars. It's a semi-circle driveway. There's an important person there that I'm not supposed to know is there. I promise I won't tell. They let me go. I shouldn't have been there at that time, because the other person came and didn't know I was coming. It's a person I wasn't supposed to see or know about. And I see him. And I see his car. It's concealed to some extent, because of the circular drive-way. It's a big, long car. It's black, dark.

GWEN: Had you seen it before?

NOREEN: No, I had just heard about this person.

GWEN: Had you met him before? Did you know who he was?

NOREEN: I knew him from the town—we're not in town now. I know who he is. He's the person in the other picture I drew that they don't recognize. I can identify this person. He's a very powerful person with this group of people that I shouldn't have been hanging out with.

GWEN: What happened at the Desert Castle?

NOREEN: Things are happening there. I shouldn't have gone at that time. There are people there. There are things happening there when we get there that I shouldn't have seen. I shouldn't have been there. It was not the right time.

I just want to get out. I don't want any more to do with it.

I don't know why everybody seems so mad at me. There's an argument of some sort. I tell them there's a friend I have to meet. Once I get back, I still have a little way to drive. It's important. I have a friend to meet.

I tell the people at the Desert Castle my friend is expecting me, I have to leave. So I get to leave, but everyone seems to be angry with me.

GWEN: Tell us about the argument.

NOREEN: The argument was just . . . I told them people knew I was coming there . . . they expected me back for dinner . . . that they knew I was going there. I

lied. No one knew I was going there. I lied about .
several things to several people. I'm sorry I lied.

GWEN: How long were you there?

NOREEN: Maybe an hour and a half.

GWEN: How did your male friend act while you we
there? Toward you and toward the other people?

NOREEN: He's mad at me. He seems to be mad at me
don't know why he's so mad at me.

    I go. I go with my friend. I calm down. I'm okay. I
drops me at the mall, and I get in my own car and go
my girlfriend's house. When I leave there, I'm kille

GWEN: Driving?

NOREEN: Yes.

GWEN: How far from your friend's house had you gotte

NOREEN: I was followed before that. Because the peop
knew where I was going. I told them I was going ther
I think someone was sent after me. Someone follow
me. I felt fear and danger when I left the hill. I met r
friend. I tried to act as normal as possible. She was ir
good mood. I leave her—and I'm cut off.

GWEN: What do you want to tell us about that? Concer
ing how many people were in the other vehicle?

NOREEN: I only see two. I was cut off. They're coming
both sides of the car. They want me to roll the wind
down.

GWEN: Are you still driving?

NOREEN: No, I've stopped. They've cut me off.

GWEN: Who are these people?

NOREEN: People sent from the hill.

GWEN: What is your conversation with them when th
approach the car?

NOREEN: Just "Roll down your window." I'm shot. Exec
tion style.

GWEN: Do you see any weapons?

NOREEN: I see a gun. I see a silencer on it—this big thing on the end of it.

GWEN: Do you have any feeling about what prompted this?

NOREEN: I was at the wrong place at the wrong time. I saw someone I shouldn't have seen. I saw things I shouldn't have seen. They had to make sure there was no way I would ever talk, and this was a way of silencing me. The crime that was committed against me was to silence me.

I will never be silenced! I'm not a bad person! I was just young and I just was curious about life and people and things, and excitement and people in exciting positions were interesting to me. *I* was *good*! I *was* a good daughter to you, Mother! I told you *almost* everything. Almost.

GWEN: Is there anything more you'd like to tell your mother now that you didn't before?

NOREEN: Don't stop what you're doing. Just remember the police have fear. These are very powerful people who are involved. You may not be able to prove a lot of what you write or say, but those involved will know it's the truth. The police are frightened. They don't want anything to do with all of this. They want to mark it up as something different than it is and not to go beyond that. They have somebody to convict. They want to let it go at that.

GWEN: Besides the things you saw that night that you shouldn't have seen, did you hear anything in particular that you shouldn't have heard?

NOREEN: [her voice rises in a tone of anger and frustra-

tion:] It wasn't what I *heard*, it was *who I saw! It was wh*
I saw—who I saw—who I saw!

GWEN: Is there anything in particular you would like t⟨
tell your best friend?

NOREEN: My best friend would be my mother.

GWEN: Is there anything you'd want to tell Susan or you⟨
boyfriend?

NOREEN: I'm mad at my boyfriend. I'm still mad at him⟨
My girlfriend—I love *her*.

GWEN: Will you be continuing to help your mother wit⟨
this case?

NOREEN: I still live. [Long pause] Yes . . . yes.

The tape ended, and I continued to sit without moving⟨
too emotionally drained to get up from my chair. Hearin⟨
Kait's words, uttered with Kait's inflections, by the husk⟨
voice of a middle-aged stranger, had been the most bizarr⟨
experience of my life. And they *were* Kait's words. I didn'⟨
have the slightest doubt of that. The "shopping mall with
C in it" was Coronado Center, the largest mall in Albu⟨
querque, only blocks from our home. And how many teen⟨
agers other than Kait addressed their mothers as "Mother"⟨
All her friends had called their mothers "Mom." Even th⟨
flowery term *Desert Castle* sounded right to me, since Kai⟨
had had a tendency toward romantic exaggeration. The out⟨
burst of irritation had been familiar to me also—"It wasn'⟨
what I heard—*it was who I saw—who I saw—who I saw!*"⟨
knew without having to hear it the accusatory statemen⟨
that would naturally have followed: "*Mother, you're just no⟨
listening!* Don't you *ever* pay attention?"

Who was the man Kait saw at the house in the moun⟨
tains? And who was the alternate love interest who ha⟨
driven her up there, a person I hadn't approved of and ha⟨

met once or twice? Which of Kait's many past boyfriends had I seen so infrequently? Usually they'd settled in like members of the family.

My mind flew back to the very first boy Kait ever dated. His name had been Rod, and she had brought him over two times. I'd tried to discourage the relationship, because Rod was too old for her, a former high-school dropout who had returned for a degree. I'd been afraid he would take advantage of Kait's starry-eyed romanticism, and as it turned out, I was right to be concerned. She had bought him a silver bracelet with their names engraved on it and, the very same day she gave it to him, had discovered that he was involved with another girl.

She had cried herself to sleep that night, and as far as I knew, she'd never dated Rod again.

But that had been four whole years ago, it *couldn't* be Rod. Perhaps it was Tuan, whose number had appeared in her phone directory? But, no—I'd met Tuan more than twice. How often had I met Khanh? And what about Nam? Would Kait have been foolish enough to confide in one of Dung's friends? It was hard to imagine, but I wouldn't have put anything past her at that point in her life. According to Betty, Kait had "trusted all the wrong people" and "exposed herself at every turn," so who knew where she might have turned for emotional support?

The phone rang, and I reached automatically to answer it. It was the psychologist friend who had given me *Many Lives, Many Masters*, calling to tell me about the success she'd been having using past life regression to help certain patients discover the roots of their phobias.

Any other time I would have been eager to hear about this, but at that moment I needed to talk myself. Interrupting her in midsentence, I poured out everything that had been happening, including Noreen's description of Kait's "Desert Castle."

"I think I know where that is," my friend said. "There's a mansion that fits that description near the base of the mountain trail where my husband and I go hiking. It's the closest thing to a 'castle' I've seen in New Mexico."

"How do I get there?" I asked, and she gave me directions. If it hadn't been late in the day, I would have gone right then, but in November the night comes early, and I didn't like the idea of being caught in the foothills after dark.

I decided to postpone my search for the Castle until morning.

23

I found the Mediterranean mansion without any difficulty, although the distance from Kait's death site was much more than twelve miles.

It sat, nestled in the foothills, overlooking the city of Albuquerque, exactly as Noreen had described it, with the Sandia Mountains a snowcapped backdrop.

I parked my car a little way down the dirt road, slung my camera around my neck, and approached the building by way of a rocky footpath on the north side. The gate was locked, and I didn't see any sign of life; no cars were parked in the courtyard or in the circular driveway.

I climbed over the gate and walked across the courtyard. When nobody appeared to confront me, I continued on under the archway and up the tiled stairs to the bronze-mounted doors of the main building. The term *castle* suited the place perfectly, and it even had four outbuildings, including an animal house and a cabana for the swimming pool.

I peered in through the windows and saw that the residence was furnished, but there was a feeling of vacancy about it, with deck chairs blown over by the wind, scum in the swimming pool, and tumbleweeds lying in drifts among the marble statuary.

I decided that if I hadn't already set off a silent alarm I was probably safe enough, so I strolled through the grounds, snapping pictures from every angle. Then I climbed back over the gate and drove back to town, where I had two sets of prints made, one to show Don, and the other to send to Noreen.

When I got back to the town house, I found a message on my answering machine to phone Barbara Adams, secretarial assistant to the psychic Nancy Czetli.

"Nancy got your letter," Barbara told me when I returned her call. "The moment she opened the envelope she got this big rush of fear for you. She got some very strong feelings about what happened to your daughter. She feels your daughter was killed because she observed drug transactions. Nancy feels there's a drug runner involved who was crossing state lines and was involved in a transaction with some sort of VIP. Nancy says to tell you you're playing with fire and to be real careful."

"Will Nancy be willing to work with us to find out more?" I asked.

"Nancy doesn't like to work directly with families," Barbara said. "The request has to come from the police."

"There's no way we can get the police involved in this," I said. "They won't consider anything except 'random shooting.'"

"Typically Nancy does not work with families," Barbara said. "Their emotional involvement can get in the way of her objectivity. Another problem is, she may be able to tell you who the killer is, but you won't be able to do a damned thing with the information. You can't go into a court of law and say, 'This is what a psychic says,' so it can't be used as evidence. When she works in conjunction with the police, she gives them leads, and they physically follow up on them to establish proof."

"APD won't do that," I said.

There was a moment of silence.

Then Barbara said, "If that's the way it is, I don't suppose the police would furnish you with photos of the crime scene?"

"No," I said, "but we have them on a videocassette. Our oldest son taped the television news shows."

"Let me check back with Nancy and get her reaction," said Barbara.

The following day she called back.

"Nancy says get out of the way before they get you next," she said. "She says what you've got to do is try to get the system to do the work for you. She is really concerned that you don't keep pushing on your own. There's heavy-duty drug traffic going across state lines and well-to-do people are involved—be real careful of that—she's real concerned, she says *leave that alone.*

"What you want is to get the FBI involved. Do you have proof that the police have removed stuff from the files and that sort of thing? If the police are saying to the FBI, 'We'll handle this, stay out of it,' then your hands are tied unless you can prove shoddy police work or a possible cover-up. *Then* they can get involved in the case."

"We can't do that unless we have more information," I said.

After another exchange via Barbara, Nancy did break down and agree to work with us directly, but only if I promised not to pursue things she told me not to follow up on.

"She doesn't want to be responsible for your being killed," Barbara said. "She's really concerned about that."

"I don't much like that idea myself," I assured her.

"Then send her a photograph of your daughter, showing the eyes," Barbara said. "Send the video of the crime scene, a map with the spot marked where your daughter was killed, the exact date of the shooting, an article of clothing or an intimate possession that belonged to your daughter, and a sample of her handwriting. Then I'll set up a telephone appointment for you."

I sent a box with the video, one of the flyers that showed Kait and Dung together, a city map with the murder site marked with an X, a page from one of Kait's school composition books, and the teddy bear that she had continued to sleep with even after Dung moved in with her.

Barbara called to tell me when the box arrived, and we set up my interview with Nancy for December 4.

Nancy's approach was very different from Noreen's. Crisp and businesslike, she clicked off her reactions in an objective, no-nonsense manner:

NANCY: The videotape was real helpful. I feel that money changed hands. I get that from the scene in the courtroom. I sense it was about a thousand dollars.

I don't know how it all fits together, but I got one brief glimpse on the videotape of the Vietnamese boyfriend leaving the funeral home, and along with a sense of grief, he gave off anger and satisfaction. I feel there was some connection between him and these others. I cannot tell how—there was just a brief flash there, before he realized he was being filmed—but there was a sense of having gotten even with her. It's not enough to go on in terms of accusing him of having hired somebody, but *somebody* did. I feel very certain that the people who did this were paid, but they're not about to admit that, because a conviction for murder-for-hire could bring them the death penalty.

LOIS: So you feel the Hispanics did do it?

NANCY: Yes, I do. I detect the feeling of their presence on that street. I also don't buy it as random at all, because it comes across very strong to me that somebody was checking her license plate against a number that was written on a piece of paper. They also seem to have known about where she was supposed to be and approximately the time she was going to be there.

Besides, if this were a random shooting, they would just have been joy-riding around, firing, but I feel sure she was followed and chased. Had she had a more powerful car, she might actually have gotten away from them, because I sense they were having problems with their car. From seeing her car on the video I got a feeling of her fear and desperation. She was being followed, and she guessed she was going to be killed, and she seemed to know very much that it had to do with information she had about this boyfriend or his cronies. It's some kind of illegal activity that she had recently become aware of and which she had threatened to expose. She didn't want to go through with that, because unfortunately she was more in love with him than she could afford to be.

LOIS: What else do you get about the boyfriend?

NANCY: It's distinct from the teddy bear and from the residue around the car on the videotape that she's angry and she's seriously considering turning this Vietnamese fellow in. Had she done it, he might have been charged with a felony-level crime and probably deported.

He also seems to have been having a great deal of

trouble emotionally. I detect it even in the photograph
you sent of the two of them together, and it is certainly
in his photograph on the TV, that he's having a lot of
trouble handling her independence and the fact that
she was more intelligent than he was. There was a crisis
reaction in terms of the way she was threatening his
manhood and there's a feeling in him of "I'm going to
teach her a lesson—I'm going to teach her who's boss."
He didn't want to lose control of her.

LOIS: Barbara Adams said you think this is drug related.

NANCY: I think your daughter was a very nice person, she
was just naive. She did not realize that from the moment she caught on to what was going on, her life was
in danger. She should have gone to the federal authorities immediately. She shouldn't even have bothered
with local law enforcement, it would have been too
risky. Unfortunately, she sat on it. If she had not sat on
it, she would have had a chance, but they would probably have had to put her in the Witness Protection Program. Whatever she stumbled onto involved drug deal-
ings involving a lot of money.

The likelihood of a conviction in this case is very
poor, because the prosecution doesn't have anything to
link these Hispanic guys with the Vietnamese, and
their witnesses are not very strong.

Now, there is another person out there still, someone who overheard a detailed discussion of how this
was set up and he's been very uneasy about that. He's
not into killing and has a reverence for women that the
killers do not have, and he was quite disturbed from the
outset. I also get the impression that this person called
Crime Stoppers but never identified himself.

If this person would come forward, they could nail

the killers, because this man is credible and doesn't have the erratic patterns of the other witnesses. He is afraid to come forward, because of the nature of what he overheard. The fact that your daughter observed evidence of such magnitude of criminal activity that people would take a contract out on her is frightening to this man. It's not that he would not care to help, he would very much care to help, and he feels a certain civic obligation to do so. The problem is that he's afraid he also will be killed, and he has a family. He's done a lot of wrestling with his conscience. His testimony would be really, really good, because he was around a series of times when the killers discussed the money they had been paid and gave some information about the man who hired them. With this man's testimony it would be clear it was not a random shooting.

LOIS: It's hard to think that this group who are running drugs interstate would hire stupid, bumbling kids to do the hit for them.

NANCY: Actually, it would be a pretty good setup, because these guys are known for odd violence, so it could be believed to be a more wanton killing, which is how they wanted it to appear. They would have absolutely no concern about these gentlemen talking, because if you trade the rate of the sentences around, the sentence for a random shooting is going to be a lot lighter than sentences for interstate drug transportation or murder-for-hire.

LOIS: Barbara said you thought Kait was witness to a drug deal.

NANCY: I think she had knowledge of drug exchanges that had been going on for a while, and that may have been

what she was trying to collect more information about
the night she was killed.

LOIS: Do you see the threat of a knife involved in any of
this?

NANCY: I associate that with the Vietnamese. I see periodic
violence in Kait's experience. I get the feeling from
that teddy bear that she had experienced violence on a
number of occasions.

LOIS: Do you have anything else for me?

NANCY: I think that things are going to happen around
this Vietnamese man that will shed a more realistic
light upon his possible involvement in her death. So I
don't think it's necessarily over with, but it may be
some time before that happens. I also don't have much
hope about the trial of Garcia.

It's my feeling that this was set up with Hispanic
hitmen, because if any Oriental person had been seen
around her with a gun, the whole mess would have
come out immediately. So they used a completely different racial setup to distract.

But they *did* have some kind of connection. And I
don't know if it was the boyfriend himself or through
his network, but I feel that they had a connection to
Hispanic hitmen. Within a drug network you can ask
people to do things.

LOIS: Do you feel these Hispanics have killed before?

NANCY: I feel they may have been involved in some kind of
incident in which a federal officer was either killed or
badly hurt. That would have been down near the Mexican border.

LOIS: How in the world do you get such precise information?

NANCY: By far the most helpful tool in this instance was

the video. I work best from the crime scene itself. When people become frightened, they leak a lot of information mentally, and somehow it gets stuck in the cells of the environment. I don't understand exactly how it works, except that I know that cells can, in fact, store information. I'm sure of that. They reflect scars from the scenery that stay a long time. Old battlefields do it. Really brutal murder scenes. There's a memory almost of what happened.

The other thing was Garcia's eyes. Once I saw those, I recognized the thought pattern from the murder scene. Each time I looked at the murder scene on the video, I was getting the feel of the killer. Then, when I saw the men in court, there was a very good shot of Garcia where I could see his eyes real clearly, and I recognized the pattern—it was the same thought pattern I'd picked up from the crime scene. From the time I locked eyes with Garcia, I was sure they had the right person.

LOIS: Thank you very much for doing this for us.

NANCY: There's one other thing I would like to say to you as a mother myself and as someone who has had these odd abilities all her life. I hope you know that your daughter has an existence now. It's not at all the same as what it was, but her soul has an awareness of how much you care and how much you're hurting, and when you think loudly about her she is very much aware of what you're thinking. I get the distinct impression that she is trying very hard to communicate with you through dreams and even directly. She's trying to make you feel and realize that her soul has continued.

She really seemed frustrated, when I felt her, about

the fact that there are occasions when you doubt this. She's determined that you know that this isn't your imagination—it isn't just your wishful thinking—she really has been trying to communicate with you and other members of the family. She's trying to get through friends too. And she's been real concerned about her father's reaction. She's worried that he's going to hate because of this, and she doesn't want either one of you damaged in that way. She's concerned that his anger isn't resolved. You've turned yours into action, as women often do, but he hasn't. It's harder for a man to do that.

I have the feeling that her father may have sensed a lot of danger from this Vietnamese man and now feels guilty that he didn't say more to his daughter to try to protect her. He must understand that this wasn't his responsibility. As independent as she was, even if he had said more, she would not have listened. She believed in the basic goodness of human beings, and that naiveté is the wrong thing to carry around with you when you're dealing with people like this, because they use it against you.

Nancy opened new doors in our collective thought processes. Don admitted that he had never felt good about Dung, but had concealed his dislike because he didn't want to be regarded as racist.

Robin reacted to the suggestion that the suspects might have been involved somehow in some incident where a federal officer was injured and asked me to check the police file to see if either man had an FBI identification number. I consulted the file and found that both of them did, but it didn't say what they were for. Marty Martinez, the boy in the backseat, had no FBI number.

For me, Nancy had answered the question of why the truck driver, Eugene Lindquist, who had nothing to gain by deception, had reported seeing Hispanics in a Camaro that matched the description of Juve's chasing a girl in a Ford Tempo west on Lomas, long before Kait left Susan's house.

If their assignment had been to kill a girl in a Tempo, Lindquist might have seen the killers checking the license-plate numbers of *all* girls driving Tempos on that area of Lomas. And the cars they would have been checking at that time would have been headed *west*, because at nine-thirty Kait had been driving *to* Susan's house, not leaving it. Betty's statement that Kait had kept consulting her watch with the time nine P.M. in mind had made no sense to us when we thought Kait had gone to Susan's at six-thirty. But our discovery about Kait's three stolen hours changed everything. She might well have been running late for a nine P.M. appointment.

And the tipster who had phoned us about the drug transaction and might also have sent the postcard to the attorney general? From then on, whenever we spoke of him, we referred to him with sympathy and affection as "the Good Man Who Is Afraid."

24

Our second Christmas without Kait was fast approaching, and none of our children wanted to come back to Albuquerque. Don and I had accumulated enough frequent-flyer miles on our respective business trips to give us three bonus plane tickets, so we decided to spend the holidays with my stepmother in Florida, and give Donnie one of the tickets so he could join us there.

The week before we left, I phoned Betty Muench. The information we'd gotten from Noreen and Nancy had been so similar in content that I couldn't resist getting input from our "resident psychic" to see if her reading supported those of the others.

It had been six months since I'd spoken with Betty. Now I asked her if she could get answers to three more questions for me, and she said she would take a shot at it, despite the fact that the questions themselves made no sense to her.

She typed out the reading and read it to me over the telephone:

QUESTION: WHAT MAY WE KNOW ABOUT KAIT'S EXPERIENCES ON THE NIGHT SHE DIED BETWEEN THE TIME SHE LEFT HER PARENTS' HOME AND ARRIVED AT SUSAN'S HOUSE?

ANSWER: Kait comes across very strong. She comes across up close and there's a burning heat to her presence. She senses this and backs off, so as not to come across as overwhelmingly intense.

"Usually when I get people it's on the left side and it's at least an arm's length out," Betty said. "Kait was pressing in real close. This connection was powerful."

ANSWER: There is an intense pressure on the top of the left side of the head, and this will show that there will have been some deep thinking going on in her on the day in question. There will be this that she will have come to realize, and she will have made several attempts to find the tangible manifested proof to support her thoughts.

"She was thinking about something, and she was going a couple of places to find out if she was thinking correctly," Betty said.

ANSWER: On the night in question there will be a time frame which will have allowed her to be in the presence of several people. She will have known the visit with her parents, and then there will have been two other stops before she will have arrived at the house of Susan. There will have been a stop which will seem to have had her sitting alone in her car, and this will have been in view of something that she will have been thinking about. It is as if she will have backtracked to where she had been before she went to her parents' house, and she will have seen something which will have caused her alarm, and yet she will have thought at that time that there was surely an explanation.

"I had the idea she went back to her apartment and watched something," Betty said.

ANSWER: There will have been what she will have perceived at that time as a kind of double-cross, someone will have said something and then changed, will have promised something and was obviously not in the process of keeping this promise. She will have been noticed, and there will have been her moving from this situation, and then she will have made another stop, a stop which will have shown that she was tentative about claiming what she had seen. There will be this left-side energy which will have been her intuition working very strongly in this time frame in question. She was in the process of making a decision that would put not only herself in jeopardy but all who knew her. This was the point of her dilemma at the time of her death. The places will be places in which she will have often been —her own home place, and another place of high authority.

"So, she went back to her apartment," Betty said thoughtfully. "There she saw somebody—her boyfriend, maybe?—doing something he'd promised he wouldn't do. She didn't want to believe it unless she had to, so she went someplace else to check out what she'd seen. Do you suppose she was considering turning him in to the police?"

"Let's wait to discuss it until after you're finished," I said.

QUESTION: WHAT MAY WE KNOW ABOUT THE DESERT CASTLE, THE OWNERS OR OCCUPANTS, ON THE NIGHT OF KAIT'S DEATH?

ANSWER: There's a sense of something sliding across the chest—across the heart chakra—and going up the right side of the neck. It will be as if there was a very masculine feeling about this place.

"The right side is the masculine side," Betty explained to me.

ANSWER: There is this energy around this Desert Castle that will show that there will be in a very near time something that will come up about this place that will show that what went on there on the night of Kait's death will be something that will occur more often than thought.

There is a sense about this place that the subject of death is quite often spoken of, and there is some manner of connection with death. This will seem to be very male oriented, and there is in this some kind of cultlike energy which is so strong around this death subject that it hits one directly emotionally.

There will be in this place one who will claim to be the possessor of this place, but this is a lie. This one is not the owner of anything and will be a fraud from all descriptions.

There is a sense of illegitimacy about this place and the proceedings in this place. This is a meeting place for those who would have ideas about a misuse of power. There is a thought that anything is permissible as long as it serves the immediate purposes of the group. This is a place in which those will be found who will work with death and who will do so for money. The ownership is in question, and it has a sense of having been abandoned out of fear of this group of occupants, occupants who are illegitimate in their actions and in their possession of this place. The essence is a cult gang energy.

"I get the feeling that the people in this 'Desert Castle' are the ones who issued the hit order," Betty said. "It also sounds like they're going to do it again. At least, that's how I interpret that part about something soon happening at that place that 'will show that what went on there on the night of Kait's death will be something that will occur more often than thought.' I think we need to get braced for another murder."

QUESTION: WHAT MAY WE KNOW ABOUT THE PERSON KAIT OBSERVED IN A DRUG TRANSACTION?

ANSWER: The person Kait observed buying drugs on the night of her death is a person of some importance. This one covets his reputation and is usually very careful about his actions, yet there will have been an instance in which a certain urgency will have overcome him, and so there will not have been the usual caution. There is a dread of discovery which will border on paranoia, and this will be part of his fear about this observation by Kait. He will not have had anything to do with the actions after that, but his followers will be involved, and this is what must be considered in the death of Kait.

"This man didn't order Kait's killing, but his presence is what triggered it," Betty said. "Where did you ever come up with such far-out questions?"

I told her about Noreen and Nancy, feeling as guilty as if I were confessing to having invited three dates to the same dance. Betty surprised me by saying she thought getting input from several sources was an excellent idea.

"Psychics aren't all alike," she said. "Our abilities differ, and we utilize different forms of energy, so mixing and matching will give you a better-balanced picture."

She expressed an interest in Noreen's sketches and asked me to send her copies. When I put those into the mail, I also mailed our second set of Desert Castle photographs to Nancy Czetli and asked her if this was the place where Kait had seen the drug transaction.

Don and I left for Florida on December 14, and the mere fact of being out of Albuquerque and away from the memories it held for us was enough to make us lightheaded. In a way the happy memories were more painful than the sad ones, because they were part of a past that could never be relived.

First we flew to Orlando, where we spent two days touring Epcot and Universal Studios like children on a holiday, enjoying the sunshine and flowers and eighty-degree weather. Then we rented a car and drove to nearby Maitland, so I could interview Noreen Renier for my *Woman's Day* article.

Noreen turned out to be a handsome dark-haired woman, with a strong-boned face and the lithe, trim build of a tennis player. She told us she'd had no psychic abilities as a child, and had become interested in the paranormal when she was working in public relations at a Hyatt hotel and was asked to do promotion for a lecturing medium.

"Just being around that woman had a strange effect on me," she said. "She was very powerful, or maybe I was very sensitive. She kindled my interest, and I started reading up on the subject and began to do meditation with two of my woman friends.

"One afternoon we were meditating with our eyes closed, when all of a sudden my body felt as if somebody had plugged it into a wall socket. I heard my voice start talking all on its own, and I thought I was going crazy! I opened my eyes, and my friends were staring at me in horror. One was sipping from my coffee cup to find out what the hell I was drinking, and the other was crying because I'd given her a message from her dead mother!"

Noreen said she went through five years of laboratory testing at Duke University and at the Psychical Research Foundation before going into police work.

"At Duke they hooked me up to an EEG machine," she said. "First they had me just be myself, and they monitored my brain waves. Then they asked me to psychomotrize an object, and they discovered I was using another part of my brain. The psychic comes from the emotional side. You don't find as many men psychics as women, because men have been trained from childhood to suppress their emotions."

I asked if the pictures I'd sent her were of Kait's Desert Castle.

"I don't know," she said. "I get impressions in a trance, and when I come out of it I don't remember a thing. I went back and listened to the things I said on the tape, and the place does match my description, but unless I'm channeling Kait, I don't have any way to verify it."

Back in our rental car I asked Don, "How did you feel about her?"

Lois Duncan with psychic Noreen Renier in Maitland, Florida

Christmas 1990 in Florida. Standing: Don and Lois. Second row, seated: Brett; Robin; Donnie; son-in-law Ken with Erin, 5. Seated on the floor: Kerry with Brittany, 3.

"I liked her," he said. "And I appreciated her honesty; she doesn't pretend to be anything more than she is."

That Christmas was less traumatic than the previous one. We rented a couple of rooms near my stepmother's apartment, and Robin and Brett drove over from the East Coast to join us. Even our Jewish contingent came for the holidays, dutifully terming their trip a "winter excursion." We decorated an evergreen tree with seashells and poinsettias and, after the gift-opening ceremony, spent the day on the beach.

I decided to take advantage of being in Florida to research the circus book and spent a morning interviewing the "Great Wallendas." Carla, the tightrope-walking five-year-old in my father's photographs, was now a grandmother who owned her own circus and had fascinating stories to tell about her European ancestors.

"My grandparents would transport their circus by horse-drawn wagon from one little town to another at night," she told me. "Between the towns they would sometimes be attacked by wolves. What they'd do would be cut loose a horse and shoot it and leave the carcass to divert the attention of the wolves while the performers got away."

I suppressed a shudder as my mind flew back to Brett's essay about the wolves who had broken into our flock and made off with a lamb.

Upon our return to Albuquerque we found a message from Nancy Czetli on our answering machine:

"I got the pictures you sent, and you don't have the right house."

Disappointment crashed down like a landslide. I had been so *certain*! Yet, when Don got out a city map and extended a line twelve miles to scale in a two-thirty o'clock direction, I could see that the mansion I'd photographed was too far north. With the map as our guide we spent most of New Year's Day driving along the base of the mountains, photographing houses. There were a number of impressive residences with stucco walls, flat roofs, and semicircular driveways, but none of them could legitimately have been called a "castle."

"There's no way to know the origin of that term," Don reminded me. "It might be a code name. Or maybe the owner referred to it as his 'castle' because it was so expensive to build."

We took three rolls of pictures and mailed them to Nancy.

The following day we experienced another disappointment. I had a call from Paul Becht, who had heard from our private investigator in California. He had done a very poor job. Not only had he been unable to find out anything about R & J Car Leasing, but instead of investigating the lawyer, Minh Nguyen Duy, in an undercover manner, he had confronted him face-to-face at his new office in Van Nuys, California, and demanded to know what his connection was with Business Management Systems. Duy had adamantly denied ever having heard of the business, and the investigator had accepted that statement without question, despite the fact that the business was at the same address and had the same phone number as Duy's former law office.

"I'm sorry this didn't work out like we hoped." Paul said.

"At least we tried," I said. "And something else has come up now that makes me believe the insurance scam is the tip of the iceberg."

I told him about the call I'd had from the tipster who told me that Kait had witnessed a drug transaction. I was tempted to add that three different psychics who knew nothing about the phone call had told us the exact same thing, but I didn't want to risk my credibility, so I let the tipster's statement stand on its own.

"I think we should take that phone tip seriously," Paul said. "It came at exactly the time the new directory came out, which makes me think the informant probably wanted to call sooner but didn't know how to reach you when your phone was unlisted. But the tip's not of any use to us without the names of the people involved. There's a lot to suggest that Kait's boyfriend or his friends may be drug runners, but we don't have the concrete evidence that would be necessary to get a conviction."

"I have plenty of proof that they were crossing state lines to commit insurance fraud," I said. "And I have Bao Tran's check to prove that he financed the car wrecks. Neither the police nor the FBI will follow up on that. Is there *any* way we can force the authorities to do *anything*?"

"The insurance companies might be able to do that," Paul said. "Which ones covered the 'injured parties' through the rental companies?"

"National General, State Farm, Progressive, and Farmers. And all the fake injuries were treated at Humana Hospital."

"I know some people at several of those companies," Paul said. "I'll pass along what you've got and see how they react to it. But even if Bao Tran and the others are arrested and convicted of insurance fraud, you aren't going to get them for murder unless you get more proof."

25

Several days later Nancy Czetli's secretarial assistant called to say that Nancy had looked through our new batch of photographs and reacted strongly to two of them. Our first reaction was to think she was hedging her bets, but when we examined the negatives we discovered that the pictures she had selected were two very different views of the same house, one taken from the front and the other from the side as we drove past it on our way down the mountain.

I set up another phone appointment with Nancy:

NANCY: After looking at the photos I think Kait had been in the area of this house and possibly in it that evening and other times and was aware that drug activities were going on there. This was a part of the activity she was going to expose.

   An odd thing about it is, when the exchange is taking place, she's not in the house, she's outside. The people involved in the transaction aren't the people who own the house. I don't know whether the man is a friend and can come over or is renting or what, but it isn't his house. And I do not believe the person who owns that house knew anything about these activities. This home was being used as an exchange point, but as near as I can tell, the owner was out of town at the time.

Some of the occupants at the time of this exchange were two small, slightly built Oriental men, and a man who's Caucasian. He's middle-aged, heavyset, and has shiny black hair.

LOIS: Do you feel these Orientals were the suppliers of the drugs?

NANCY: Both the Oriental men were involved in importing them. I get the feeling that Albuquerque is the hub of a multiveined network and drugs are being imported from at least two states.

LOIS: What do you feel about that house now?

NANCY: It seems to be a clean house now. They don't use it as a drug pickup point anymore.

LOIS: How did they get in there?

NANCY: With a key. The white guy had a key. He must know the person who owns the house, because he had a key and authorization to be there.

LOIS: Do you feel this was the man who put out the hit order?

NANCY: No, definitely not. This man was not in any way responsible for Kait's murder, nor does he necessarily realize that the murder was connected with what he did. Knowing that she was killed and knowing who she was involved with, it did cross his mind back there in the beginning that something might be connected, but he's now accepted the public solution of what happened. He did not order her killing, I want to be very clear on that.

LOIS: Right after Kait was pronounced brain dead, a call was made from her apartment to somebody in Santa Ana. Was this connected with the drug trafficking?

NANCY: I think that man is the one who put a contract out on Kait. And when the contract was completed, the guy was notified, and there was another exchange of money. There had been a prepayment, and then another payment was made. But I don't feel the second payment ever got to the killers. That money was stolen in transit.

LOIS: What was the connection between these Vietnamese and the killers themselves? We need to establish a link.

NANCY: My feeling is the only link is drugs. Hispanic guys act as transporters from a different section of the network. It's a Latin part of the transport system. And when you're in this kind of a network, you don't say no to the boss, or you turn up dead. So it's not like they had a whole lot of choice. They were told what to do and they did it. But they were paid for it and blew the cash very quickly.

LOIS: What about Juve Escobedo, who supposedly drove the hit car? Do you have any idea where he is?

NANCY: I sense that he's in northern Mexico right now. He's been coming back and forth, though. He's remained pretty free, because he knows nobody's really looking seriously. He should be back in town probably late next week.

LOIS: Do you sense a police cover-up? Was somebody paid off?

NANCY: Actually, no, I don't feel that any money changed hands. Something occurred early on—I don't know what it was—that kept the investigation from going in the right direction, but once the police identified the Hispanics as the killers, most of the Homicide Department became convinced it was random. Cops can be very blind when they think they've figured something out. It's not exactly a cover-up, although it certainly can look like one. It's like they've solved this case, so why are you still fussing?

I think there is one of the detectives who really does agree with you. He doesn't dare say so, but he agrees with you. There were just too many things about that boyfriend that didn't wash. He has continued to pursue this, but he doesn't want anyone knowing he's doing this. But you've got one investigator who still isn't satisfied.

LOIS: Are you sure it's a man? [I was hoping it was Sergeant Lowe.]

NANCY: Oh, yes, definitely, and he's a very good investigator. He's a psychical person, although he would never use that word. He knew the boyfriend was lying over and over again, and he found that highly suspicious. So this investigator keeps thinking, if he didn't have something to do with this, why would he have lied? This guy is good at reading character. He knew what he was looking at.

LOIS: Do you think he's going to be successful?

NANCY: I think the tragedy of it is that the puzzle will not be broken until after another murder has occurred. This detective has checked on the boyfriend and I feel that he has notified some of his friends in Vice that he thinks he may be involved in drug dealing. The day may very well come when they set him up.

I also think one of the anonymous phone calls that the police department got telling them where to start looking for these hitmen was from one of the people who hired them. They hired away from their own, because they were going to set these men up. That way they were able to stop the investigation. If the investigation had gone on, it would have uncovered the rest of the stuff involving the Vietnamese. What's horrifying to us who live regular, conventional lives is how easy it is to get a contract hit. It's not even very expensive.

LOIS: I gather Juve, the driver, is not going to turn up?

NANCY: Oh, they're going to get him eventually, but I don't believe he will be found before this summer at the earliest. Still, as I said, he'll be in the area toward the end of next week. If they check his regular haunts, they might catch him.

LOIS: Do you think Kait had a sense of what was going to happen to her?

NANCY: From what I get from Kait, she had nightmares about it—about being chased by a car and about hearing the shots and knowing immediately she was not going to get away. That's why she really floored it when she saw the car behind her, because she remembered the dream and she tried very hard to get away.

LOIS: Do you feel Kait still has an existence as Kait, not just as an energy?

NANCY: She exists as more than Kait was. Because when you cross that dividing line between this dimension and the dimension in which souls rest between lifetimes, you have more knowledge and more understanding of the evolving process of the soul than we can possibly have.

LOIS: Do you think we ever again get back together with the people we love?

NANCY: Definitely. When you cross over you are met, and you're met inevitably by someone you will recognize and be comfortable with, because that's the purpose of meeting you. They don't want you to be afraid.

LOIS: I wonder who met Kait.

NANCY: I have the feeling there was a gentleman there—
would say by his age he had probably been a grand‐
ther—who really helped her tremendously, because s‐
still was very frightened. She didn't realize she w‐
dead and kept trying to run.

He was with two women. Kait knew one of the‐
and the other she hadn't met personally, but she kn‐
instinctively who she was. She wasn't alone for a‐
length of time. They were there right from the begi‐
ning.

LOIS: My father died when Kait was fifteen, and Do‐
mother when she was eleven. My own mother di‐
three years before Kait was born.

On the morning of the day Kait was shot, she ca‐
over to our house and wanted to look through the ‐
family albums. That surprised me because she'd nev‐
been interested before. I got them out and sat do‐
with her, and she kept picking out pictures of ‐
mother and saying, "Why, Mother, she looked just li‐
you!" Do you think, subconsciously, she was trying ‐
establish a bond with her?

NANCY: She recognized them all somehow. She knew wh‐
their place was relative to hers. She did not understa‐
the significance of it at first—why they were there, w‐
she was there, what exactly had happened—but, at lea‐
they were able to reach her mentally and get h‐
calmed down.

LOIS: Do you get any feeling about how she is now?

NANCY: I get the feeling that she is very excited about wh‐
is now possible for her. She is very disappointed ‐
herself and in how she lived her life. She feels that s‐
let you down and let herself down. But she will gr‐

past that. She's a very curious person. She has a tremendous sense of curiosity, and she is very interested in what she can learn now. She likes to learn.

LOIS: Is she following what's going on here?

NANCY: Very definitely. And she says to tell you, "Don't worry. Even if they're not convicted, it doesn't matter." And I know what she means by that, because when you cross to the other dimension, you have to face yourself. I guess, in a sense, that's what is meant by Judgment Day. Everything you've done is known to God, and you have to give an accounting of how you have and haven't grown karmically during your past lifetime. So she's not going to be that upset if these people aren't convicted, because she's sure these men will get what is coming to them eventually.

What she *is* concerned about is more murders. That bothers her a lot.

LOIS: Murders of members of our family?

NANCY: No, murders in general by this particular group of drug dealers. She's very concerned that they're going to kill someone else. She has discussed this with the people who are helping her learn how to communicate again.

LOIS: What do you mean by "helping her to learn to communicate"?

NANCY: Telepathy has to be learned. Kait can receive, but she has difficulty sending.

LOIS: Is there anything I can do to help her to communicate?

NANCY: Possibly, as you heal, you'll be able to help her. The mind has two states, sending and receiving. You know how, when you lose something and you look and look and look for it and can't find it, when you give up and are walking away, you immediately know where $ is? What causes that is you've kept your mind in sending state, but when you unblock, the informatio comes through. It's a subtle difference in the way yo think. Meditation helps you to be better able to achiev it.

LOIS: We don't know when the trial will be.

NANCY: They'll keep postponing it.

LOIS: We're worried that we're going to be kept out of th courtroom.

NANCY: Actually, that would be just as well. I always advis my clients—not that they listen to me, but I advis them—to stay out of the courtroom, because what goe on in there is not about the truth, it's about who pu on the best performance. The theory upon which ou justice system was built is a good one, and if peopl acted in the way it was intended, we'd be fine, but that not how it is.

Let me give you another piece of advice. Try t mend your fences with the prosecutors. I feel you hav a difficult relationship with the police right now. Th prosecutors are very wary of you, because you've bee labeled something of a nut. They think you're so ma you might hurt their case. If you demonstrate to the that that's not your intent, they will be more cooper tive. Right now they have a pretty jaundiced view you.

We wanted to know who owned the Desert Castle, even he was not involved in the drug ring and had abandoned h home "out of fear of this group of occupants."

When I couldn't find the house in the city directory,

asked a friend in real estate to see what she could find on it, and she got me the name of the owner.

According to the tax rolls he was the only occupant.

I gave this information to my friend at the credit bureau, who pulled the man's credit file. It was very unusual. In the year and a half since Kait's death he had applied for credit four times, and on each occasion he had given a different address, none of which was the address of the Desert Castle.

I got out our map of the city and went out with my camera to photograph each of these residences, with the idea of sending the pictures to Nancy to see if she could solve the mystery of what this gentleman was up to. The streets appeared on the map and were easy to find but they all dead-ended slightly short of the house numbers. The owner of the Desert Castle did not seem to want to be located. None of the addresses on his credit applications existed.

26

February. The nastiest month of the year. Autumn lon gone and spring still too far away to contemplate.

The duck pond in the park behind the town house froz over, and the ducks waddled pathetically about on the blue black ice, unable to understand why they weren't paddlin in water. Don's car wouldn't start unless he jumped it ever morning. Donnie injured his knee and had to have surgery I started work on the text for *The Circus Comes Home*, wrot another article for *Woman's Day*, and submitted the pape Dr. Roll had requested for his parapsychology journal.

We received an offer for our house, and our realtor ad vised us to take it, although it was for much less than we ha hoped. She said the publicity about Kait's death had had negative effect upon potential buyers who were morbid concerned about "which room the murdered girl slept in. We accepted the offer and closed on the house, consolin ourselves with the knowledge that we now had one le thing to worry about.

Donnie announced that he was planning to move to Flo ida, because Albuquerque no longer seemed like home t him, and, despite having just received an award of excel lence from the Department of Energy, Don decided h would take early retirement so we, too, could leave at the end of the year.

We didn't know where we would go, just "somewhere away."

According to the DA's office the trial still hadn't been scheduled. All anyone would tell us was that the continual postponements were "by mutual agreement." Juve Escobedo was still not in custody, although half of Albuquerque seemed to keep bumping into him. A stranger, who recognized me from television, came up to me in the grocery store to tell me she had called APD to report that Juve was at his girlfriend's house, but nobody had come to pick him up.

On February 14 I went to the cemetery and was surprised to find an arrangement of flowers on Kait's grave. It was a sweetheart bouquet, with forget-me-nots and a rosebud, and a little pink heart poised pertly on top of a pipe cleaner. At first I thought Dung must have left them there, but then I remembered Kait's telling me that the Vietnamese men didn't understand the concept of Valentine's Day. Was it possible Kait's "other boyfriend" had been there grieving for her?

I sat down on the brown matted grass and wept for all of us.

That night I dreamed about Kait. She was about ten years old and was standing next to my bed.

"I need two sheets of your good paper to write to my friend Greta," she said.

The dream was so clear in my mind when I woke up in the morning that I wondered if it held a meaning. I got out Kait's weekly planner with the phone numbers in it, but no "Greta" was listed.

Then it occurred to me that she might mean Greta Alexander, the one psychic who hadn't responded to my letter. I mailed her a second letter saying Kait was asking for her.

Greta phoned me.

"I'm sorry I didn't call before this," she said. "Your first letter got buried in my mail pile. I'd like to talk with you some evening, if that would be possible."

"That would be fine," I said. "I think my daughter wants to channel a message through you."

"She tells me, 'When it's dark, when the light is in the sky,' " Greta said. "That's when she is to speak."

"You've already communicated with her?" I asked incredulously.

"You bet."

"When would you like to schedule it?"

"I'll have to ask my angels," Greta told me. "I did five police cases yesterday, and I'm emotionally down right now. I'll just have to play it by ear and see what comes to me."

I had thought I was conditioned to psychics, but obviously I still had plenty to learn.

Dr. Roll received my article and called to thank me.

"May we be on first names?" he asked. "I would like very much for you to call me Bill. I found Noreen's sketches fascinating. Also very educational. I'm assuming that the man in the picture is not, in fact, the true killer?"

"We have no reason to believe so," I said. "It's Noreen's feeling that this was Kait's way of telling us it was a drug-related hit. Nancy Czetli also thinks the murder was drug related."

"How much information did you give these psychics when you wrote to them?"

"They specifically asked that I not tell them anything," I said. "The only things they wanted were some of Kait's possessions and pictures of the crime scene."

"And the police aren't involved in this endeavor?"

"They would never accept it."

"You're probably right," Bill said. "My experiences working with police have been very disappointing, as most can't take in the fact that ESP is not an exact science. In everyday life we're used to focusing on the subject in which we're most interested, and everything else goes into the background. ESP doesn't seem to work that way. It's often quite hard for a psychic to focus on the target, and what comes to mind may be anything related to the situation.

"When you give a task to a psychic, the way to focus her is to supply her with objects. That does help as a rule. But even then there is an inherent uncertainty that we haven't yet overcome, because we're not sure exactly how ESP works yet. In lab experiments that uncertainty is called 'displacement.' Instead of hitting the target you hit somewhere around the target. So then the question is, why would Noreen have displaced to that picture? The reason you give could be very appropriate—that there is a message—that the drug connection is the significant thing and that is what Noreen got onto."

"There was something else she didn't get right," I said. "At one point she *became* Kait and described her last moments, and she said Kait was cut off by another car. Then she said the killers came to either side of her car and shot her 'execution style.' From everything we've been told, that isn't what happened."

"I know Noreen," Bill said. "She works by psychometry. I imagine she was holding an item Kait was wearing when she was killed?"

"Yes, she was holding Kait's cross."

"And might there have been another car on the road?"

"It's possible that there was a VW bug."

"Then, perhaps Noreen displaced to what Kait was thinking in that moment of crisis. The VW bug cut her off, and she thought, *I can't get away!* and visualized the execution scene, and that vision was part of the mental images the cross absorbed. As I said before, ESP is far from an exact science. Using several psychics to get a majority opinion is a fine idea. Just don't expect all the details they give you to coincide."

By now I had read most of the books in the New Age section of our chain bookstores. Some seemed contrived and fabricated, but others were mind provoking. I was intrigued by Dr. Raymond Moody's interviews with children who had survived near-death experiences; by Dr. Roger Woolger's accounts of past-life regression; by Robert A. Monroe's experiences with astral projection; and by Jane Roberts's dialogue with a spirit guide.

Having covered everything available in the mainstream stores, I visited a metaphysical bookstore and found the works of Alice A. Bailey. Betty Muench had told me she found Bailey's books meaningful, so I bought the one on telepathy. Although the publication date was forty years ago, it contained material that supported one of Nancy's theories.

In citing the difference between emotional and mental telepathy, Bailey noted that the former could get in the way of the latter. It was her belief that with mental telepathy, as compared with gut animal instinct, "the more emotion and feeling and strong desire can be eliminated, the more accurate will be the work accomplished. . . . An attitude of nonattachment and a spirit of 'don't care' are of real assistance. . . . Emotion and desire for anything on the part of the receiving agent create streams of emanating energy which rebuff or repulse that which seeks to make contact.

. . . When these streams are adequately strong, they act like a boomerang. . . . In this thought lies the failure on the part of the receiving agent whose own intense desire to be successful sends out such a stream of outgoing energy that the stream of incoming energy is . . . driven back whence it came."

That could explain why both Kait's brothers had experienced visitation dreams, while her sisters, who were more emotionally involved, had not. It would also explain why Noreen had evicted me from the conference call.

On the night of February 28 I had trouble sleeping, and at one-thirty A.M. I pulled a ski jacket on over my pajamas and went for a walk. It was a starless night, yet a full white moon peered out through a space between the clouds and created a pathway of light, which I followed to the far side of the pond where the ducks were sleeping in a row at the edge of the ice. One gave a drowsy quack, as though stirred from a dream of a summertime lake filled with water bugs.

I stared up at the blue-veined moon and the realization struck me—"It's dark and a light is in the sky!" Why had Kait given Greta Alexander that message? Was there something about the moonlight that intensified her energy?

The cloud bank slid across the moon, and the night went black; tree branches creaked in the wind, and I was suddenly freezing. I groped my way back to the house, tripping over shrubbery now concealed by the darkness, and crawled back into bed next to Don, who was sleeping so soundly, he hadn't even realized I was gone.

I knew that the phone was going to ring, and it did.

"There's more to Kaitlyn's death than meets the eye," a woman's voice said when I lifted the receiver.

"Greta?"

"Of course," Greta said. "This is the night my angels brought Kaitlyn."

"Please, hold for a minute," I said. "I have to switch phones." I hurriedly crossed to my office, snatched up the extension, and turned on the tape recorder.

"I've been thinking a lot about Kaitlyn tonight," Greta continued. "I feel that her boyfriend may have had something to do with her death. She was used as a—I don't know how to say this—used like, 'You either do as I've told you to do or else.' He was involved in situations that were not ethical. Kaitlyn knew some things, but I don't think they killed her just to keep her quiet. It happened because of her boyfriend, but not necessarily to keep her quiet. She *was* going to spill the beans, but there was more to it than that.

"She's still at unrest. You can feel it. That's why this has been bothering you so bad. She's been trying to tell you something. I think she feels very sad she didn't pick her friends better. And she feels bad to think that you might believe you could have done something and didn't, because you could have done nothing. She tells me she was a very firm-willed child and that you allowed her to be her own person. I'll keep in touch with you, honey."

Click—she hung up.

"Your friends do call at odd hours," Don remarked at breakfast.

"This one was Marcello's supersleuth," I told him.

"Did she charge like a supersleuth?"

"She didn't ask for payment. Still, I can't imagine why Kait was so anxious to get her. She didn't tell me anything important."

When I talked with Robin, she disagreed with me.

"Greta's the first to suggest that the motive for Kait's murder was more than just to silence her," she said. "That part about Kait being *used* makes a lot of sense to me. When Kait used your credit card to rent a car for Dung's wreck, she probably considered that naughty, but not really terrible. It was an offbeat way to help poor Dung earn money, and his friends were doing it. But once she dealt herself in, it started to snowball. Maybe the next thing Dung wanted her to do was rent a car for a drug run."

"The charge would have shown up on our credit-card statement," I said.

"Not if Dung paid in cash when he took back the car."

"Kait would have drawn the line at doing something that serious."

"We don't know what kind of pressure those guys were applying, Mother. Nancy talked about violence; Noreen said there was a knife. They might have been threatening the lives of other members of the family. Was there ever a time after Kait and Dung moved in together when she disappeared for a couple of days and you didn't know where she was?"

"She came over every day—" I began, and then stopped. "There was one occasion—I wondered about it at the time—"

"What happened?"

"Kait had just gotten her apartment, so the nest was empty, and Daddy and I took a four-day vacation trip to San Diego. Brett took the dog to his house, and Kait promised to come over every day to feed the cat. We also asked her to record the last segment of *L.A. Law* for us. We got home on a Sunday night." The memory was more vivid now. "It was evident Kait hadn't been over, because the poor cat was starving. And she hadn't taped *L.A. Law*, she'd had one of her friends do it."

"What was her explanation?"

"She said she'd just gotten busy. She'd set a big pan of dry food out for the cat, and it hadn't occurred to her that all the strays in the neighborhood were going to descend on it. And she told us her VCR was broken, so she couldn't tape the show."

"That VCR was brand-new! She got it for graduation!"

"And after she died, Brett brought it to our house. There's never been a problem with it."

"If Kait deliberately set out enough food to last the cat four days, she didn't 'just get busy,' " Robin said. "She knew in advance that she wouldn't be coming over. It sounds as if she was gone all the same days you were."

"You're right, it does." How could I have missed something so obvious!

"How about this for a scenario: Dung took Kait out to Orange County, and they rented a car from R & J Car Leasing to bring back drugs."

"The leasing service that we think may have served as a cover for the insurance scam?"

"That's been one of our theories, but it's never been proven. Maybe R & J was a perfectly legitimate business, but just happened to be where Dung rented the car to do a drug run."

"The rest of the Vietnamese men may have been doing that too!" I exclaimed. "When Kait and Dung went to California in March, An Le flew out there with them. He was supposed to return on the same flight they did, but when I picked them up at the airport, he wasn't with them. Kait said he'd turned in his ticket and driven back instead."

"I bet he drove back in a rental car!"

"And Tuan may have done the same thing! He was out there too. Kait said he flew first class and stayed only one night."

"If she told you that, she hadn't become aware of the drug running yet, or she wouldn't have been so open about Tuan's being out there. She probably found out about that after Dung moved in with her and she discovered he was out every night until dawn. Noreen said Kait 'did some work' for a man who 'worked at and was part owner of a disco.' Is it possible that the work was delivering drugs?"

"Perhaps Kait wanted to pull out, but Dung wouldn't let her," I said, picking up the scenario. "She told me Vietnamese men expect their women to obey them. That may have been the thing that was 'threatening Dung's manhood.'"

"Maybe he placated her by promising to go straight," Robin said. "Then, when Laura and her boyfriend came over to watch videos and Dung took off on them, Kait realized he still must be dealing. They had another showdown, and he told her too much in an effort to convince her that he had no choice in the matter. Kait probably reacted by telling him that if he didn't get out of the drug scene she'd blow the whistle on that as well as the car wrecks.

"The next night, before going to Susan's, she swung back by the apartment to check on what Dung was doing. She saw him leaving with somebody, possibly An. She was afraid to follow them alone, so she called somebody she thought she could trust to drive her up there. Have you come up with any ideas about who that might have been?"

"The only person who fits the specifics of Noreen's description is a boy named Rod," I said. "He's ancient history, Kait hadn't seen him in years. So I guess it must have been one of the Vietnamese."

"Well, whoever it was, they met at Coronado Mall and drove to the Desert Castle," Robin continued. "What if Dung and An were at the Castle, involved in a drug transaction? Kait threw a scene—didn't Noreen quote her as shrieking, 'I don't want anything more to do with it!'?—and somebody tried to intimidate her by threatening her with a knife. Then the mysterious second boyfriend took her back to the shopping center, and as soon as Dung was out of earshot, one of the others phoned the hitmen."

"That's setting things up awfully fast."

"Not if the wheels were already in motion and this just served as the catalyst to make them move quickly. Mike told you that Dung had been out with a guy named Adrian, tailing Kait to see if she was being followed by a VW. If he did that, he must have been aware that her life was in danger."

At that instant the room disappeared and was replaced by a flowering orchard with lacy pink blossoms blowing in the breeze. Then the vision was gone as quickly as it had come.

"I think we've got it," I said shakily. "Kait just handed us a bouquet. What I don't understand is why she didn't come to Daddy and me."

"I think she *was* coming to Daddy and you," Robin said. "Why else would she have left Susan's to go back on the road that night? She wasn't headed for her apartment, she was headed for *your* house. Betty said Kait was 'in the process of making a decision which would have not only put herself in jeopardy but all who knew her.' The decision she made was the right one, but she made it too late."

There was an article in the paper that night about the conviction of several members of an El Paso drug organization that had been operating in three states since 1987. The states were New Mexico, Texas, and California. The drugs were shipped by unsuspecting truck companies in huge wooden crates doused with chlorine to avoid detection at the border and stored in warehouses in Albuquerque to be picked up by buyers in their own trucks.

According to Nancy Czetli, Kait had stumbled onto a multiveined network that overlapped three states, and we knew that two of those states were California and New Mexico. Was it possible that the third was Texas?

I decided to do some research on the drug scene in El Paso.

27

When I went to the university library and dug out back issues of the *El Paso Times*, I was stunned by the magnitude of the narcotics trade that interconnected Albuquerque, El Paso, and Los Angeles.

One article titled "Police Benefit from Sale of Drug Assets" began with the statement "Thanks to drug dealers, the El Paso Police Department is $325,493 richer" from funds that were the result of asset seizures and forfeitures of property involved in illegal drug trafficking in the El Paso area.

Another article, dated February 15, 1991, concerned an El Paso resident arrested on charges of drug smuggling. This man had bragged to an informant that he was the primary money-launderer for a crime organization that had moved 60 tons of cocaine and $80 million in cash between El Paso and Los Angeles in 1989. Charges stemmed from a 21-ton cocaine seizure near Los Angeles in September 1989, only two months after Kait's murder.

When I pulled up articles from that date on microfilm, I discovered that the drug haul had set a world record. A DEA spokesman was quoted as saying, "This is not just powder on the table, it's more like powder on the football field. This seizure should put to rest any further speculation that Los Angeles is, in fact, the major pathway for cocaine entering the country." In keeping with Betty's reading that said a "serpent's head" was "a symbol of some great clan or force . . . which will have to do with a certain Vietnamese group which will hold power," Oriental smugglers of drugs and illegal immigrants were known as "snakeheads."

According to one article, one of the vehicles used to transport the cocaine had New Mexico license plates.

Not only did this account pull Albuquerque, L.A., and El Paso into a triangle of drug interaction—Betty had said there was "an overlay of a kind of triangle"—the self-proclaimed big time money-launderer was identified as being the *administrative manager and part owner of a disco.*

Could this be the disco owner Kait "did some work for"?

I copied the articles and took them home for Don to read.

"This is too right-on-target to be a coincidence," he said. "If Dung forced Kait to go with him on an L.A. drug run, they could have made the delivery to El Paso as easily as to Albuquerque."

The DA's office had told us that the trial of Miguel Garcia was scheduled for Monday, March 11, and had assured us that we would be notified if there was a postponement. On the appointed day Don and I went down to the courthouse to watch the selection of the jury and were told that the trial had been postponed. Don called the DA's office to ask what had happened, but he couldn't find anybody there who knew anything about it. Finally, on Thursday, he did get through to Susan Riedel, who told him that neither side was ready to go to court yet and the trial had been tentatively rescheduled for early April.

Something was going on, but we didn't know what. People from the DA's office and the office of the defense attorneys kept phoning our out-of-state children and asking them questions about Kait's activities, personality, and friendships. An investigator from the DA's office called me to ask if Kait had repaid us for the charges she had made on our credit card, but wouldn't tell me why she needed the information. Brett had a call from a friend who worked at the jail, who said it was rumored that Miguel Garcia was going to be released and that Dung would be arrested in his place.

He also had a call from a former roommate, who had moved into Kait's old apartment and become friendly with her neighbors.

"The neighbors say that the day after Kait was shot, when she was in a coma and Dung was at the hospital with us, the other Vietnamese guys threw a party at the apartment," Brett told us. "You'll never guess what the party game was. They were out in the parking lot, spray-painting a beige VW black."

"There was an entry in the police report about their painting a car," I said. "It said it was 'a small car,' but didn't specify a VW, and it said the incident took place a full week before the murder."

"The car was a beige VW," Brett repeated. "And, according to Kait's neighbors, they painted it the day *after* she was shot."

April arrived, and there was still no word of a new trial date. When Don called to ask about it, he was told that the trial had been rescheduled, but the information about it was on the desk of Assistant District Attorney Charlie Brown, who couldn't be disturbed because he had guests in his office. Nobody else had access to this information, and every time Don phoned, Brown was occupied with guests.

Finally, on April 23, we were called to the DA's office to meet with District Attorney Bob Schwartz, Charlie Brown, and Susan Riedel.

Schwartz told us that the charges against Miguel Garcia and Juve Escobedo were going to be dropped.

"The defense attorneys have turned up new evidence," he said. "We've been in touch with law enforcement agencies in California and are going to have Sergeant Lowe start looking into some things that you folks have expressed an interest in. We'll be calling you in next week to help us do some brainstorming."

But when Schwartz rushed off to another appointment and Charlie Brown took over, it was clear the two men hadn't gotten together on their script.

"We're sure that Garcia's guilty, but our case has eroded," Brown said. "The two children who originally testified they heard Garcia say he killed Kait now say they didn't believe him, that 'Mikey was always lying about things like that.' And the neighbor who reported seeing Garcia hand a gun in through his kitchen window to his mother or sister has turned out to be highly impeachable. She hates the Garcia family and would blame them for anything.

"Meanwhile, the defense has concocted a ridiculous story about your daughter's alleged involvement with the Vietnamese mafia. That's absurd, of course, but since our case has been weakened, it wouldn't take much to cause dissension among the jurors. Once a suspect is tried and found 'not guilty,' he can't be retried for the same crime even if he confesses to it, so, rather than risk a verdict of 'not guilty,' we're withdrawing the charges. We're ready to reinstate them when we get new evidence."

"You *are* going to keep investigating, aren't you?" Don asked him.

"The case is still open and active."

I decided to grab this opportunity to tell the prosecutors

about the three-hour time gap that had been camouflage
in the police report by misquoting me as saying Kait at
dinner at our house.

Brown's only reaction was to the term *camouflaged*.

"The police make mistakes like that all the time," he sai
"There are often statements in their reports that aren't ac
curate, but that doesn't mean they're deliberate fabrica
tions."

"It wasn't my intention to disparage the police," I sai
hastily. "My point was that, even if the misquote was a
innocent mistake, the end result was that it *did* serve t
camouflage the fact that three hours of Kait's last evenin
are unaccounted for. She went somewhere and did some
thing she didn't want anyone to know about, and it seems t
us like that has to have some sort of significance."

Neither Brown nor Riedel responded to this statement

Then, realizing this might be our last chance to get any
thing on record, I told them we had a copy of Bao Tran
check.

They expressed no interest in seeing it.

"Please, keep us informed," I said as we got up to leave
"We've felt so out of it, with nobody willing to talk to us.

"We'll call with a progress report every two weeks," Rie
del said. "In return, we want you to promise not to talk t
reporters. The media is going to have a field day whe
Garcia is released, and we'd rather they didn't quote state
ments from the family of the victim."

Don and I promised not to give interviews, and we kep
our word. In fact, I spent the next week in Dallas with Kerr
and her family in order to avoid having to field questior
from friends in the media.

As expected, our local newspapers ran banner headline

Albuquerque Tribune, April 24, 1991:

POLICE BLASTED ON ARQUETTE CASE

Two defense attorneys say Albuquerque police conducted a "shoddy" investigation into the shooting death of Kaitlyn Arquette.

The investigation focused on two innocent men and ignored a possible connection to Vietnamese gang activity, attorneys Joseph Riggs and Michael Davis said.

District Attorney Bob Schwartz said the decision to drop the charges was partially based on an investigation by Garcia's attorneys. They discovered that Arquette's relationship with a group of Vietnamese under investigation in a multimillion-dollar insurance scam may have led to her death.

Had the case gone to trial as scheduled next week, Davis said, "We were going to kill them on the stand, really do a number on the state's case."

He said the scam involved filing insurance claims on accidents with rental cars. A car rented with Arquette's credit card was involved in a California accident. After the accident a deposit of $2,000 appeared in Arquette's bank account.

Schwartz declined comment on the quality of the police work.

Albuquerque Journal, April 24, 1991:

DA DROPS CHARGES IN ARQUETTE SHOOTING

One of the men accused of killing Kaitlyn Arquette, Miguel Juan Garcia, 19, walked out of the Bernalillo County Detention Center at about four P.M. (today) after fifteen months in jail. Carrying a Bible and a garbage bag full of his belongings, Garcia said he felt "blessed" to be free.

Jail employees and inmates waved to him from the windows as he hugged his mother, Maggie, and other family members.

"I thank the Lord and two great lawyers," Garcia said, his voice choked with emotion.

District Attorney Schwartz said he dropped the charges because "there's been some erosion in the state's case . . . and then there seemed to be this other angle while the state's case was dwindling."

He said the new angle was "the emergence of these other facts regarding her association with this group of Vietnamese. She had a clear association with that group."

He said he informed police homicide Sgt. Ruth Lowe Tuesday that he was dropping the charges and that Lowe said "they would be very interested in looking at the new angle."

Riggs said private investigators Dennis and Tanya Hicks were able to provide new evidence indicating detectives failed to investigate other avenues.

"Our investigators found that Kaitlyn Arquette's boyfriend Dung Nguyen actually fabricated a love note and told police she wrote it," Riggs said. "I think the prosecutors are saving the [homicide] detectives some embarrassment from having to own up to serious mistakes at the trial."

APD officials have said any comment would have to come from the prosecutors.

Albuquerque Tribune, April 25, 1991:

FORMER SUSPECTS STILL UNDER SCRUTINY IN ARQUETTE SLAYING

Although authorities have dropped murder charges against two men in the Kaitlyn Arquette case, they remain suspects in her shooting death, police say.

Arquette's former boyfriend, Dung Ngoc Nguyen, also is a suspect, Deputy Police Chief Nick Alarid said Wednesday.

When asked why Garcia and Escobedo are still considered suspects, Alarid said, "Everybody's a suspect. This is still an open investigation, and everyone's suspect."

He declined to elaborate.

Defense attorneys accused police of conducting a "shoddy" investigation for focusing on what the attorneys called two innocent men and ignoring a possible connection to Vietnamese gang activity.

But police defended their investigation.

"The investigation is a good investigation," Alarid said.

He did not know whether there were any Vietnamese gangs in Albuquerque.

Alarid said the attorneys' claims concerning Vietnamese gang activity may be nothing more than "smoke."

There was a photograph in the *Journal* of Miguel Garcia tearfully embracing the sister who we believe had made the threatening phone calls to us. The child I had heard babbling in the background during her phone calls was cuddled in her arms.

On April 25 a feature article appeared in the *Tribune* describing how Garcia had found God during his incarceration. "I gave my life over to the Lord and he was telling me not to worry, that he was going to get me out of that place," Garcia said. He also said he now planned to become a minister. He reported that after his release from jail he went outside and hugged his family, spent most of the evening talking with his girlfriend and visiting with his eleven-month-old son, born while Garcia was in jail, watched a gospel show on television, and fell asleep at ten-thirty.

The release of Garcia was frightening to the state's witnesses.

"We are so afraid," said the woman who allegedly saw him pass the gun through the window. "There's already been threats made against me and my mother."

She said Garcia's family had told her they were going to burn down her house with her seventy-two-year-old mother in it.

Another witness, who demanded anonymity, said she was terrified for her children, because one of the suspects knew what school they went to.

"He has our address," she said. "I don't know what I am going to do."

On April 26 the burglary-related charges against Garcia were also dropped. Assistant DA Charlie Brown declined comment on the reason for this.

Two weeks passed, and we didn't get the promised call from the district attorney's office.

Four months went by, and nobody contacted us.

Finally, Kerry ran out of patience and phoned Tanya Hicks, one of the private investigators for the defense.

After talking with Tanya, Kerry phoned me with her report.

"She's a very nice woman and told me a lot," she said. "The reason the defense attorneys never talked with you and Daddy is because the police warned them not to. They said the Arquettes were—and I'm quoting her exact words —'hostile and uncooperative, and everything they say is totally ludicrous.'

"And there's something else the police don't want us to

know about. A Vietnamese informant has told the Hickses that An Le has been arrested for murder in Oklahoma. Tanya says the informant told her it was the same type of drive-by shooting as Kait's."

28

"I feel like the second shoe has dropped now," I said. "Both Betty and Nancy predicted another murder."

"And the fact that this information came from a Vietnamese informant is in keeping with Betty's prediction that the person with the most guilt would be 'sacrificed by the community,'" Kerry said. "The Hickses didn't follow up on that information, because by then they were no longer working for Miguel's attorneys. While they were on the case, though, they turned up a lot.

"Tanya thinks Kait was killed because of the car wrecks. The insurance scam brought in fifty million dollars per year. Tanya says Bao Tran is what's called a 'capper' in the Asian mafia, which means he's up at the top and sets everything up. She says it's a very incestuous group, and she thinks the gang members were ordered to take out any round-eyes who knew about the scam. She thinks Dung may have tried to get around that by taking Kait to California with him, possibly hoping to get her involved so she wouldn't be a threat to them.

'Tanya said the same thing that Dung's friend Ray said about Dung's friends out there being suppliers of cocaine. She says Los Angeles is one of the major pathways for getting cocaine into the country. The method for getting it in is called 'the Trampoline.' The coke gets bounced from Colombia to Mexico and is transported across the border by Mexican nationals."

"Juve Escobedo is a Mexican national!" I exclaimed. "When Betty said one of the suspects had relatives in the L.A. area, we jumped to the conclusion it was Miguel, but maybe *Juve's* the one who has relatives there. If Kait ran into either one of those guys when she and Dung were in California it would explain the reading that said, 'There will have been some kind of other encounter at another time,' and 'They will seem to have some way to fear that something is known about them by her and thus now by others.'"

"Tanya says she has a video of Dung selling drugs," Kerry said. "He's all dressed up like an Asian godfather, flanked by a couple of strong-arm henchmen to beat up the customers who don't pay. She says he's utterly vicious, but an excellent actor. Her husband is a Vietnam veteran, and when *he* did the interrogation, Dung had no problem with the language, because he knew Dennis Hicks could switch over to Vietnamese. But when they held the interrogation in the DA's office, Dung suddenly was hardly able to speak English. Susan Riedel felt so sorry for him that she wouldn't let anyone pressure him and told him he didn't have to answer 'uncomfortable' questions.

"The Hickses don't understand what's going on with APD. Tanya said she tailed Dung one night when he went out to sell drugs and watched him make a sale standing under a streetlight. A police car was parked a couple of yards away from him, and the cop just sat there and watched and never did anything.

"Dung told APD that on the night Kait was shot, he and his friends were at the Firehouse restaurant. Tanya says that's not true. The Firehouse is a tiny place that's not frequented much by Vietnamese, and the lady bartender told her that if those guys had been in there that night she was sure she would have noticed them.

"Tanya said that she and Miguel's attorney, Joe Riggs, sat down with the prosecutors and went over all the evidence they had against Dung. That's when the prosecutors decided to drop the charges against the Hispanics. Riggs then offered to hand everything over to APD so they could use it to start a new investigation. Nobody's ever bothered to come and get the tapes and things, and she considers that a sign that the investigation's over.

"Oh, and one other tidbit that will make you want to vomit—Miguel is planning to sue APD for false arrest."

When I repeated that news to Don, he actually started laughing.

"He'd better consult Betty Muench before he tries that," he said. "If Juve is 'rearrested' and 'comes forth with all manner of confessions,' Miguel is going to wish he'd left well enough alone."

"How can Juve be rearrested when the charges have been withdrawn?"

"They can get him for breaking probation and running out on a bench warrant and withdraw *those* charges if he agrees to say what they want him to. They must have had some reason for keeping him on hold, otherwise they'd have picked him up a year ago."

"You think the police would actually cut a deal with him?"

"Don't tell me there's still a part of the file you haven't read!"

He dug out the transcript of a tape of Detective A. V.

Romero interrogating Robert Garcia, the "witness-who-wasn't-there."

"We might be able to work out a deal with Juve," Romero told the teenager in an effort to get him to testify against Miguel. "Chances are we might be able to cut him some slack, cut him loose and not charge him at all."

"That does sound like their ace-in-the-hole," I conceded.

"Their other plan was to manipulate us," Don said. "It's obvious Bob Schwartz had no intention of calling us in to brainstorm, and Susan Riedel hasn't given us one single progress report. They made those promises to keep us from talking to the press and leaking the fact that the 'new' information the police profess to be so eager to follow up on is the same information we gave them the day after Kait died.

"I think it's time we got together with the Hickses."

We arranged to meet the detectives at a restaurant for lunch, but the four of us got so busy talking that we never even opened our menus. It was evident they were emotionally invested in Kait's case and were frustrated and furious that APD didn't want to use their evidence.

"We just don't get it," Tanya said. "There were no arrests for six months after the shooting, during which time those Vietnamese men were the only suspects, yet Steve Gallegos admitted in the DA's office that he never investigated *one single thing* in California."

"But Sergeant Lowe told me he checked out everything in my letter!" I exclaimed.

"He didn't check anything that had to do with Vietnamese activities."

"Not even the phone numbers called from Kait's apartment?"

"Not those—not *anything*. We've got his statement on tape."

"Then what was APD doing all that time?" Don demanded.

"Who knows?" Tanya said. "There were no formal interviews conducted during that time period, and after he typed his report, Gallegos destroyed all his notes. When Joe Riggs asked him about the interview in which Dung's friend, Adrian, described how Kait was being followed by a beige VW, he said he couldn't remember anything about it. He didn't tape the interview; the report was omitted from the file; Adrian disappeared right after he was interrogated; and with the notes destroyed, there's no way to document the content of Adrian's statement."

"Did he ever get the Vietnamese letters translated?"

"He said his superiors wouldn't let him, because there was a budget crunch."

"*A budget crunch!*" Don exploded. "It wouldn't have cost them a penny! We've been trying for two full years to get those letters back so we could get them translated *at our own expense*! And what about the man on the force who speaks Vietnamese? The only reason Lois gave those letters to the police was because she was told there was a man on the force who would translate them!"

"That's bull," Dennis said. "There's nobody on the force who knows enough Vietnamese to translate those letters. Changing the subject—have you ever seen the accident report for the wreck when Kait was driving?"

"No," Don said in surprise. "You mean there *was* such a report? Gallegos told us there was, but he never produced it, so we chalked it up as another of his inaccuracies."

"From what we've been told, the report does exist," Dennis said. "It's not in the file, though, and we haven't been able to find a record of the accident."

"If Kait wrecked a car, it wasn't in March," I said. "If she

d it during spring break when Dung staged his wreck,
an's check would have been for three thousand, not fif-
en hundred. It's possible Dung took her out there again in
ay. If they did stage another accident, it was probably
en."

"There's something else we're curious about," Tanya
id. "It's why Dung came back to Albuquerque after recov-
ing from his stab wound. Why didn't he run to a safe
use?"

"What's a safe house?" I asked.

"It's a hideout for Vietnamese fugitives. The mafia has
em scattered all over the country. When gang members
t in trouble, they hole up in the safe houses until they can
ange their identities and get new Social Security num-
rs. Dung could have done that easily, yet he returned to
buquerque and remained in close touch with the police.
cording to Gallegos, he phoned several times to inquire
out the status of the investigation.

"Another question—why did Dung spill his guts about
e insurance scam? He was read his rights and didn't have
admit to anything, but he spouted names and addresses
e they were going out of style. He even handed over Bao
an's new business card, showing that he's now vice-presi-
nt of Japan Life Sleeping Systems."

"Is Dung still in town?" Don asked.

"We have no idea. The police let him walk out the door,
d now nobody can find him. That's another odd thing—if
ung was planning to skip town, why did he confess to the
r wrecks before he left? Why didn't he run *before* he got
lled in for questioning?"

In the car on the way home I said to Don, "I have a
eory about why Dung came back to Albuquerque. Re-
ember Carla Wallenda's story about her grandparents?

When they felt the wolves closing in, they'd shoot a hor
and leave it behind to distract them while the circus g
away."

"You think Dung was stationed here to keep tabs on t
investigation and confessed to the wrecks to divert attenti
from the drug running?"

"If so, it worked!" I said. "With the Hickses and ev
with Mike! They all believe Kait was killed so she would
expose the insurance scam. Everybody has been so mesme
ized by the car wrecks that nobody's bothered to look ve
hard at the possible drug running."

"How do you feel about Gallegos's statement that I
superiors are the ones who didn't want the Vietnamese l
ters translated?"

"I'm willing to buy that," I said. "He's a pawn in t
bureaucracy. We don't know what sort of pressure was b
ing applied to him." I remembered the day that I'd tak
Gallegos the items from Kait's desk and he had sa
"Would you believe there are people in this departme
who still insist your daughter's shooting was 'random'?" F
incredulous tone had proclaimed that idea preposterou
Something had happened after that to turn him around, a
because the man was so likable on a personal level, I w
eager to believe that throughout the botched investigati
he had been acting on the orders of less ethical "superiors
who, perhaps, may not have wanted the activities of Du
and his friends investigated.

When we got home I phoned Mike to see if he had hea
anything about An Le's arrest. He told me he'd heard t
rumor and had been trying to follow up on it but was havi
no luck because An had so many aliases.

"I'm sure the FBI could find him," Don said when I tc

im that. "I'd give a lot to know why they've chosen to stay
ut of this."

An idea suddenly occurred to me.

"I bet Gary could find out for us!"

"Who?"

"Gary Miller, who took me to my first school prom.
Don't you remember? You met him at my high-school re-
nion."

"The tall, thin guy with the red hair?"

"Yes, that's the one. It blew me away when he told me he
as an FBI agent. I'd always thought he'd be something
thereal like a poet."

"Do you know where he lives?"

"No, but somebody on the alumni committee will."

I made a few calls, got Gary's address, and wrote him a
tter describing our situation and asking if he could find
ut why the FBI had been unwilling to get involved in the
vestigation.

Gary responded with a phone call.

"I checked with the FBI office in Albuquerque," he told
e. "They've been very aware of the case and wanted to
ork on it. They told APD they would be willing to help in
ny way, that it looked like a major case that would involve a
t of questioning and they wanted to offer their manpower
nd the use of their laboratory. The Homicide Department
ld them to butt out. The FBI can't step into a case on
eir own, Lois. Once we present our credentials, it's up to
e locals."

"Why would the police refuse to accept their help?"

"There's a lot of political jealousy between locals and
ds," Gary said. "Locals don't like the feds to help out with
eir cases for fear the Bureau will solve them and reap all

the glory. They've even been known to hide or destro
evidence rather than let the FBI solve a case for them. If th
feds get the credit, there aren't any stats for the locals."

" 'Stats'?"

"Statistics on how many crimes they've solved. Every po
lice officer has to show results. It's like working in a factor
and having to account for how many doghouses you mak
each month. These guys are being pressured by their super
visors to rack up stats or get the hell out of the departmen
That's why they don't like to work on complicated case
No police department in the country has enough mone
and if they can't solve a case right away, they're pressured t
close it, so they don't have to use their resources for
prolonged investigation."

"Do you think that's why APD kept insisting this wa
'random'—they wanted to get a 'stat' with a minimum o
effort?"

"That may or may not be true in this particular case,
Gary said. "But there definitely are occasions when marl
are set up for arrest, and even if the feds know it, there
nothing we can do about it except make anonymous calls t
the suspects' defense attorneys.

"At this juncture, though, with the locals' case down th
drain, maybe you and your husband can get something go
ing on your own. Do you have any proof that there wa
interstate crime involved?"

"Yes, and we've already sent it to the FBI in Orang
County," I said. "They never even acknowledged that the
received it."

"You should have sent it to the L.A. office," Gary tol
me. "Resident agencies get to be their own little kingdom
and sometimes the guys in charge of them are less tha

adequate. Contact the special agent in charge of the FBI office in Los Angeles and tell him what you've told me. Then set up an appointment with the SAC at your local FBI office and tell him the same thing.

"If you deal with the SAC in L.A., I guarantee that you'll get a response of some kind. They can't open an investigation unless it seems to be a real federal case, but the SAC is in a position to make that determination. If you can present him with hard evidence that these people are going across state lines to conduct insurance fraud or to carry narcotics, the case will come under the jurisdiction of the Bureau. If the SAC decides there's interstate crime involved, the FBI can step in without permission from APD. But you have to understand, their primary objective will not be to investigate your daughter's murder, because that's not a federal crime. They'll be investigating interstate drug trafficking and insurance fraud, and if information about Kait's murder happens to surface, that will be frosting on the cake."

We didn't know how much evidence the SAC would require, so we thought that we'd better accumulate as much as we could. We had formed a grudging respect for Miguel Garcia's aggressive attorneys, and since Joe Riggs had selected the Hickses as his investigators, we decided we'd follow his lead and hire them ourselves. I suspected also that they were the people Mike had shared his information with at the point at which Betty said he "would seem to quit." My reason for thinking this was that the defense attorneys had been quoted in both papers as saying the car wreck participants were paid $2,000, an inaccuracy that had appeared in my letter to Mike. We had learned later that the actual amount was $1,500, but the erroneous $2,000 figure kept being referred to by the defense, who could only have gotten it from my letter. I trusted Mike's judgment, and if he'd had enough confidence in the Hickses to have passed along information for them to follow up on, I had to believe they were decent, trustworthy people who would not intentionally endanger us.

Knowing that the detectives had an initial loyalty to Riggs, we didn't feel right in asking them to get us the Garcias' phone bills, so we restricted our requests for information to Vietnamese activity. We asked them to try to confirm An Le's alleged arrest, to get information about Dung's friends in California, and to continue to work on digging up the missing accident report. The fact that this particular report had mysteriously vanished, while the other accident reports had been left in the police file, suggested that it might contain information the police wanted hidden. Had Kait and Dung rented their car from R & J Car Leasing? Was the name of the second party in the wreck significant?

"It's too bad we don't have the name of that kid who contacted Riggs," Tanya said in a casual aside to her husband at the end of our meeting.

"What kid?" Don asked.

"There was a boy who turned up at Riggs's office and told his secretary he wanted to meet with him. He said he was a former boyfriend of Kait's and they'd started dating again only weeks before the murder. The kid was crying and sounded flaky, and since Riggs already had what he needed to get Miguel off, he didn't bother to set up an appointment. Chances are it wasn't on the up and up anyway."

"Did the boy say he knew Kait in high school?" I asked, struggling to keep my voice from reflecting my excitement. Could this be the person Kait had met at the Coronado shopping mall—the romantic relationship that continued without my knowledge?

"Riggs didn't say," Tanya said. "But he did mention one thing—the kid had a silver bracelet with his name and Kait's on it."

29

Every time one of the psychic readings proved accurate I was just as stunned as I had been back when I discovered R & J Car Leasing listed in the Orange County phone book. No matter how much evidence I was confronted with that psychometry, telepathy, and clairvoyance were a reality, a lifetime of skepticism had structured my mind-set and I needed continual confirmation that my belief in them was justified. If I had lived in the time of Christ, I would have demanded to see the nail holes in His palms and then been equally astonished by the nail holes in His feet.

"It's Rod!" I said to Don when the Hickses had left. "I remember that bracelet! I was there when Kait had it engraved!"

"Do you remember his last name?"

"No, it's been too long."

"What kind of car did he drive? Did it have four-wheel drive?"

"I never saw his car. Kait wasn't supposed to be dating boys who were old enough to drive, so he never brought it over."

If I could come up with Rod's name and the Hickses could find him for us, he might be able to provide all the answers we were looking for!

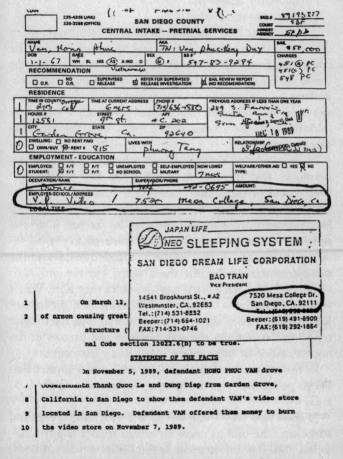

SAN DIEGO COUNTY
CENTRAL INTAKE — PRETRIAL SERVICES

BKG # 89193577
COURT SDF
ARREST AGENCY SDPD

NAME				AKA			BAIL
Van, Hong Phuc				TN: Vay Phuc Hong Duy			$ 50,000

DOB 1-1-67 | RACE WH BL HIS (AS) A IND O | SEX (M) F | SS # 597-83-9294 | CHARGES 451(a) PC 451(c) PC 548 PC

RECOMMENDATION   Vietnamese

☐ O.R. ☐ NO O.R. ☐ SUPERVISED RELEASE ☑ REFER FOR SUPERVISED RELEASE INVESTIGATION ☑ BAIL REVIEW REPORT (NO RECOMMENDATION)

RESIDENCE

TIME IN COUNTY Orange Cal 2yrs | TIME AT CURRENT ADDRESS 6 mrs | PHONE # (714) 636-8880 | PREVIOUS ADDRESS IF LESS THAN ONE YEAR 249 S. Farris Santa Ana Ca Sun Afer AUG 18 1989

HOUSE # 12581 | STREET 9th st. | APT # C 202
CITY Garden Grove, Ca. | STATE | ZIP 92640

O | DWELLING: ☐ NO RENT PAID ☐ OWN/BUY ☑ RENT $ 815 | LIVES WITH phuong Tang | RELATIONSHIP (SHERWOOD, Deputy)

EMPLOYMENT - EDUCATION

O | EMPLOYED: ☐ F/T ☐ P/T ☐ UNEMPLOYED ☐ SELF-EMPLOYED STUDENT: ☐ F/T ☐ P/T ☐ NO SCHOOL ☐ MILITARY | HOW LONG? 7 mrs | WELFARE/OTHER AID ☐ YES ☒ NO TYPE:

OCCUPATION/RANK Owner | SUPERVISOR/PHONE self 42-0695 | AMOUNT:

EMPLOYER-SCHOOL/ADDRESS   V.P. Video / 7520 Mesa College, San Diego, Ca

LOCAL TIES

1   On March 12,

2   of arson causing great

structure (

nal Code section 12022.6(b) to be true.

STATEMENT OF THE FACTS

On November 5, 1989, defendant HONG PHUC VAN drove

7   codefendants Thanh Quoc Le and Dung Diep from Garden Grove,

8   California to San Diego to show them defendant VAN's video store

9   located in San Diego. Defendant VAN offered them money to burn

10 the video store on November 7, 1989.

The video store arsoned by Van Hong Phuc had the address
that was on Bao Tran's business card.

Mother wouldn't like him.
Mother's changed her mind, Kait!
I could see her disapproval.
Mother *approves* now!
The fact that Rod had gone to Miguel's attorneys, when
the natural thing to have done would have been to go to the
police, suggested that whatever evidence he had to offer
would incriminate somebody other than Miguel and Juve.
Perhaps he *had* gone to the police and they had turned him
away, as they allegedly had turned away other would-be
informants whose stories didn't mesh with the random-
shooting scenario.

I drove over to Kait's old high school and perused the
yearbooks that spanned the years when Rod would have
been a student there, but I couldn't find his face in any of
the photographs. The fact that he was older than most of
his classmates probably had curtailed his interest in school
activities, and apparently he hadn't bothered to get his senior picture taken. I scanned the hundreds of names on the
school registration list for those years, but the only two
"Rodneys" who were listed were no older than Kait. Was it
possible "Rod" was either a middle name or a nickname?
Kait's friends from that era had scattered, but I set about
trying to locate them through teachers and parents in the
hope that one of them might recall Rod's last name.

In the meantime Dennis Hicks, who was a former San
Diego policeman, was dredging up information in the L.A.
area.

"I know now why Dung was so free with those names and
addresses," he told us upon his return from a trip to California. "All that information he fed Gallegos was outdated.
By the time Dung was finally interrogated in July 1990, Bao
Tran had moved from the address on South Fairview, and

there apparently was no attorney named Minh Nguyen Duy at the address for the law office on Tran's business card. However, I did find an attorney named Minh *Buy* Nguyen at that address and also in Van Nuys, although Minh *Buy* Nguyen denied ever having heard of anybody named Bao Tran.

"The other business card Dung gave Gallegos showed Bao Tran as vice-president of Japan Life Sleeping Systems, with a branch office called San Diego Dream Life Corporation at 7520 Mesa College Drive. City Licensing showed that no license was ever listed for that corporation and it was arsoned in November 1989. And get this—the business at that Mesa College address had two identities! It was also identified as a video store owned by a man named Hong Phuc Van, who was listed as living at the same address on South Fairview that Bao Tran did."

"Hong Phuc Van," I repeated. It sounded familiar. Then it hit me. "Mike was told that Tran's unlisted phone number was in the name of 'Van Hong Phuc'! He must have gotten the names out of order!"

"They probably were given to him in a jumbled order," Dennis said. "These people make a habit of rearranging their names. For example, in the Little Saigon phone directory, there's a listing for 'Nguyen, Duy Minh' at the address I was given for Minh Nguyen Duy. There's nothing illegal about that, but it does make it difficult to keep track of people.

"Hong Phuc Van has served a prison term since Kait's death. Four months after her murder, he hired two young Vietnamese men to burn down his video store, at the same location as San Diego Dream Life Corporation. In the course of setting the fire, the boys caught fire themselves. They informed on Van, who was arrested and convicted of

Arson with Bodily Injury. He was incarcerated from November 1989 to August 1990.

"I couldn't get much on the mysterious R & J Car Leasing except that it went out of business right after Kait's death. Nobody seems to know where the owners disappeared to. The people who now run a car leasing business at that address say the police must have come by and asked for R & J personnel at least a dozen times, but the police wouldn't say what they wanted them for.

"I checked out all the addresses listed on the accident reports. None of the people who claimed to be injured in the wrecks involving Dung and An Le lived at the addresses they gave the police. In fact, a number of the addresses don't even exist.

"But, despite all this, I've changed my mind about the motive for Kait's murder. I now think she was onto something even more serious than insurance fraud. After her death Dung's friends in Orange County appear to have panicked. They deserted their homes and businesses and simply evaporated, which indicates to me they were afraid that Kait might have left behind information that was inflammatory enough to get them deported.

"It's now my belief that Kait found out about a massive drug ring and that Dung's friends were runners between L.A. and Albuquerque. When Tanya talked with An's landlord, he told her that as soon as Kait died all hell broke loose at that apartment complex. Things got so loud and violent that he evicted An. He said that while An was his tenant, he was hardly ever there; he spent all his time going back and forth to L.A., and every time he came back he had a huge wad of bills on him.

"When the San Diego Police Department found out who it was I was investigating, they offered to give me a permit to carry a concealed weaapon. They said that particular bunch is notoriously dangerous and it's worth your life just to stick your head in their territory. They're not only into insurance fraud, but extortion, arson, and paid assassinations, and they run one of the biggest crack-smuggling outfits in the country. Detective Franks of the Westminster Police Department's Gang Unit told me he spoke on the phone to a detective at APD and tried to explain to her how ruthless and widespread the Vietnamese gangs are, but he got the feeling she wasn't taking him seriously.

"APD appears to have dropped their investigation of Kait's death. The L.A. police say they never were contacted about the insurance fraud, and they're not at all happy about that, becuase they would have liked to have interrogated Dung. They're right in the middle of a big undercover investigation that's targeted at doctors and attorneys who are bilking insurance companies, and the names Dung might have supplied for them could have been invaluable."

After Dennis left I told Don, "I think it's time to end my book now. I'm going to call it finished on Kait's twenty-first birthday."

"But that's next week!" Don exclaimed. "The story's not over yet!"

"Maybe the book will bring us an ending," I said. "We've reached a dead end as far as our personal investigation goes, and there still are so many questions we need to have answered.

"Who was responsible for Kait's murder, and who was the triggerman? If, as the police are so certain, Miguel Garcia was the person who shot Kait, did the Vietnamese hire him? Is it possible to establish a link between these two sets of people? Were Dung and An Le involved in a drug ring, and if so, did this have anything to do with Kait's death?

Does either Miguel or Juve have relatives in California? Where is the statue of the snake head 'under which there are held many meetings,' and what Oriental clan has adopted it as their symbol? Has An been arrested for murder? If so, where is he? Who was the VIP Kait saw buying drugs? Did Dung really try to kill himself, or did somebody stab him?

"There must be people out there who can give us some answers, but first they have to know what information we're looking for. It's even possible that Rod will read the book and contact us, or that the Good Man Who Is Afraid will gain the courage to come forward. And there still are predictions of Betty's that haven't proven out yet. Remember how she said there would be 'media shows from the national level' and 'Mike can be instrumental in getting this into that view'? No national television show is going to be interested in covering the outdated story of the death of a teenager in Albuquerque unless we do something to thrust it into the limelight. And in her very first reading, Betty predicted that there would be 'one who will be as a kind of undercover person, and there will be in this then the ultimate knowing in this case.' That person won't know that we need him unless our story gets out there.

"Kait wants us to finish this up so she can move on."

"She's sent you another dream?" Don asked.

"She wrote me a good-bye note."

I knew how ridiculous that sounded, but Don didn't smile; he simply nodded and waited for me to continue.

"In the dream I was seated at a desk in a junior high classroom, leafing through a book about the Civil War. I turned a page, and out fell a note in Kait's handwriting. It was all folded up like one of those origami paper puzzles, and when I finally got it open, there were only four sentences:

> *I wanted to leave a note to tell you good-bye. I'm sorry things turned out like they did. I never told you how much I liked you. You were my favorite teacher.*

"At first I thought she'd left it for one of her schoolteachers. Then I realized she meant it for me."

"It's not very sentimental." I could tell that Don wanted more for me, something effusive to cling to when grief overwhelmed me.

"Kait was my student before she was my daughter."

"Why do you think she left the note in a history book?"

"I think the significance must be the War Between the States," I said. "In the Civil War our nation was divided against itself. In her final days that's just how it was with Kait—she was torn between her love for Dung and her commitment to doing what she knew in her heart was right."

The next time I talked with Robin I told her the book was almost finished, and she said there was something more she wanted me to add.

"The way Kait died was written into her script," she said. "There was nothing that you or Daddy could have done to prevent it."

"If we hadn't let her go out—if we'd physically restrained her—"

"Nothing you did would have made any difference," Robin said. "If it hadn't happened that night, it would have happened the next night. I saw the hole in her face when I told her good-bye, Mother. The bullet that hit her cheek went straight into God's fingerprint."

* * *

It is September 18, 1991.

Kait is twenty-one years old today.

I have brought my gifts to the cemetery—a huge pot of yellow chrysanthemums and the manuscript box that holds her story.

"The ending will come," I tell her. "There *will* be an ending."

I have come equipped with a note that I tape to the grave marker: *Rod—Get in touch with Kait's parents!* He probably won't remember the date of her birthday, but there's always a chance he might bring another bouquet.

I open the box and read Betty's prediction aloud:

It will come that there will be the unveiling of the truth. . . . There will be those who will be caught and exposed, and it will be for this family to come to see and know what it is that Kait will have been dealing with in her final day.

"You did a good job," I tell Kait. "You made some mistakes, but you cleaned up after yourself. I'm proud to be your mother."

The purpose of Kaitlyn is not lost in this time. . . . She will have been true to herself to the end, and this also she must accept.

"It's time for you to go on to whatever comes next for you."

Can I really exist in a world that doesn't have Kait in it?

I can do that, I tell myself.

Given that there's no choice, then, I can do that.

A breeze, still soft with the lingering sweetness of summer, moves through the branches of the elm tree that shadows Kait's grave, and a leaf breaks free and sails down to land on the manuscript.

Just another small death out of season.

I strain to hear the lilt of Kait's voice in the breeze, but, of ourse, I do not. All I hear is the rumble of cars on the freeway—the raucous squawks of a nasty brigade of crows—the rattle of a plastic windmill on a neighboring grave.

I don't have the powers of a medium; I am only a mother whose psychic abilities end at the edges of the heart.

But I do have one thing going for me, I am a writer, and I have the ability to create scenes. I close my eyes, and on the darkened screen of my eyelids, I produce the image of my daughter as I most want to see her. Tall and strong and lovely, Kait stands before me; her eyes sparkle with unquenchable mischief, her glorious honey-colored hair is splashed with sunlight, God's fingerprint is once again just an innocent dimple, oddly positioned on the ridge of her smooth, tan cheek.

She raises her hand in a comical half salute, just as she did on the night she walked out of our lives.

Later! I'll see you guys later!

"Good-bye!" I tell her. "Try to stay out of trouble, honey! Next time I want you to keep an eye out for wolves!"

I am wasting my breath, for she is already striding away from me and my words go fluttering after her like a battalion of butterflies. Impatient for new adventure, she eagerly pushes aside the veil and, without so much as a backward glance at the teacher, steps joyfully, confidently forward into the light.

Kait Arquette at age 5. "God's fingerprint," the indentation on the left cheekbone, is where the first bullet struck.

Epilogue

When you reach an advanced age and look back over your lifetime, it can seem to have had a consistent order and plan, as though composed by some novelist. Events that when they occurred had seemed accidental and of little moment turn out to have been indispensable factors in the composition of a consistent plot. So who composed that plot? . . . Just as your dreams are composed by an aspect of yourself of which your consciousness is unaware, so, too, your whole life is composed by the will within you. And just as people whom you will have met apparently by mere chance become leading agents in the structuring of your life, so, too, will you have served unknowingly as an agent, giving meaning to the lives of others. . . .

It is even as though there were a single intention behind it all, which always makes some kind of sense, though none of us knows what the sense might be, or has lived the life that he quite intended.

Joseph Campbell

People arrested in insurance-fraud case in OC

■

State grand jury indicted each of the following on three counts of conspiracy to commit insurance fraud/grand theft, two counts of insurance fraud, one count of felony "capping" and one count of attempted grand theft. Bail is set at $250,000 for each person, except where noted.

■ Arrested at the law office of James MacPhee, 14541 Brookhurst, #C1, Westminster: James Michael MacPhee, 42; Duc Minh Nguyen, 32, allegedly brought in accidents for all the clinics and law offices ($1 million bail); Quy The Nguyen, 37, administrator; Phuong Thi Bich Vo, 31, office manager; Lam Hoang Luu, 30, administrator; Michael Gomez, 41, client administrator

■ Arrested at the Cooper Medical Clinic, 10550 Westminster Ave., Garden Grove (no longer doing business at that location): Brenda Espinoza Gonzalez, 24, secretary

■

These Orange County residents were arrested in San Diego on suspicion of one count of aiding and abetting a fraudulent vehicular collision and one count of filing a false insurance claim:

■ Son Van Nguyen, 38, of Huntington Beach (bail unknown)
■ Phong My Quach, 28, of Garden Grove (bail unknown)

Source: Orange County district attorney

SAN DIEGO DREAM LIFE CORPORATION

BAO TRAN
Vice President

14541 Brookhurst St., #C1
Westminster, CA. 92683
Tel.: (714) 531-0002
Beeper: (714) 664-1021
FAX: 714-531-0746

7520 Mesa College Dr.
San Diego, CA. 92111
Tel.: (619) 292-0695
Beeper: (619) 491-8909
FAX: (619) 292-1864

The law office of James Michael MacPhee, who, along with the Vietnamese paralegal Duc Minh Nguyen, was arrested for insurance fraud in January 1993, was at one of the addresses shown on Bao Tran's business card.

Afterword

The hardcover edition of *Who Killed My Daughter?* was published in the United States in June 1992, and Lois toured the country with the book. Starting with *Good Morning, America* and *Larry King Live*, she appeared on radio and television shows from coast to coast to relate Kait's story and plead with informants to come forward.

And information did trickle in to fill in some of the gaps in the Arquette family's scenario.

An occupant of an apartment complex across from Kait's high school wrote to say that one of the Hispanic suspects knew the Vietnamese through parties held in an apartment there. He also said that at the time of Kait's murder, the tenant in whose apartment the parties were held was driving a VW bug without an engine cover that matched the description of the car seen fleeing the murder site.

Lois passed this information on to the district attorney, as it seemed to provide a possible connection between Dung Nguyen's friends and the Hispanics.

Nobody followed up on it.

In July 1992, Marty Martinez phoned the police and voluntarily confessed to murder-for-hire, saying he and his friends were hired by the Vietnamese to kill Kait. The confession was not made public until ten days later when a newspaper reporter stumbled upon the police report. It was five more days before Marty was finally interrogated, at which time he recanted, saying he was drunk when he confessed. He was not arrested and was not given a polygraph test.

Sergeant Lowe told the press, "We're not working on anything now. . . . [The Arquette girl's murder] is kind of sitting on the back burner."

After reading the book, investigators at the National Insurance Crime Bureau and the Fraud Division of the California State Insurance Agencies contacted Lois for more information about the car wreck scam.

On August 5, 1992, two lawyers in Orange County were arrested and charged with spearheading a major auto insurance fraud ring. One lawyer was also under suspicion of solicitation to commit murder by putting out a contract to kill a witness who had been shown how the car wrecks were set up.

California State Insurance Commissioner John Garamendi stated that this breakthrough was significant, because although lawyers are often at the heart of fraud rings, they are seldom charged because they delegate the work to subordinates and then deny any knowledge of the crimes.

In reporting the arrests on the CBS Evening News, news anchor Connie Chung cited *Who Killed My Daughter?* as "a true story in which a grieving mother claims her daughter was murdered when she was about to go to the police."

One prominent California law firm that represents insurance companies in connection with fraudulent claims involving auto accidents purchased thirty copies of the book to distribute to contacts throughout the insurance industry and in law enforcement.

On January 13, 1993, there was a record-setting crackdown in Southern California that led to over forty arrests of people involved in four loosely connected insurance fraud rings. An additional seventy suspects were under investigation. Many of those arrested were doctors and lawyers in Orange County, and several of the Vietnamese car wreck "victims" were from Albuquerque.

One of the lawyers arrested in this bust was James Michael MacPhee, who had his practice at 14541 Brookhurst, Westminster, California, *an address that appeared on one of Bao Tran's business cards.*

Bail for MacPhee was set at $250,000. Bail for the Vietnamese paralegal who allegedly set up the car wrecks was set at one million dollars. As this book goes to press, MacPhee has not yet gone to trial, *but the paralegal has been tried, found guilty, and sentenced to prison.*

On January 27, 1993, the television show *Unsolved Mysteries* ran a dramatization of Kait's story. Mike Gallagher made his files available to the producers and was instrumental in providing background information. All parts were cast in Albuquerque except for Kait's boyfriend. Although many Vietnamese actors were registered with Albuquerque talent agencies, they refused to audition for parts in the "Kait Arquette Story." The part of Dung Nguyen had to be cast in Hollywood.

Lois was interviewed on the show, as were Mike Gallagher and Detective Steve Gallegos. Their statements were as follows:

Detective Gallegos: "I don't think that the Vietnamese connection is related to this case. Thus far I have not received any information that would indicate—*positively*—that the Vietnamese are involved in this homicide."

Mike Gallagher: "I think it's important for the police to remember, and for anyone else who looks at this case to remember, that Kaitlyn's boyfriend's friends were involved with large-scale organized criminal activity in Los Angeles and with multimillion-dollar insurance fraud. I don't think the police ever took that seriously."

Lois: "Our family doesn't know for sure who pulled the trigger on Kait. The thing we feel very strongly about, however, is that she was not shot randomly by people out on a spree having fun shooting a pretty girl in a red car.

"We believe Kait was killed because she was getting ready to expose illegal activities involving her boyfriend and his companions. It might have been that she was shot by the Vietnamese; it might have been that they hired someone else to shoot her. But the one thing we're absolutely sure of in our own minds is that this was *not* a random shooting— Kait was *assassinated*."